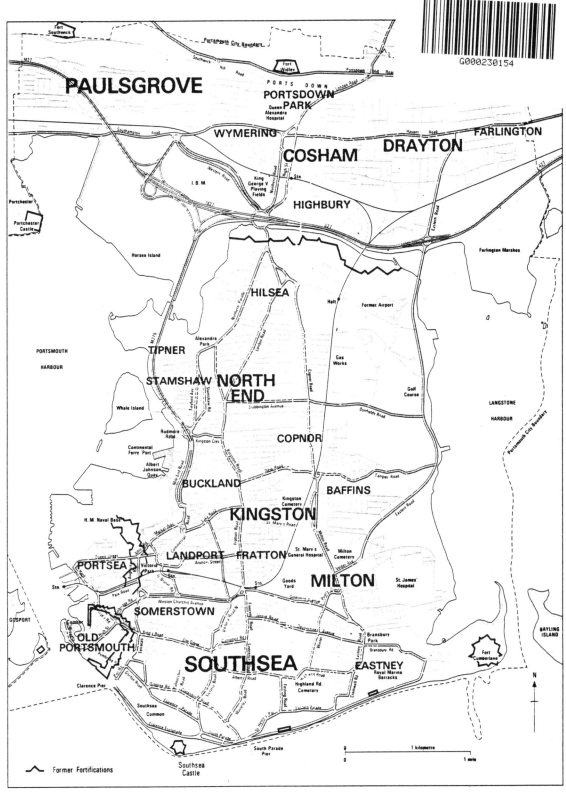

Modern road-pattern and place-names on Portsea Island.

The Spirit of
PORTSMOUTH

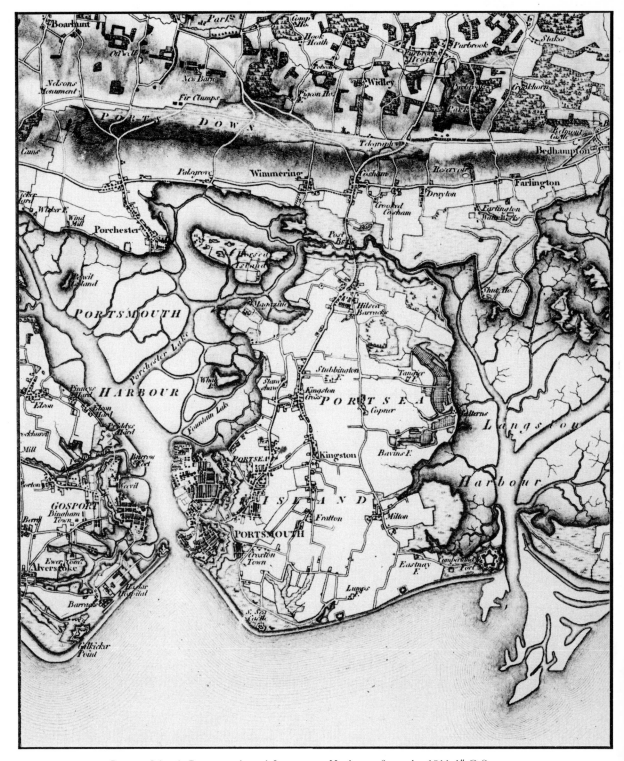

Portsea Island, Portsmouth and Langstone Harbours from the 1811 1″ O.S. map.

The Spirit of
PORTSMOUTH
A History

J. Webb, S. Quail, P. Haskell and R. Riley

Phillimore

1989

Published by
PHILLIMORE & CO. LTD.
Shopwyke Hall, Chichester, Sussex

ISBN 0 85033 617 1

Printed and bound in England by
STAPLES PRINTERS ROCHESTER LIMITED
Love Lane, Rochester, Kent.

Contents

List of Illustrations

Acknowledgements for Illustrations

The authors wish to thank the following individuals and organisations for permission to reproduce material in their possession as text illustrations: Lord Dartmouth and the Staffordshire County Record Office, No. 3; The National Maritime Museum, No. 5; The British Library, No. 6; Portsmouth City Museums and Art Gallery, Nos. 9-11 and jacket pictures; *The News*, Portsmouth, Nos. 32, 54 and 57; The Provost of Portsmouth, No. 34; Mr. Peter Rogers, No. 44; Portsmouth City Records Office for all remaining items.

The authors are grateful to a number of individuals who have assisted them in the preparation of this book, and in particular they would like to thank Mrs. Elizabeth Dunk, Miss Rosemary Phillips and Mrs. Brenda Worton of Portsmouth City Records Office, Miss Sarah Lewin of the Hampshire Record Office, Mr. Alan King and the staff of the Local and Naval History Section, Portsmouth Central Library, and the Librarian and staff at The News Centre, Portsmouth.

Finally, the authors would like to thank Mr. Roger Skinner and the staff of Portsmouth City Council's Reprographic Section, especially Miss Kate Foster, for all their hard work preparing illustrations for publication.

Acknowledgements

The authors are grateful to a number of individuals who have assisted them in the preparation of this book, and in particular they would like to thank Mrs. Elizabeth Dunk, Miss Rosemary Phillips and Mrs. Brenda Worton of Portsmouth City Records Office, Miss Sarah Lewin of the Hampshire Record Office, Mr. Alan King and the staff of the Local and Naval History Section, Portsmouth Central Library, and the Librarian and staff at The News Centre, Portsmouth.

Finally, the authors would like to thank Mr. Roger Skinner and the staff of Portsmouth City Council's Reprographic Section, especially Miss Kate Foster, for all their hard work preparing illustrations for publication.

Preface

This new history of Portsmouth, based on a thematic rather than a conventional chronological approach, examines in the light of much recent published and unpublished research certain major aspects of the city's development, some of which have previously been neglected by scholars. An attempt has been made throughout to put greater emphasis than hitherto on the former rural settlements which are now part of the heavily built up city, since it is not always realised that until the 19th century Portsmouth, despite its world-wide fame as a naval base, was still in part a farming community closely associated with its agricultural hinterland. In our decision to isolate certain themes, we were conscious of the danger of failing to provide a proper understanding of Portsmouth's overall development. The first two chapters, however, which deal with the principal features of the area and the way the modern city has evolved, should obviate this problem and enable the topics dealt with in subsequent chapters to be seen in context. Inevitably, certain familiar events and landmarks in English history have found no significant place in our scheme, but it is hoped that new insights and interpretations, and a greater appreciation of Portsmouth's heritage and the way of life of its people over the centuries, will more than compensate for any omissions. If we have been able to capture for the reader something of the unique spirit of the city, our aims will have been fulfilled.

Portsmouth
January 1989

J.W.
S.Q.
P.H.
R.R.

Chapter One

Marsh and Water

Long before Portsmouth existed, marsh and water were the dominant influences in shaping the landscape. The skeleton of this southernmost part of the Hampshire Basin is chalk, visible in the great white pits scarring the rounded green bank of Portsdown, to the north of the city, and dipping beneath Spithead to rise again to the Isle of Wight on the southern horizon. Seventy million years ago when this skeleton was laid down, much of Britain and Europe lay deep under water. Jacquetta Hawkes liked to think '. . . of the seas where chalk was forming clouded with white as though from a snow storm – a fall that lasted thirty million years and lay to a depth of a thousand feet'.[1] At the same time were created the flints found in the shingle beaches along Portsea Island's southern shore '. . . compacted of sponges that once stood delicate but rigid in the brilliant underwater world of Cretaceous times'.[2] Gradually the seas regressed, the land mass emerged and slight folding and tilting of the chalk took place, followed in what is now southern England by a warm period and the creation of swamps and lakes. Cycles of sedimentation in which the seas alternately advanced and retreated left mud, sands, clays and gravels in marine and fluvial deposits above the chalk. These Eocene beds, whose strata now dip southwards from Portsdown, form the foundation of Portsea, Hayling and Thorney Islands and the neighbouring coastal lands to the west. About twenty-five million years ago the Eocene layers were tilted on end by the outer ripples of the great earth movements that threw up the Alps. As the land buckled the South Downs were made, with their characteristic steep northern and gentle southern slopes.

About two million years ago began the succession of arctic and warm interglacial periods that brought both polar and near-tropical climates to Britain. The fluctuating sea levels that resulted gave the final shape to the local landscape, eroding the southern slopes of Portsdown and covering the Eocene beds to a depth of three feet or more with superficial deposits derived from shifting rivers and floods. Most significantly, the islands and harbours now emerged. Until the final post-glacial period the coastal plain was continuous and formed the northern bank of the so-called 'Solent River', while the Isle of Wight was still embedded in the broad southern bank that extended from Dorset to Sussex. As coastal erosion progressed and the last ice-sheets melted, the sea rose and drowned the Solent River estuary and its tributaries, creating the Solent and Spithead, Southampton Water, and Portsmouth, Langstone and Chichester harbours.[3] The deep-water channels now followed by shipping trace approximately the courses of these earlier rivers, and the site on which Portsmouth was to grow became a low, marshy, pear-shaped island some five miles long, cut off from the mainland by a strip of the sea, its southern coast flanked by narrow channels soon widening into broad tidal bays. Surrounded then by natural defences of mud, marsh and water, Portsea Island discouraged permanent early settlement. Today, when almost completely covered with buildings, its margins are encircled by stone and concrete barriers constructed over centuries to deter invasion by men and the sea.

The shaping of this coast formed what was to become one of the world's great anchorages. Sheltered from the south by the Isle of Wight, the Solent's twin entrances create a convenient tidal pattern at Portsmouth, with a seven-hour flood and a five-hour ebb. As the water retreats from the 15 square miles of Portsmouth Harbour it scours the narrow entrance channel and then turns sharply south-east to sweep along the coast to the southernmost tip of the island by Southsea Castle and on out to the Nab. On the Gosport side the Spit Sand protects the harbour mouth from the rough seas beating up from the south-west, while the extensive Horse and Dean Sands, with No Man's Land and the Mother Bank, give large areas of comparatively calm sea around the deeper anchorage of Spithead. Visiting Portsmouth in 1552, Edward VI noted that '. . . the mouth of the Have[n] is not past ten score over, but in the middle almost a mile over, and in lenght for a mile and a hauf, hable to beare the greatest ship in Christendome'.[4] In 1793 Thomas Pennant judged the entrance channel to be 'about as broad as the Thames at Westminster'.[5] Immediately inside, the water spreads behind the curving shingle hooks of Fort Blockhouse and Portsmouth Point; on the west, past the submarine base into the winding channels of Haslar and Alverstoke Lakes, and on the east into the little commercial harbour of the Camber and formerly into the Mill Pond. Beyond the dockyard the harbour widens sharply and divides into two main branches separated by a three-mile expanse of mudbank surrounding Pewit Island. Fareham Lake slants north-westwards for about four miles up to Fareham Quay, where the small Wallingford River runs in from behind Portsdown. Portchester Lake stretches northwards to the castle, and then used to bear east round Horsea Island into Port Creek, where it met the tide flowing from Langstone Harbour on the other side of Portsea Island. Numerous small creeks diverge from the main channels, with evocative names like Bombketch, Spider, Weevil and Half Ebb Lakes.[6]

The strategic value of Portsmouth Harbour over the centuries changed according to the prevailing continental enemy. Late in the third century the Roman fort at Portchester was the westernmost of the Saxon Shore forts built from the Wash around the south-eastern coast to repel invaders. In the fourth century, as the empire crumbled, the nine-acre fort, whose great encircling walls still stand, formed the base for naval patrols of oared galleys which put to sea as marauding pirates approached. Although there is evidence of extensive civilian presence at Portchester from the sixth century onwards, and it is listed as a fortified town in the 10th-century Burghal Hidage, nothing is known about the military use of the harbour during the Saxon period.[7] With the Conquest attention shifted to France, and there was much coming and going between England and Normandy, at first mainly through ports in Kent and Sussex and from Southampton, while in the 12th century Henry I became the first of many monarchs to make Portsmouth Harbour his customary place of departure or arrival. As the Norman and Plantagenet kings first administered their territories in France and then fought to regain them, the harbour was used for three centuries as a major collecting point for the transport fleets. In the 12th century a castle was built in the north-west corner of the Saxon Shore fort to provide a royal residence and military base easily reached from Winchester, while the Roman walls were repaired to enclose an extensive outer bailey in which an army could conveniently be assembled. It was often easier to raise the men than to find enough ships to carry them, and before an expedition the sheltered waters of the harbour and Spithead filled slowly with the king's ships and requisitioned trading vessels, waiting for a sufficient fleet and a favourable wind. Then as now, Portsmouth was a convenient departure point for France, which could be reached the following day if the wind was right. The port was much frequented in the next 150 years, but Henry V collected expeditions at Southampton rather than Portsmouth and for the rest of the 15th century the harbour was relatively little used.[8]

It was not until the early Tudor period that Portsmouth was once again the scene of major activity, mainly focused on the development of the dockyard. In Elizabeth's reign, when Spain succeeded France as England's major adversary and action moved to the Spanish Netherlands, Deptford, Woolwich and Chatham became strategically more useful than Portsmouth, while West-Country ports were better departure points for raids on the

1. Portsea Island, Langstone and Portsmouth Harbours. Aerial view from the north, 1983.

2. Langstone Harbour. Aerial view from the south, 1986.

Spanish coast or Spanish fleets in the Atlantic. Portsmouth took little part in the Armada campaign of 1588, and in view of this lengthy English neglect it is interesting that the Spaniards had not lost sight of the harbour's advantages. In 1597 Spain prepared an even larger armada, and its commander ordered a survey of the principal English ports with a view to establishing a base if invasion proved successful. Portsmouth was reported to have a very good harbour, capable of holding 4-500 vessels, with four fathoms at low water at the mouth and up to six fathoms within. Between Portsmouth and Southampton was a very fine bay where ships could cast anchor in all winds except from the south-west.[9] Contrary winds were proving a major disadvantage of the Thames yards, where ships could be prevented for weeks from getting round into the Channel to sail westwards. The Duke of Buckingham, appointed Lord High Admiral in 1617, used Portsmouth as the base for his expedition to La Rochelle in 1627. Once again Spithead and the harbour witnessed the gathering of a major fleet, and nearly one hundred ships, including 40 of the king's, sailed at the end of June to a disastrous conflict at the Ile de Rhé. Preparations for a second expedition brought Buckingham to the *Greyhound Inn* in the High Street in August 1628, where he was assassinated by John Felton.[10]

In the 1630s Charles I built up the ship money fleet to counter the growing naval strength of France and the Netherlands. Although many of the ships were victualled and repaired at Portsmouth, the initial rendezvous for the annual Channel patrol was generally in the Downs. The growth of the Thames and Medway yards, especially Chatham, was seen as a threat to Portsmouth, and in 1634 a report on the harbour recorded that it could receive more than two hundred sail and emphasised its strategic importance as 'the readiest inlett or outlett Eastward or Westward':

> A fleet (especiallie of great ships) shall arrive sooner in Spaine from Portsmouth then come from Chatham to the Isle of Wight, and consequentlie in all suth voyages a monethes victualls and wages will be saved his Majestie . . . and the difference for readines to doe service, betwixt this place and Chatham, is so much as for one to have his sword drawne in his hand, whilst another's rustie in his scabard.

Enemy attack on any point along the south coast was most likely in a northerly (i.e. an off-shore) wind, which similarly served best to bring the defending fleet out of Portsmouth Harbour.[11] Viscount Wimbledon, Governor of Portsmouth, advocating a general levy for repair of the kingdom's strongpoints, argued that 'No place deserves more charge to be bestowed upon it than Portsmouth, both by reason of its situation and its being the frontier town, as it were, upon the Low Countries, France and Spain'.[12]

Before the construction of dry docks, ship repair and maintenance had to be carried out with the vessel afloat or beached in a suitable creek, temporarily walled off at low tide. In 1634 Portsmouth Harbour was judged adequate for most practical purposes, though the lack of a dry dock was regretted: 'Within the Harbour the tides heave enough to grave all such shippes as for their mould underwater or waight overhead are fitt to lye with the ground, and the graving place at the docke firme and good'.[13] In 1662-3 construction of a wet dock at Portsmouth was under consideration, but surveyors reported that two creeks on the eastern side of the harbour, Pool Head and Land Deep, were capable of receiving 30 frigates of the 4th, 5th and 6th rates, being 'convenienter' places than any wet dock, and saving some £15,000 by costing nothing to fit up.[14] Ten years later the protection afforded by the harbour and its approaches was recorded in accounts of 'a very great storm' from the south-south-west, in which the payhouse chimney was blown down and a hulk set adrift, but which inflicted no damage on the warships in harbour or at Spithead.[15]

In the second half of the 18th century improvements were made to the dockyard, and a detailed report in 1774 on 'the principal Navy Port in Great Britain' was prefaced by a glowing account of the harbour and Spithead:

It has a more spacious and safer Roadstead before the Harbour than any other in England or indeed than any other known in the World, so that the greatest Fleets and Convoys may Rendezvous and lay there in perfect safety.

Capital ships can pass into and out of the Harbour with less intricacy and danger than at any other Port, and the Harbour it self is entirely safe and convenient for every Naval purpose.

As naval ships increased in size it became more difficult to lay them up at Chatham, and the report listed moorings for 62 ships in Portsmouth Harbour as follows:

Vessels: Ships of the Line, 44; Ships of 50 guns, 6; Large frigates, 4; Small frigates and sloops, 6; Hulk and yacht, 2.
Location: Fountain Lake, 6; Portchester Lake, 11; West Shore and Blockhouse Mooring, 29: East Shore, 16.

The accompanying map shows 42 swinging and 20 head-and-stern moorings, the latter mostly in Fountain Lake and the further recesses of Portchester Lake.[16]

In the same year a description of the harbour as seen from Portsdown Hill by William Gilpin, a New Forest clergyman, showed that most of these moorings were currently occupied:

Besides innumerable skiffs and smaller vessels plying about this ample bason, we counted between fifty and sixty sail of the line. Some of them appeared lying unrigged on the water, others in commission with their colours flying. Beyond Portsmouth we had a view of the sea, which is generally crowded with ships, especially in the road of St Helens, where some men of war are commonly waiting for the wind.[17]

Contemporary prints and paintings bring visual confirmation of these descriptions. A view of Spithead in 1729, for example, shows it crowded with the sail of a united Dutch and British fleet,[18] while in 1790 a pair of pictures was painted from a viewpoint in the middle of the harbour, showing the ships moored to north and south of the artist's vessel.[19] In the Napoleonic Wars the harbour was crowded with captured French warships used as prison hulks, their masts removed and decks cumbered with ungainly huts for the guards, and in 1810 an oil painting attributed to Louis Garneray, temporary prisoner of war and eventual French court painter, depicted this scene.[20]

Naval use of the harbour severely limited the development of Portsmouth's commercial port, which remained largely confined to the Camber, a little inlet near the mouth on the eastern side. Close to the deep-water channel and protected by a shingle spit, this sheltered bay was probably a major reason for the location of the new town late in the 12th century. For more than six hundred years Portsmouth was a member of the port of Southampton, like Titchfield, Cowes and many other small ports in south Hampshire, and although little is known of the town's early trade, the Camber was physically a typical medieval harbour.[21] In the 16th century the earliest maps show the shingle spit, later known as Point, as a long thin sickle with a couple of houses but no quays, curving to enclose the Inner Camber, whose narrow entrance lay between the tip of the sickle and the Town Quay, a two-pronged projection on the eastern side, at the end of Hog Market (now Warblington) Street. At this time the Outer Camber was a relatively spacious part of the main harbour, its east bank running along the town wall northwards to the Mill Pond.[22] As de Gomme showed in 1668, however, low tide left 'the kamer' and the whole area between Point and the dockyard a continuous expanse of mud, apart from the three thin channels draining the Camber, the Mill Pond and the Mast Pond.[23] Within the harbour various encroachments for military and naval purposes gradually reduced the space for mercantile manoeuvre. By 1687 the Camber Bastion jutted into the Inner Camber, while the Victualling Quay, far larger than the Town Quay, obstructed its entrance. To the north the Old Gunwharf had projected into the main harbour from the early 18th century, while the New Gunwharf, constructed on reclaimed land during the Napoleonic Wars, massively occupied most of the former mudlands south of the Mill Dam.[24]

In 1836 the Committee for Improvement of Trade and Fishery complained of

> ... the almost total want of Wharf or Quay Room for landing and shipping merchandize, there being no accommodation at the present Quay in ordinary tides for even one Vessel drawing more than 6 or 7 feet water, and room only for two or three of that draught; indeed Portsmouth, although the first naval port of the Kingdom, has less accommodation for Mercantile business as respects Wharfs and Docks, than any other place in the British Channel, however insignificant its pretensions.[25]

Goods were put into lighters instead of being landed directly, leading to delay, damage and loss, particularly of perishable groceries. The lack of a dry dock for repairs made many ships avoid the port altogether.[26] In 1839 the town clerk noted that no significant addition had been made to the Town Quay (only 250 feet long) in the past 150 years, and that the Camber was 'as it has been for several centuries, an extensive bed of mud in the midst of the buildings of the Town, by which it is nearly surrounded on all sides, into which the principal sewers of the Town discharge themselves'.[27] In 1836-9 various improvement schemes were drawn up, culminating in an Act providing for the deepening of the Camber and the construction of over twelve hundred feet of wharves along the eastern side and around the East Street area of Point. A swivel bridge across the mouth of the Inner Camber connected the old and new quays, while a repair slipway beside White Hart Row replaced a proposed dock, dismissed by the Treasury Commissioners as too speculative an undertaking.[28] Untypically for the period, these improvements were financed not by private capital but by the borough council, who borrowed heavily for the purpose. The local merchants not only vigorously opposed the passage of the Bill but brought actions for compensation for damage to trade while the work progressed, and objected to increased wharfage dues. The improved Camber was formally reopened in 1843, but plans for a dry dock in the Outer Camber were not approved until 1859.[29]

As steamships developed, Southampton's docks expanded but Portsmouth lagged behind. The search began for a more capacious commercial harbour, and in 1857 the Council proposed to convert the Mill Pond into a steam depot and dock. George Rennie and others praised the convenience of this extensive site, capable of accommodating 30 large ships, near a railhead, close to Portsmouth, Portsea and Landport, and protected by the fortifications. Government assent was sought by arguing that the harbour entrance would become less congested, and that an auxiliary fleet might be swiftly and secretly armed for war in the new depot. An impassioned letter from the mayor, Benjamin Bramble, protested that, while neighbouring ports prospered, Portsmouth's inhabitants 'have been hitherto debarred by hereditary naval prejudices and objections untenable in the present day from availing themselves of the legitimate advantages afforded by their maritime position'. The Board of Ordnance remained adamant, however, and the plan was rejected.[30]

Portsmouth's 19th-century import trade consisted mainly of coal, building materials and groceries,[31] and as the population expanded from about fifty thousand in 1839 to 94,500 in 1861 further shipping accommodation became necessary. Plans for new quays along the north and west sides of the Inner Camber parallel with East and Broad Streets were supported by the Harbour Master, who described in 1868 how colliers crowding along the Outer Camber wharf obstructed the approach to the Inner Camber, where vessels were often moored three abreast, discharging over each other. Ships might wait a week or more for a berth, and were ordered away from the harbour by an uncompromising Master Attendant and hampered by naval moorings. Portsea's small landing place had been engulfed by dockyard expansion at the New Buildings and replaced by Anchor Gate Wharf, itself lost to further expansion in 1864. In compensation the Admiralty provided Flathouse Wharf farther up the harbour, and when the corporation decided to extend this and charge higher dues, there was again sustained objection from the principal users, particularly the Gas Company.[32]

Langstone Harbour, on the eastern side of Portsea Island, appears superficially to offer opportunities for commercial shipping, but has major physical disadvantages and has therefore developed very differently. Here about three-quarters of the area is exposed at low tide, leaving wide expanses of mud and sand dotted today with small craft and sea birds. Within the harbour Langstone Channel runs north-east to join Chichester Harbour around the northern end of Hayling Island; Broom Channel branches north-west to join Port Creek; while Sinah, Russell's, Velder and Eastney lakes are shallow areas of uneven depth. The approaches to the harbour entrance have long had an unenviable reputation based on the shallow and variable depth of water across the bar, which is flanked by the East and West Winners, extensive sand and gravel banks exposed at low water. The powerful ebb tide, sometimes reaching four and three-quarter knots, can combine dangerously with on-shore winds.[33] In 1747 Desmaretz had marked the sandbanks east of the entrance as being 'A hard Sand dry at low Water of Spring Tides whereon there generally runs a great Sea'.[34] A survey in 1782 reported the entrance as being 'almost barr'd up with banks' and perilous for ships without a pilot.[35] In 1908 a report on abortive plans for mercantile development judged it 'unsafe for vessels to enter the harbour drawing more than 13 ft. at springs or 10 ft. at neaps, and then only at the top of the tide'.[36]

Since the entrance remains largely unimproved the present use of the harbour is mainly recreational, apart from two quays dealing in dredged sand and shingle. Small yacht clubs line the western shore; dinghy racing, water skiing and wind-surfing are popular summer activities; bait-digging and fishing mirror the state of the tides. Above all, the harbour is one of the great southern wintering grounds for wildfowl and waders. Arriving in hundreds in August and September, the flocks of dunlin, teal, widgeon, shelduck, oystercatchers and lapwings rise to thousands by mid-winter, while the concentration of thousands of brent geese is the largest on the south coast. Rare passage migrants often appear at the nature reserve on Farlington Marshes, where a partly reclaimed area of freshwater marsh and rough grazing land extends for about a mile into the harbour from the northern shore. Beside it to the east four small islands (Long, Baker and North and South Binness) provide high-tide roosts for many winter waders. Protected now, the sea-birds were once an important part of the local economy. In the early 17th century on four acres called the Pewit Ground some three hundred dozen pewits were annually bred and sold at 10s. a dozen, with another forty dozen from Warblington Manor. Here also was

> . . . a creek or peece of ground flowed with the sea at every full sea called the foulling grownds wherein ar yearely taken to the use and profict of the lord of the said manor winter foulle, that is to saye duckes, mallards, wyggenes and other fouls called wide foule of great profict and compoditie to the lord of the manors.[37]

The wide shallow lagoons of the two harbours, the gently flowing tides of their upper reaches, the flat coastlines and breezy open skies were all favourable to the practice of one of the most ubiquitous of early coastal industries, evaporating sea water for salt. In Hampshire, many pre-Roman salt production sites and 11 of the 26 Hampshire Domesday saltpans lay around the two harbours. Their total value in 1086 was £3 9s. 9d., compared with only 8s. 4d. for the other fifteen. Bedhampton's two pans, yielding 37s. 8d., and the pair belonging to Boarhunt, at 22s. 6d., were the highest valued; the Copnor saltpan, ancestor of the later Portsea salterns, yielded only 8d. in 1086.[38] Lymington was the main medieval Hampshire salt-making centre, though, as Camden noted in the 16th century, 'In many places along this coast salt is made of the sea water collected. It is first of a palish green colour, which they have a method of boiling to the purest white'.[39] At about this time 'A note of the saltworke at Porsey' records that in 40 acres there were '240 Boune Bryne and pickell pannes made in the ground . . .'. Repaired by early May and filled with sea water they were left for a month's evaporation. From June until September 80 pans were drawn three times a week, giving 300 tons of brine to produce 30 weys of salt of 40 bushels each. The estimated cost of making such a saltern was £700, less than two years' net income.[40] Robert Bold, who bought Portsea manor in 1598, was the Copnor saltmaster until 1626, and in the early 1630s Charles I granted leases of the 'coppner groundes alias le Sault pitts' to various projectors.[41] In 1666 the Great Salterns works were established when Richard Alchorne dug salt pits in about one hundred acres of the reclaimed Gatcombe Haven. Summer evaporation was followed by a longer season of brine-boiling and 'having good skill in Chymistry' he made refined salt which brined meat for long sea voyages more reliably than dry-salting. Great Salterns and Copnor supplied Portsmouth's Navy Victualling Department, and improved many acres of land that would otherwise have lain waste upon the coasts.[42] In the later 17th century Portsea Island salt production ranked second in the county.

Less necessary than salt, but a welcome part of the local diet, were oysters, whose discarded shells appear in many old gardens. In the 19th century they sold for a shilling a hundred, but Portsmouth's trade was then declining. In 1836 a trade and fishery committee estimated that oyster grounds of 300,000 acres lay around the Solent and its harbours, but lamented destruction done by dredging in the breeding season from May to August 'at a period when it is necessary for its existence, the Oyster should remain quiet'. Before 1815 two hundred to three hundred boats had arrived at Portsmouth annually, bringing valuable trade for several months, but by that date few came, and the committee fruitlessly pleaded for enforcement of a close season.[43] In Langstone Harbour David Russell owned the New Milton Fishery with 18 acres of beds in Russell's Lake, guarded by a watchman's house still visible on a small island by Farlington marshes. The fishery took oysters from Langstone and Emsworth Channels and the neighbouring rithes, and claimed that its reserve stock of large oysters seeded the whole harbour at spawning time. Established in 1820 and dealing also in winkles and clams, this business flourished for nearly a century.[44] In 1902 the deaths of the Dean of Winchester and others from typhoid after eating Emsworth oysters at mayoral banquets at Winchester and Southampton demonstrated the tragic consequences of pollution of the harbours by sewage from the expanding local communities.[45] Russell's fishery was certified uncontaminated, while improvements in sewage disposal and post-war trade led to revival after 1918.

Salterns and oyster farms exploited natural products without substantially disturbing the environment, but in the 19th and 20th centuries various abortive schemes applied new technologies in ways that would have radically altered the harbour and the eastern side of Portsea Island. These included a plan to dam the entrance to create a deep-water lake 'where 500 mercantile vessels may lie in perfect safety',[46] and another to load trains on to a steam ferry crossing the harbour mouth, while the narrow entrance channel inevitably tempted bridge-builders. Early in the 19th century proposals to connect Portsmouth to London led to the Portsmouth and Arundel Canal, opened in 1823. Some 86 miles of navigation via the Thames, Wey and Arun were already completed or under construction by 1816, and a further canal joined the Arun with Chichester Harbour. Traffic passed by steamboat through channels north of Thorney and Hayling Islands and across Langstone Harbour to Eastney Lake, at the end of Locksway Road. Two miles of canal were cut from here to a basin at Landport. In addition to local trade it was hoped that naval and military stores and East and West India goods would be sent by this route instead of around the coast, especially in wartime. Like many late southern canals it was unprofitable, and the Portsmouth section proved inoperable since the salt water that filled it, steam-pumped out of Langstone Harbour, percolated through sands and gravels to spoil the neighbouring fresh-water springs. The canal was abandoned and Arundel Street was built over the basin, while railway lines run along the former canal bed between Portsmouth and Fratton stations.[47] Part of the towpath runs from Milton to the locks, still visible on the shore. In 1844 another canal was planned to lead from the deep-water channel west of Southsea Castle, passing inland behind Lumps and Eastney Forts to docks and basins in Eastney Lake. Designed to secure commercial development of Langstone Harbour while avoiding the awkward entrance channel, this plan came to nothing.[48] Southampton's mercantile success inspired more grandiose schemes. In 1908 it was planned to cut a channel 600 feet wide across the Langstone bar, to enable larger ships to reach tidal quays and docks at Broom Channel and Velder Lake, with rail connections to the Portsmouth-Brighton line.[49] This development mainly affected mudflats, but in 1920 another plan envisaged a deeper channel leading to more extensive jetties obliterating much of Great Salterns, including the house.[50] The quest for a major new commercial dock site never succeeded, however, and it was not until the Admiralty loosened its hold on Portsmouth Harbour fifty years later that a thriving continental ferry port developed.

For many centuries Portsea Island had little good-quality drinking water, and this led to another prolonged search. Medieval and early modern inhabitants collected rainwater, dug wells and used public pumps. More bountiful supplies were perpetuated in place-names: Fonturne furlong (1346) from the spring on the harbour shore; Landport's Spring and Fountain Streets; Hambrook Street named after the *aquam vocatam Hambrouk* (1358) running into the Little Morass.[51] In the 16th century the main source of water within the town walls became visible in contemporary maps. At the northern end of St Nicholas Street appears an oval pond surrounded by the four royal brewhouses (Dragon, Lyon, Rose and Whight Hart) clustering closely around their principal ingredient. When the pond disappeared under de Gomme's fortifications its springs were fed into cisterns, accessible by a postern gate and bridge until the 1870s.[52] Numerous wells at street corners and in gardens were covered and forgotten when piped water arrived in the 19th century, some to be revealed after wartime bombing. As the population grew, the search for more drinking water began. In 1655 Benjamin Oakshott erected two 'fresh water mils' on White Swan Field which filled cisterns with water to be distributed in casks.[53] Some townsfolk dug more wells, like the tradesman at Point who at 60 feet found mud and an antique anchor, at 80 feet sand and a little water, and who then drove a pile deep through the bottom into a spring that gave seventy feet of water in his well.[54] The shortcomings of the White Swan source were demonstrated when the Portsea Island Waterworks Company built a tank and pumped water through pipes to the town. The supply was available on two or three days a week for a few hours, and ran short in summer. One dissatisfied customer complained that whitings boiled in it came out 'red as bull's beef', another that his tea turned orange. Pike's, a major local brewer, had a whole brew spoiled by sandy water and went back to using a well near Halfway Houses.[55] In 1751 Thomas Smith, Lord of the Manor of Farlington, obtained an Act 'to supply the Town of Portsmouth with good and wholesome water', and in 1808-9 a London group bought the rights, set up the Portsmouth, Portsea and Farlington Waterworks Company, and laid six miles of mains. Water from springs on Farlington Marshes was pumped to an upper reservoir on Portsdown Hill and fed thence by gravity to the two towns. After much competitive pipe-laying with the Portsea Company, the Farlington Company achieved (September 1811) a violent discharge of rusty red water and thereafter a clearer supply. After 30 years' rivalry the companies amalgamated in 1840 as the United Portsmouth Water Company.[56]

Rawlinson's 1850 Report recommended 'a constant and cheap supply of water under pressure laid on to every house and yard to the entire superseding of all local wells and pumps'. Dr. W. C. Engledue, founder of the Royal Hospital, described the current situation:

At present the island of Portsea was one huge cess-pool, for there could not be less than 16,000 cess-pools daily permitting 30,000 gallons of urine to penetrate into the soil. Just reflect on the character of the well-water of a district which became mixed every year with 365 times 30,000 gallons of urine, to say nothing of a host of other abominations . . .[57]

By 1856 only about four thousand five hundred of some fourteen thousand inhabited houses had piped water. Few mains were laid as the town spread, although Thomas Ellis Owen supplied piped water privately to his Southsea villas from a well on his own land. From 1857 to 1908 the Borough of Portsmouth Waterworks Company effected a radical improvement by exploiting the Bedhampton and Havant springs, achieving a constant supply by 1880 and extending piped water to outlying areas from Wymering to Emsworth. By 1957 there was an average daily yield of some 23 million gallons, never falling below 14 million gallons in the driest conditions.[58] Portsmouth thus finally acquired a unique supply, no other city in the country depending entirely on a source of this kind.

Portsea Island's shores were fringed with mudflats and morasses, salt and fresh-water marshes, and deeply indented creeks and bays. Only slowly, as the human tide spread from the west in the late 19th and early 20th centuries, did the marsh and water eventually recede. As grass, trees and hedges disappeared under crowded bricks and mortar, space for relaxation and recreation was belatedly recovered from the island's margins. Drainage and reclamation were occasionally succeeded by building, for example on prime sites in Southsea, but were more often followed by the creation of parks, gardens and sports fields, so that many of these green patches around the modern city perpetuate the pattern of former ooze and waste. The value of these areas was well understood in the 17th century, when drainage for agricultural improvement was widespread. A 1626 survey of 'Ports Creeks Lakes and Lands which heretofore were surrounded and overflown with the Sea' along the Hampshire coast preceded the Wandesford Grant, ceding extensive rights over 5,189 acres of saltmarsh and mudflats in 83 parcels around the shores of Chichester, Langstone and Portsmouth harbours. Similar rights were granted over 'the Wastes of the Sea' around Southampton Water and along the northern shore of the Isle of Wight. Edward Mansell's contemporary map has not survived, but a copy made c.1665 by Daniel Favreau de la Fabvollière shows the area as it was in 1626.[59] Little of this land was drained in the 17th century and some of it remains untouched. On the eastern side of Portsea Island, however, Eastney Lake is the only truncated survivor of these tidal fleets and saltmarshes that for centuries ran deep inland. Gatcombe Haven, a great tidal lake of over 1,200 acres with a narrow entrance, was soon reclaimed and became the Great Salterns. The crown retained a 25 per cent interest in this area, but in 1663 leased 300 acres to William Quatremaine and Richard Alchorne to make the new saltworks, whose extensive pans are clearly visible on 18th and 19th century maps.[60] The rest of the land was farmed, and until 1895 remained extra-parochial. In 1830 the crown sold the Great Salterns estate to Francis Sharp, the current tenant.[61] In the 20th century the council refused permission for house-building there unless the land level was raised nine feet at prohibitive cost. They tipped refuse on neighbouring mudlands, whose owners secured £10,000 damages from the town. Simultaneously a lengthy wrangle over foreshore rights between the council, the Lords of Portsea Manor and the Board of Trade acting for the crown rumbled on from 1904-11. By 1909 the council was increasingly anxious to purchase the foreshore, to have something to show for the ratepayers' money, but was foiled by the crown's tenacity.[62] Eventually Portsmouth Corporation bought the land and allocated it for various uses: grazing, 39 acres; allotments, 75; school playing fields, 105.5; other sports, 75; and about 90 acres for a golf course with the clubhouse in the Regency mansion.[63]

Before the reclamation one deep inlet of Gatcombe Haven, with the stream that drained into it, ran halfway across the island to form the boundary between the medieval manors of Wymering and Portsea. South of the salterns there were 100 acres of 'oaze ground' in Velder Lake, of which the northern arm (drained by 1833) ran westwards beyond Baffins Pond, where ducks still dabble and splash and nest in neighbouring gardens. South of Milton Common, Eastney Lake covered nearly 170 acres in 1626, one branch running west through the present Bransbury Park to Eastney Road. Crana Lake was not dry until the 1970s, while Eastney Lake was infilled between Cumberland and Ferry Roads.[64] No creeks break the line of the long shingle bank forming the island's southern coast. Here the marshes lie a little inland, and 17th-19th century maps show the ragged edges of the Little Morass south-east of Portsmouth's sharply-angled fortifications, and the sprawling body and five spreading tentacles of the Great Morass contrasting with the tidy field boundaries of Fratton Manor. The two morasses, with Craneswater and intervening stretches of gorse, scrub, shingle and sand covered in 1785 about 180 of the 480 acres that formed the Frodington manorial waste, later Southsea Common.[65] The Little Morass was fed by the Ham Brook which rose in Landport, and until the 17th century the Becke-Kynges stream ran from Lake Lane to Sea Mill Creek (the Mill Pond). This wet ground isolated Old Portsmouth's site and probably delayed early settlement there, though later the marshes usefully augmented the defensive walls and moats. The Little Morass was drained in 1823, removal of the noxious mud proceeding slowly amid 'pestiferous fumes'.[66] Nearby, Hollingsworth's elegant *Royal Clarence Promenade Rooms* were more in keeping with Southsea's developing role as a watering-place. The Great Morass was less easily disposed of. Its various branches reached out to touch what are now Castle Avenue and Palmerston, Marmion, Victoria and Albert Roads. In the 1786 Enclosure Act it was divided between eight proprietors, with permission to drain. Little was done, however, and in 1803 a windmill was advertised for sale on a fertile island where Clifton Terrace now stands. Imperfectly drained under further Acts of 1810 and 1817, the morass still stretched up to Albert Road in 1835.[67] In the previous year Charpentier's *Guide* had made the best of the situation by extolling the area's sporting attractions: 'Nor is Southsea void of amusement in the Winter Season, when snipe are to be found in abundance beyond Southsea Castle, and every species of wild fowl that arrives on the English coast, at the shores near Cumberland Fort, give scope for the sportsman's diversion'.[68] By 1870 the western part was built upon, and as Southsea spread, substantial villas and terraces covered the former marsh. Clarendon and Waverley Gardens were laid out on the damper patches, their origins revealed by occasional flooding in heavy rainfall, and in 1884-6 an unsavoury hollow at Craneswater was converted into the Canoe Lake.

The 1785 Enclosure Act resulted from the army's wish for more clear space around Southsea Castle, and military requirements fortunately prevented building on this extensive open space beside the sea. From 1831 convict labour was intermittently used over thirty years to level and clear it. In 1922 the council bought about a hundred acres from the War Department and spent years converting this 'miniature Sahara' of shingle into ornamental gardens, bowling greens and playing fields.[69] Along the southern shore a general easterly drift rolls shingle towards Eastney, and in the 19th century there was recurrent erosion. Land between Southsea Castle and Fort Cumberland was said in 1835 to be disappearing at the rate of three feet a year, but timber groynes and pocketing, reinforced by concrete defences near Southsea Castle and a long esplanade behind the beach, held the sea at bay.[70] In stormy weather, however, especially when south-east gales combined with spring tides, tons of shingle were thrown over the esplanade, and floods sometimes reached Marmion Road. Similar problems existed at Point, where in the 18th century ships' masters were prosecuted for taking shingle for ballast. Strong westerly winds drove the tide up Broad Street, where boats plied between the houses and where boards and sand-bags were necessary street-door defences well into the 20th century. In the 19th century the corporation had an expensive setback when they lost the Great Foreshore Case. For centuries the town had exercised rights of Admiralty over land between high and low water marks, but in 1877 the Admiralty disputed this in the High Court. Judgment given for the corporation was reversed in the House of Lords, and it was later discovered that the corporation had relinquished all rights of Admiralty 150 years earlier.[71]

In the mid-16th century a long narrow two-pronged creek ran in from the harbour between the town and the dock. By 1575 two water-mills were built here and granted to the millwright, Thomas Beeston, together with 'a parcel of land commonly overflowed with the sea' called the Mill Pond, and the free fishing and fowling upon it. Often called the sea-mills, these were acquired by the crown in 1714 and rebuilt in 1774 as the King's Mill, a tide-mill grinding grain for the Victualling Office. After the mill burnt down in 1868 the Mill Pond was gradually filled, its last malodorous remnants disappearing in 1876, to be eventually replaced by the United Services sports ground.[72] Much 19th-century reclamation was effected in the dockyard with spoil from the new docks, and Whale Island was similarly enlarged. In the harbour's upper reaches, Great and Little Horsea Islands covered about a hundred and fifty acres of marshy land providing good coarse grazing, connected to Portsea Island by wadeways across the mudflats, passable at low tides. In the 1870s, as torpedo warfare developed, the Admiralty bought Horsea and constructed a long torpedo range which joined the two islands.[73] In the north-west corner saltpans once occupied Tipnor Point, while Alexandra Park was created from Stamshaw Common.

A wide bank of marsh ran across the island's northern shore, matched by a similar strip on the mainland, and the corresponding area of alluvium shown on geological maps reflects their post-glacial estuarine origins. East of Portsbridge, Hilsea salt marsh spread over 236 acres in 1626, later covered by the northern part of the airport. Desmaretz noted in 1754 that much of this land was liable to flooding, although Port Creek was fordable at low tide.[74] For much of Portsmouth's history, however, the only permanent link between Portsea Island and the mainland was the bridge spanning Port Creek, doubtless already ancient in 1510 when John Meyston of Portsmouth bequeathed 6s. 8d. for its repair.[74] John Leland found (c.1540) a two-arched stone structure, and early in Charles I's reign it was still of simple design. Its strategic importance was apparent in the 1642 siege of Portsmouth, and thereafter it became incorporated in an increasingly-complex defensive system. Except for the fortifications and the rebuilt bridge, however, the creek had probably changed little since Leland, with an ever-observant eye for tidal waters, described the scene:

> The ground is made an isle by this meene: There brekith out an arme of the mayn haven about a 3 miles above Portesmuth, and goith up a 2 miles or more by marisch grounde to a place caullid Portebridge . . . And heere I markid one arme of salte water ebbing and flowing . . . And an other creke t[hens] from the mayne se to the same bridge. And these 2 crekes meting at the bridge make the Isle of Portesmuthe.[76]

The Round Tower.

Chapter Two

Country and Town

Portsea Island is now entirely contained within Portsmouth's boundary, which also encloses the neighbouring mainland districts of Wymering and Widley, Cosham, Drayton and parts of Farlington and Portchester. Most of these, and some places on Portsea Island, perpetuate the names of medieval manors existing long before Portsmouth was founded, none of them on the town's original site. The Domesday Survey of 1086 listed three pre-Conquest manors (Bocheland, Copenore and Frodintone), lying centrally on slightly higher ground, and Wimeringes and Coseham on the mainland. Portsmouth, occupying part of Old Portsmouth's present site, was founded by John de Gisors late in the 12th century, while Buckland's lands on the island's western side also came into the town's possession and were included within the borough liberty.[1] In the same century there was a royal manor at Farlington and a grange at Stubbington. By the 13th and 14th centuries there is documentary evidence for manors at Stamshaw, Hilsea and Little Gatcombe towards the north of Portsea Island, Milton and Eastney in the south-east corner, and Paulsgove, Widley and Drayton on the mainland. Late in the 14th century the manor or lordship of Portsea comprised the manors of Copnor and Fratton, lands at Hilsea and Kingston, and rights over the southern and eastern shores.

Farming and trading were well established when, late in the 12th century, a ship-repair site was made in a creek north of the town on the site of the later gunwharf, but this fell into ruin within thirty years. After long medieval neglect Portsmouth was chosen for England's first dry dock, constructed in 1495-6 farther up the harbour. A chart of *c.*1600 shows the dock and its storehouses within a walled enclosure of about ten acres: our first sight of the nascent Royal Dockyard which was to influence the town's development so profoundly. That dock too was neglected while the Thames yards were built, and in 1623 was filled in.[2] Meanwhile Portsmouth grew slowly within its walls though Point was completely built up by the end of the 17th century, when a new town (eventually called Portsea) was developing on the common north of Portsmouth to house workers around the now fast-expanding dockyard. As population increased there began the inexorable spread of suburban housing that still continues. Landport, once called the Halfway Houses and subsequently named after Portsmouth's nearest gate, was in the late 18th century a refuge from the two overcrowded towns and later, like parts of Kingston and Fratton, a festering slum. As the municipal centre of gravity shifted north-eastwards away from hampering military restrictions, Landport housed the railway station in 1847, the new Town Hall by 1890, and shops and offices along busy Commercial Road. Southsea was a mixed area, originating with Regency terraces and artisan Croxton town *c.*1805-27, and spreading eastwards from Portsmouth along the southern shore. Elegant terraces and spacious detached houses in leafy winding roads accommodated two itinerant groups: service officers needing stylish temporary quarters, and seasonal holiday-makers in tall boarding houses. In the 1840s these four places were still separate entities, and by the 1890s, though physically connected, this was still true:

> Portsea Island is divided up into districts, each of which has a special character of its own. In the old naval phraseology Chatham and Rochester were 'the two towns'; Plymouth, Devonport and Stonehouse were 'the three towns'; while Portsea, Portsmouth, Landport and Southsea were known as 'the four towns'.[3]

The tightly packed south-western corner housed a major fortified military and naval base containing Hampshire's nearest equivalent to an industrial town, while most of Portsea Island was still agricultural, with scattered houses and hamlets. Strip cultivation (increasingly of market-garden produce) in open fields persisted into the 19th century in the west and north of the island; elsewhere fields were mostly enclosed.

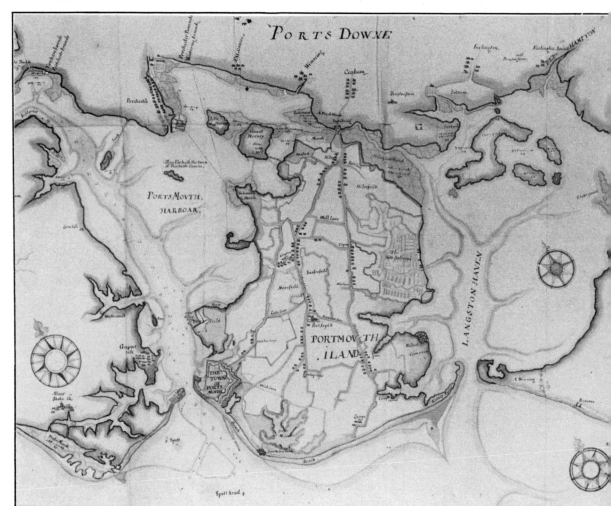

3. Portsea Island, 1678.

A 1678 map showed the London road leading south through Cosham over Portsbridge, separating at Hilsea into the three branches later named Commercial, Fratton and Copnor Roads. The western route, later a turnpike, led past 'Cole Harbour' to the Landport Gate at Portsmouth. The central route forked again south of St Mary's church into three tracks ending in the morasses. The eastern track, Velder Lane, ran through Copnor and Milton to the beach at Lumps, with a spur along Priory Crescent and Hill Lane (Winter Road).[4] In the 19th century, ribbon development along Commercial and Fratton Roads gradually connected Portsmouth and Portsea to Landport and Stamshaw, and amalgamated Fratton, Kingston, Buckland and Stubbington into a continuous strip of houses and shops. Since expansion was eastward and northward, Eastney, Milton, Copnor and Hilsea villages remained strung out along Copnor Road, widely separated by their fields, until the building tide reached them by the 20th century. From then until 1939 relentlessly uniform streets of small terraced and semi-detached houses filled the gaps between older settlements, except for a wide strip of saltmarsh and reclaimed mudlands bordering Langstone Harbour. In the 1920s and 1930s moves to the mainland resulted from municipal housing schemes at Wymering and private residential development around Cosham, while more public and private transport encouraged longer daily journeys between city-centre workplaces and ever more distant hinterland homes.

The town's expansion was formally marked by successive boundary changes. On 7 June 1566 the mayor and townsfolk perambulated the bounds of the borough and its liberty, following a circuit unaltered for 300 years. Starting at the Town Quay they went north past Chilmer Pool to Catcliffe by the Dock, and along the shore via Fountain Well to Whale Island and Tipner. Turning east to Hoxford Gate, then south to Stubbington House, they followed the eastern boundary of Beeston Field to Deadman's Lane and then back westwards and northwards to the top of Lake Lane. Zigzagging down the eastern sides of Meteland, Mere and Havencroft fields to Hambrook and the seashore, they returned to the Quay via the Platform, Round Tower and Point. The 18th-century trip included dizzying triple circuits around the main boundary marks together with much athletic climbing over sea walls and in and out of ditches. Not surprisingly the practice lapsed, to be revived by Sir John Carter, robed and on horseback, in 1807.[5] Perambulated or not, however, the borough limits remained unaltered until 1832, and it was over Buckland's open fields within this boundary that almost all Portsmouth's pre-1850 urban expansion occurred. The boundary subdivided another significant area, the ancient parish of Portsea, centred on the mother church of St Mary. This encompassed the whole island except for St Thomas's parish (c.252 acres, consisting mainly of Old Portsmouth with two detached portions in Landport); extra-parochial Great Salterns (334 acres, the 17th-century Gatcombe Haven reclamation); and that part of Wymering parish (including Hilsea) occupying 1,169 acres across the island's northern end. Everything west of the borough boundary outside St Thomas's parish was the liberty part of Portsea parish (1,278 acres); the rest was the guildable part, 3,103 acres of agricultural land with scattered hamlets and farms, relatively thinly populated throughout the 19th century.[6] The borough boundary was extended by parliamentary reform in 1832 to include the guildable; in 1895 to enclose Great Salterns; in 1904 to coincide on the north with Port Creek; in 1920 to include Cosham, Wymering and Widley; and in 1932 to encompass parts of Portchester to the north-west and Farlington and Drayton to the north-east.[7]

Until the 17th century, however, Portsmouth's population growth was rather slow, and Portsea Island communities tended to be smaller and poorer than many neighbouring settlements. The three pre-Conquest manors had a total listed population of 15 villeins, eight bordars and eight serfs, a total value of £8, and no desirable appurtenances beyond the low-value saltern at Copnor. Hayling Island, by contrast, had a recorded population of 83, also in three manors, with a total value of £20, a saltern worth ten times Copnor's, and meadows, fisheries and woodland for 21 hogs. Powerful royal and ecclesiastical overlords and South Hayling's more fertile soil probably accounted for the difference. Of the two mainland manors that ultimately became part of Portsmouth, Cosham's listed population was 25 and Wymering's (a royal manor) forty-nine. Fareham and Alverstoke each supported more people than the three Portsea Island manors put together, while Tichfield Hundred's settlements along the Meon were far more prosperous and versatile.[8]

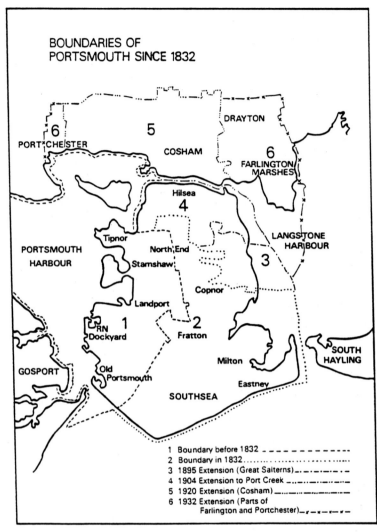

4. Boundaries of Portsmouth since 1832.

Drier gravel sites, fertile soils, neighbouring forests and chalk downland, better water supplies and easier travel along small rivers probably all helped to draw pre-Conquest settlers away from Portsea Island. When these settlements were founded is uncertain, but by 1086 some six hundred years had passed since Anglo-Saxons and Jutes began to colonise south Hampshire. Some of them (Coppa, Frod(a), Wigmaer) are perpetuated in the place-names (Copnor, Fratton, Wymering). Whether this applies to Portsmouth is doubtful, for the entry in the Anglo-Saxon Chronicle that in 501 'Port and his two sons Bieda and Maegla came to Britain with two ships in the place called Portes Mutha'[9] may not refer to Old Portsmouth's site.

The evolution of the Domesday and other manors can be traced intermittently in the relatively scanty surviving medieval sources relating to Portsea Island. One major long-term effect of medieval land-holding upon the pattern of Portsmouth's urban spread, however, is clearly visible in 19th-century maps: the contrast between crowded building on Buckland's open-field strips within the borough boundary and the later and more spacious development on the Portsea and Wymering manorial lands to the east and north. Buckland's lands included Beeston and Meteland Fields (possibly the earliest), the little Balches Croft, Pitcroft, Ropkyns and Smaldron Fields around Kingston Crescent, with Havencroft, Mere, Fountain and West Dock Fields encircling Portsmouth town. The fields illustrate Portsea Islanders' confusing habit of giving several names successively or simultaneously to the same place. Fountain (Fonturne) furlong appears in 13th-century documents and gave its name to the field lying around the prolific springs near the harbour shore. When the 15th-century dock was built, the neighbouring cultivated lands once called Westwode and later covered by Portsea town became West Dock Field, and Fountain Field, stretching north to Rudmore, became East Dock Field by the 16th century. Recurrent 17th-century plague led to the building of a pesthouse there, providing another name, and although Fountain reverted to a furlong name, Pesthouse and East Dock were used impartially until the field disappeared. To the north the little Ropkyns Field of 1469 metamorphosed into Rudmore by the 19th century. Meteland became Cherry Garden Field, and Mere (Moor, Mury) became Town Field.[10] A copy of a 15th-century rent roll of Portsmouth liberty lists over fifty landholders with properties in the town and most of the surrounding fields.[11] More informative is Richard Palshid's survey (c.1531) showing that Portsmouth's lands totalled some 864 acres, field sizes being approximately: West Dock, 105 acres; East Dock, 193; Mere, 159; Meteland, 131; and Beeston, 221 acres. Milcroft (18 acres), Ropkins Close (8), Hethfield (4) and other small parcels were probably marginal land, cleared and drained as the population grew. The larger fields were subject to common crop rotations and grazing rights, while the landholders included the Domus Dei's Guardians, the Prior of Southwick, the Vicar of Portsmouth, Thomas Carpenter of Stubbington Grange, and many townsfolk like William Byckley and Thomas Stubber.[12]

Unlike other Portsea Island manorial lands, which followed Hampshire mainland's pattern of piecemeal enclosure by agreement, substantially complete by the 18th century, Portsmouth's fields were similar to neighbouring coastal lands at Wymering, Portchester and Thorney in retaining strip cultivation into the 19th century, succumbing gradually to encroaching fortifications, housing and market gardens. In 1671-2 the crown bought some 56 acres of land 'spoyled by making new Fortifications about the Towne of Portsmouth'; and in the early 18th century it acquired property valued at £60 in West Dock Field; £2,110 in East Dock Field; £300 near the town gates; and £4,000 for Dixon's brewhouse in Pexall Ground.[13] The suburb of Portsea and its fortifications covered West and part of East Dock Fields during the 18th century, but although ribbon development was eating into the margins, other fields were substantially untouched when Winchester College commissioned new plans of Pesthouse, Cherry Garden, Town, Beeston and Pitcroft in 1792-3.[14] The Ridge family were the largest landholders in these five fields, followed by Lord Powerscourt, Winchester College and Thomas Fitzherbert of Stubbington, though the College was shedding much of its open field holdings by sale or exchange.

In the early 19th century, urban, barrack and fleet demand for vegetables, together with post-war depression, led to much market gardening. Even by 1813 under three-field husbandry the fallow field was increasingly cultivated with catch crops of greens, taken up in time to prepare the ground for seed. The assumption that this was impracticable was commonly used as an argument for enclosure: its adoption and profitability probably encouraged the retention of open fields within the borough liberty.[15] By 1838, as building increasingly disrupted common cultivation, many remaining strips on Pesthouse, Cherry

Garden and Town Fields became semi-permanent market gardens with higher rents: 40s. to 80s. an acre compared with 18s. to 24s. for open-field arable. Wrangling between the impropriator (Winchester College) and the Vicar of St Mary's over the share-out of the resultant higher tithes delayed collection under the 1838 apportionment until 1847. The practice continued well into the 19th century, and these three fields passed directly from garden and arable strips to narrow crowded streets with no intervening enclosure. Owen's 1838 tithe map shows new roads perpetuating the medieval furlong pattern (particularly evident in Cherry Garden Field), and the sale of Lord Powerscourt's open field holdings in 1849 accelerated this process.[16] Beeston and Pitcroft Fields were enclosed in 1822; buildings were creeping over them in the 1880s and by 1898 they were largely covered, except for Winchester College's share in the north-east corner.[17]

Considerable confusion has always surrounded the relationship of Copnor and Fratton manors to the manor of Portsea, which is not listed in Domesday but from which the 12th-century de Portsea family took their name. Copnor's post-Conquest overlord was Robert, son of Gerold, whose tenant Heldred also held Buckland from Hugh de Port. Nothing further is known of Copnor's descent until the 13th century, when Andrew de Portsea held both Copnor and Portsea manors which thenceforth had the same lords, including Titchfield Abbey, 1373-1537; the Wriothesleys, Earls of Southampton, 1537-98; the Bolds, Masons and Moodys in the 17th and 18th centuries; and the Leekes until the 20th century. From the Conquest until the 13th century Fratton manor's overlords were the Earls de Warenne, one of whose tenants, Hugh de Plaiz, granted half a knight's fee in Fratton to the Domus Dei. Another half a knight's fee was held by Roger de Merlay of Herbert, son of Matthew, who also held Milton and Eastney manors from King John. By 1242 Andrew de Portsea held one knight's fee in Fratton, the Domus Dei's 14th-century Fratton holding also being one fee. In 1540 the hospital's lands were surrendered to the crown. Fratton manor was granted in 1610 to Henry, Prince of Wales, and in 1622 to Robert Bold, Lord of the Manors of Portsea and Copnor, the overlordship of the three manors never again being separated.[18]

The greater antiquity of Copnor and Fratton, and the apparent absence of any substantial area identifiable as Portsea manor suggested that the latter was either once identical with Buckland, or possibly part of Fratton. There were various indications of its greater significance, however. In the early 12th century the de Portsea family controlled a large part of Portsea Island, and Baldwin de Portsea endowed the mother church of St Mary c.1164. Portsea and Copnor had a common court baron, and manorial records also referred to lands in Fratton, Hilsea and Kingston.[19] Norden's 1617 survey of Fratton explained that 'The boundes of this manor can not be sett downe for that it lyeth intermixte with the Manor of Porteseye'.[20] The apparent (and hitherto unpublished) solution to the problem was obtained in 1857 by the Leekes' solicitors, Longcrofts, who satisfied the Committee for Trade of the Lords of Portsea's title to unclaimed wreck washed ashore within the limits of the manors of Portsea, Copnor, Fratton and Milton, from the western end of Southsea Common to the Great Salterns sluice. Longcrofts' search of 14th-century rentals showed that Frodington's manorial lands in Broomclose, Murefield and Merefield, Churchfield and Hambrook; Copnor's manorial lands at Goslingscroft, Conyger Heath, Burfield, Westfield and Meremead; Hilsea lands formerly held by the Domus Dei *prope le Green Post*; and lands at Kingston and Portsmouth were all within, and held of, the Lordship of Portsea. The Lord of Portsea also owned the commons of Frodington, Goldestedde and Conyger Heaths; right of free warren within the lordship; and fishery rights at Milton, Burfield, Milersdefleete and Midomstonores fleets in and around Gatcombe Haven. Charles I's 1642 grant to Alchorne of land at Great Salterns had seized Conyger Heath, Goldestedde and Burfield fleet from the lordship, and the ancient landing place there had been damaged. At the 1622 division of Fratton manor its demesne included 40 acres in Broome Closes on the island's eastern side, and 190 acres in the common fields of Portsea. Significantly, Portsea manor's demesne lands in 1640 comprised a mansion house and about a hundred and eighty acres lying on both sides of Deadman's Lane, including Church Farm, also the Broome Closes and Conyger pasture extending to Langstone Harbour. Other closes included Great Domers, Merks and Hop Gardens, lying in Fratton, Copnor and Milton.[21] The demesne's central position next to the church endowed by Baldwin of Portsea, Fratton and Copnor's status as manors held of the Lord of Portsea, and the extent of the lordship's lands all suggest that this was not a minor holding but the island's principal manor.

Enquiries among solicitors and local inhabitants identified unfamiliar place-names in the 1393 description of the boundary ascribed by Longcrofts to the Lordship of Portsea. According to their interpretation it began at the shingle bank running eastward into Langstone Harbour at the south end of Goldestedde (the deep-water channel in Gatcombe Haven where the Domus Dei's tenants landed coal and gravel), then ran northwards through the water to the south-east corner of South Breach, along the northern boundary of Great Salterns, and via Gatcombe to Langstreete (the London road at the Green Post). Turning south, it followed the ditches bordering 'Tenthenoup' to 'Schildewell' (at North End) and Westfield, continuing westwards along the Beckynge ditch (the stream running from Lake Road to the Mill Pond), and thence to Hambrook. Following this watercourse to the sea near the Little Morass, it returned eastwards along the shore to Goldestedde. The south-east portion of this boundary and some perquisites in Langstone Harbour were shared with Milton and Eastney manor (formerly attached to Warblington), and in 1852 the Leekes bought this lordship and its remaining rights.[22] If this interpretation is correct, the boundary coincides with that of the guildable part of Portsea parish, and adjoins the borough liberty. Longcrofts' chief purpose, however, was to prove entitlement to wreck, and although the coastal boundaries were established, the landward bounds may follow another line. Further work on Portsea manorial records may eventually resolve this uncertainty.

The third focal point of medieval landholding, religion and population was Wymering, containing Cosham and Hilsea, the parish (c.3,079 acres) spanning Port Creek and uniting Portsea Island with the mainland. Wymering, a royal manor in 1086, was subsequently held by many owners (including the Albemarles, Brunings and Uvedales) as a unit or in portions, until Thomas Thistlethwayte bought the whole manor in 1821. Cosham, part of Domesday Wymering, became separated until the Brunings held it in the 17th century, and thereafter followed the same descent. Land in East Cosham granted to Tichfield Abbey passed to Henry Wriothesley in 1607 and was bought by the Thistlethwaytes in 1821. Hilsea was probably part of Wymering manor until 1730, passing by sale to William Padwick and then returning to Wymering under the Thistlethwaytes in the 19th century.[23] Despite some early enclosure, Wymering retained much open-field cultivation until about eight hundred acres of arable, waste and marsh were enclosed in 1812.[24] The strategic importance of Portsbridge, carrying the only road to the mainland, led to successive strengthening of its fortifications, involving substantial government land purchases. In 1758 roughly ninety-six acres of Hilsea Common's 204 acres were taken, to the fury of those with pasture rights. In 1814 the government paid £128,225 for land at Hilsea, though work on the Lines was delayed. Wymering's tithe apportionment (1839) showed the Board of Ordnance owning around seven hundred and forty acres, exceeded only by Thomas Thistlethwayte with about eight hundred and seventy-nine.[25]

We do not know whether a community already existed there when John de Gisors granted, c.1180, land called Sudewede to the Southwick canons for a chapel dedicted to Thomas of Canterbury. If so, they would have found it convenient, for St Mary's, endowed c.1164, was two miles distant near the pre-Domesday manors. If not, it grew fast: before 1194 de Gisors referred to 'my town of Portsmouth' when granting the canons the tithe of his water-mill 'next the arm of the sea' to the north.[26] Rebellion against Richard I cost de Gisors Portsmouth, Buckland and Titchfield, and although escheats to the crown were usually sold the king 'retained in our hand our Burgh of Portsmouth' and built a royal residence at Kingshall Green, east of St Nicholas Street. Richard I's 1194 charter, granting a Thursday market, annual fair, exemptions from tolls and other privileges, encouraged trade and further settlers. In 1198 and 1229 Kingston (formerly Buckland) was described as 'a member of our town of Portsmouth', marking the town's increasing predominance over the earlier manor. Acquisition of a gild merchant in 1256, development of harbour jurisdiction, successive confirmations of its charters, appointment and election of civic officers and members of parliament consolidated Portsmouth's position.[27] A 13th-century bishop of Winchester founded the Domus Dei, a combined hospital, poor-house and travellers' rest, and the chancels of its chapel and St Thomas's are the town's only two surviving medieval buildings, for Portsmouth paid a heavy price for equipping armies against France. Inadequately fortified, it was repeatedly burnt in French raids from 1338 onwards, and remained relatively depressed into the 16th century.[28] The town's medieval topography thus remains obscure apart from the location of religious buildings; Quarr Abbey's High Street cellar; and a large water-cistern, stores, dock and quay along Oyster Street's Camber waterfront.[29] A 1469 rent roll of Portsmouth liberty lists some seventy tenements and 11 crofts, many outside the town, together with 28 vacant places and pieces of land, probably within the walls. There were houses in St Thomas's and Penny Streets, in 'Hoggeseres Lane', near the High Hall, and in the market place, with four shops in the Butchery.[30]

Tudor monarchs used Portsmouth as a victualling base, starting c.1492 with a brewery (possibly the *Greyhound* in High Street), augmented during Henry VIII's French wars with the Four Houses (1512-13), and the Anker bakehouse (1513) in St Thomas's Street. High temperatures in 1513 threatened to spoil the beer, buried in thatched trenches until the Camber quay storehouses were built in 1514. The Cowdray painting (1545) shows men shifting casks from store to ships, the crane wharf near 'the stoore broomhowses', and the Swanne bakehouse (1544) just inside Point Gate.[31] The walls protected the victualling base rather than the town, and the earliest extant Portsmouth map (1545) shows improved fortifications and the town in ground-plan: the first of many surveys making Portsmouth 'one of the best mapped towns of its size anywhere in the world'. The familiar grid street plan, hardly altered today, shows that only the lower High Street had houses continuously on both sides. St Thomas's and Penny Streets were sparsely inhabited, though buildings lined the eastern Camber shore, with a cluster inside Point Gate.[32] Leland's description was clearly accurate: 'There is much vacant ground within the toun waulle. There is one fair streate in the toun from west to north este'.[33] Edward VI wrote in 1552 that 'within the walls are faire and large closis and much vacant rome'.[34]

Tudor Portsmouth did not expand. Spain replaced France as the major threat, the Netherlands attracted the crown's attention more than Normandy, and Portsmouth dockyard was neglected for the Thames yards. Richard Popinjay's map (c.1584) shows little development after forty years, and two significant losses: areas marked 'burned' record the destruction in 1557 of the quayside victualling stores and cooperage, and in 1576 of the King Street storehouses containing burgesses' goods valued at £2,200. Although Elizabeth permitted a national appeal for compensation, there was little response.[35] Despite these losses and the smallness of the town, which in 1565 probably contained only 85 households, some merchant burgesses were prosperous. Popinjay's map labels the buildings with their owners' or occupiers' names, showing the Byckleys, townsfolk since the 15th century, holding 17 houses and Camber stores. Henry Byckley, dying in 1570 on his Chidham estate, a wealthy man, was mayor three times and M.P. for Portsmouth in 1553. The Town House in the centre of High Street round which the Thursday market was held had recently been provided by 'one

Carpenter, a riche man', probably Thomas Carpenter, the lessee of Stubbington Grange. About one hundred and thirty buildings appear on Popinjay's map, as well as God's House, secularised after the Dissolution and now the governor's headquarters. Popinjay was Surveyor of the Works, planning the new defences, and his map is probably accurate: nothing in the contemporary grants of town lands suggests significantly greater domestic building activity.[36]

During the 17th century Portsea Island's population increased significantly. Buckingham's expeditions, Charles I's ship-money fleets, Interregnum and Restoration sea warfare against the Netherlands and the post-1688 French struggle made Portsmouth an operational base, provisioning and maintaining fleets. Periodic sales of prizes and surplus stores stimulated trade, and shipbuilding and repair expanded the Dockyard workforce. Attempts to quantify the early-modern growth of Portsmouth meet various obstacles, including incomplete 1525 lay subsidy returns and the absence of parish registers before 1654. Partial counts of houses and people for ecclesiastical and fiscal purposes give some indictions of pre-census size, though so many uncertainties are involved that these calculations should be regarded with caution, often only as a starting point for discussion.

The 1603 survey of Anglican communicants provides (if all the incumbents followed the same procedure) a count of adults aged about sixteen and above in the parishes, and illustrates Portsmouth's comparatively small size among the communities in the Winchester Archdeaconry. Portsmouth (469) and Portsea (305 with two recusants and nine other non-communicants) had together less than half the numbers in the six town parishes of Southampton (totalling 2,138). The extensive rural parishes of Titchfield (823) and East Meon (1,031) were much larger than Portsmouth town, with Havant (451) and Hambledon (467) about the same size.[37]

The 1665 Portsmouth Hearth Tax return lists 651 units with a total of 2,558 charged hearths and 115 with 'Hearths not chargeable'.[38] Strangely, the 1674 return also lists 651 taxable units: 453 in Portsmouth, 140 on Point, 10 at the Dock and 48 certified exempt with no location specified. The Portsmouth total comprises High Street, 232; Oyster/St Thomas's Street, 81; St Mary's Street, 65; Warblington Street, 48; Hogmarket Street, 23; Lombard Street, four. The apparent omission of Penny and St Nicholas Streets, occupied in the 16th century, is puzzling. Land grants, 1640-1700, record vacant plots being taken and de Gomme's map of about 1678 shows many houses in this north-eastern sector. Peter Christie's calculations from these figures are suspect on several grounds. Even if any of these returns could be trusted, including 115 buildings with 'hearths not chargeable' from the 1665 return when calculating the overall 1674 total probably leads to double counting.[39] Normal nine-year mobility, high plague mortality in 1666, and a total of 175-250 burials annually in St Thomas's parish in the early 1670s[40] would make some non-paying 1665 units identical with tax-paying or discharged 1674 units. Christie uses Laslett's 4.75 mean household size multiplier on the combined 1665 and 1674 figures to give an estimated population of 3,679. The lower multiplier of 4.3, now thought more appropriate, applied to the 1665 total (766) gives three thousand, two hundred and ninety-four.

Christie's conclusion that 'Portsmouth townspeople were evidently richer on average than town-dwellers elsewhere at this period' is also suspect, being based on a calculated average of 3.45 hearths per Portsmouth household compared with 2.6 for Exeter and 3.0 for Bury St Edmunds. These towns retained many medieval dwellings, while Portsmouth's 14th century destruction and late development led to house construction here when building materials and style commonly resulted in more fireplaces per house. Moreover, much of Portsmouth's economy was founded on providing temporary shelter and alcohol for large periodic influxes of transients, and in this specialised environment multi-hearth units were not necessarily permanently occupied by large households or more than intermittently

the Marish.

ʒ Canber.

ʒ Mill pond.

5. Portsmouth town, *c.*1678.

prosperous. High Street's 23-hearth inn and many six-hearth taverns, and Broad Street's 8-11 hearth beersellers exemplify this feature. Not until 1724, after more wartime overcrowding and heavy drinking, did Defoe comment that the presence of the fleet and many merchant-men 'has really made the whole place rich, and the inhabitants of Portsmouth are quite another sort of people than they were a few years before the Revolution'.[41] The 1676 Compton Census lists 2,652 communicants at St Thomas's and 132 (less than half the 1603 figure) in Portsea parish, giving estimated populations of 4,270 and 220 respectively, using a multiplier of 5/3 to convert adults to total population. The peculiar nature of Portsmouth often resulted in the presence of many adult males without their families, so that any generally applied multiplier may overestimate the population. If these figures seem a trifle high, the 1725 visitation return of about eight thousand 'souls' in Portsmouth parish is incredible, especially compared with the 1801 census enumeration of 7,839, following 76 more years of war and population growth with houses packed into every available space.[42]

Point, almost empty in the 16th century, was largely built up by the 1670s. In the 1590s waste ground was granted for merchants' and military storehouses. Early 17th-century tenements were built on substantial plots by a cordwainer, sailor, gunner and shipwright, while by 1610 four inns appeared along Broad Street. Fishermen and seamen increasingly inhabited the peninsula around Smock Alley, and grants of beach ground marked the colonisation of the southern shoreline.[43] In 1674 Point had 140 hearth-tax paying units averaging 3.5 hearths per household, though even less than in Portsmouth town did this imply wealth. The earliest surviving Poor Rate Book (1730) lists 159 rateable properties on Point, many probably storehouses. Of these 81 were assessed at 6d. (the lowest level), 50 at 1s., while the highest valuation was 4s., only five being assessed at 2s. 6d. or more.[44] Some prime sites housed prosperous businesses. A wharf and storehouses at the Camber entrance were built and occupied (1656-77) by Nicholas Peirson, shipowner and timber merchant, and were subsequently used to store weapons and ammunition from decommissioned ships. Andrew Lindegren, Swedish iron-ore merchant, thrived there as Navy prize agent and East India Company representative during the French wars, auctioning at the neighbouring *Star and Garter* cargoes of wrecked and captured vessels, and was succeeded by his son, vice-consul for Sweden, Denmark, Norway and Brazil. From 1885-1960 the property housed the offices of ferry and steam packet companies.[45] Many houses in Broad Street were originally built on plots running through to Bath Square, with stores and workshops behind, many now rebuilt as fashionable dwellings.[46] This stable shingle bank provided good foundations, and although the sea rose easily into cellars, and at times of spring tides and low pressure overflowed over ground floors, the shingle was quick-draining and seawater preserved timbers from dry rot. As population increased, many houses were extended on piles over the beaches of Point and Dirty Corner. Quebec House, sole survivor of many weather-boarded houses, was built in 1754 as a seawater bathing house in Bath Square. The forecourt of the 18th-century *Still* nearby, licensed to open at 4 a.m., housed the former High Street fish market.

Described in 1729 as 'the Wapping of Portsmouth' and likened to Gomorrah, Point had numerous drinking-houses (41 in 1716 and 53 by 1784), open day and night and catering for lower ranks at ground level and officers upstairs.[47] Separated from the town by the guarded King James's Gate and a moat across Broad Street, it was an ideal area for containing roistering sailors, easily brought from Spithead in liberty boats to the common sally port. Pressed men, few of whom could swim, could not easily desert from Spice Island, where most of their needs were met: 'Liquor-shops, contract taverns; Jew slopmen, taylors, and drapers; jostle Christian pawnbrokers, watch jobbers, and trinket merchants, cook shops, eating houses, and ordinaries, vie with each other to entertain all classes . . .'[48] As steam replaced sail more ships anchored inside the harbour and Portsea increasingly became the Navy's recreation area. With boat-builders, sail-makers, marine engineers, shipping offices, coal and ballast merchants and fish markets, however, Point remained a working sea-going community well into the 20th century.

In Portsmouth, the 1730 Poor Rate Book listed 435 rateable properties. Some, especially around the Camber, were stores, workshops and stables, and how many households were omitted we do not know. Many were taverns: in 1715 there were 51 inns, brandy-shops and coffee-houses in the town, over half in High Street.[49] Three of the largest Portsmouth breweries (Deacon's, Pike's and the later Brickwood's) were in Penny Street, flourishing on naval contracts and tied houses.[50] Robert Wilkins' satirical account of *The Borough* (1748) depicts a community of small shopkeepers living comfortably by buying each others' wares, over-charging strangers, and profiting handsomely from smuggling. Commenting on the lack of propertied men, he defines the town's élite:

> A rich Burgher is one, who has met with so much Success in the World, as to be able to purchase the House he lives in, and if, by a further Improvement of his Stock, he is afterwards in a Condition to buy a Publick House (which is always both Tavern and Ale-House) and supply it with his own Merchandise, we then esteem him a very great Man.[51]

The new town hall, still in the middle of High Street, built in 1738 to replace its 'old and ruinous' predecessor, was flanked by the butchers' shambles (removed as a nuisance in 1827) and the fish market. Demolished as a traffic obstruction in the 1830s it was succeded by another next to the *Dolphin*. Contemporary prints show an elegant steet, and Charpentier's 1842 panorama can be used with directories and census returns to reconstruct the town centre.[52]

The 1841 census enumerated 9,354 people in Portsmouth parish, with 1,094 inhabited houses within the fortifications, housing 6,586 people, and 80 inhabited houses outside the walls, housing 410. Institutions (barracks, hospitals, workhouse and gaol) contained another 1,962 males and 396 females. Two houses were under construction and 95 uninhabited. There were 10 unoccupied houses in High Street, one being built, and 149 inhabited by 978 people. Of these 28 per cent were children and young people under twenty, not apprenticed or employed; 24 per cent servants (overwhelmingly female); and 19 per cent people aged 20 and over with no listed occupations (mostly housewives and spinsters). Independent and professional people and service officers totalled nine per cent; craftsmen and retailers 16 per cent; hotel keepers, victuallers and those engaged in transport two per cent; the remaining two per cent being clerks, officials, teachers and other service ranks. Ten years later the High Street population was 940 out of 10,329 in Portsmouth town, the occupational proportions having altered little. High Street's low, gabled dwellings had been replaced by substantial three- and four-storeyed houses; fewer than thirty survived wartime bombing, among them Nos. 12, 13, 60 and 132, inhabited in 1851 by prosperous professional men with four to five children and three to five servants. The *George*, *Dolphin*, *Fountain* and *Wellington* each housed between five and 17 family and staff, but only 12 visitors between them, mostly commercial travellers at the *Fountain*. The upper end consisted mainly of private houses; banks, official residences, tailors and jewellers predominated in the centre, with builders and beersellers nearer the sea. At No. 64 lived Vincent Pappalardo, consul for Brazil, Spain, Sardinia, the Two Sicilies, Uruguay, Parma and the U.S.A.[53] Guidebooks claimed that the 'very handsome street' was 'adorned with many excellent shops: indeed its general appearance may rank it among the finest streets out of London'.[54] Thomas Roscoe, visiting *c*.1840, gave apparently independent confirmation, but actually transcribed the local guides.[55] A more critical visitor in 1847 thought Portsmouth and Portsea 'anything but beautiful', enumerating the chief buildings and concluding 'if they are equal in merit to the average of provincial towns, it is as much as we can say for them'.[56] Sir Frederic Madden, former resident, was similarly unimpressed in 1866: 'The street leading from Point looked more miserable than ever . . . The Parade and High Street seemed deserted . . .'.[57] Portsmouth's population peaked in 1871 at 11,569, but many prosperous citizens and service officers had moved to more spacious surroundings. By the 1880s the administrative and commercial centre had moved north to Landport, Portsmouth continuing as a religious, legal and educational centre, acquiring the Royal Naval Club, and retaining the garrison headquarters.

Further development around the old town was impossible since civilian building was forbidden near the fortifications, which were bordered by the Little Morass and the Mill Pond. Portsmouth's next suburb, therefore, developed on the common waste and open field to the north between the town and the Dock. A survey of 1697 maps the first houses already constructed in St George's Square, Butcher and Kent Streets, describing them as 'the Workmen's houses belonging to his Majesty's yard and is their freehold, permitted to be built by the Lieutenant Governor and his predecessors'. A 'publick house' was strategically sited beside the Mill Gate. East of the Yard, extending to Jenen's Marsh on the harbour shore, was 'the most properest land to build houses on, and sufficient for all the workmen which belong to the Yard'.[58] This included the site of the New Buildings, surprisingly near the outworks, and some of these were erected while a prolonged debate rumbled on about the relative claims of housing, future dockyard extension and strengthened defences. Thefts from the yard led in 1700 to closure of the north-east gate, and by 1705 these artisan dwellings provided concealment for 'embezzled' materials passed out through holes in de Gomme's decayed timber palisade.[59] Some, often misleading, indications of the Common's 18th-century development appear in the poor rate books which in 1700, in addition to the 13 senior officers' houses in the dockyard, show 16 rateable properties in the New Buildings and 36 on the Common, of which some were fields. In 1704, 24 properties were listed at Pudshole, and in 1708 there were buildings in Havant, Union, Bishop, Wickham and Queen Streets, along the Hard, and in North and Prince George Streets. During the early 1720s parts of Chapel, Hanover and White's Rows appeared, and in 1725 about four hundred properties were listed on the Common outside the dockyard.[60] Early taxation lists, however, are notorious traps for the unwary, and attempts to quantify Portsea's development by poor rate records kept by a vestry have produced some extraordinary figures.[61] The vestry alone knew (perhaps) which properties were excluded and why: charges of improper exemptions were levelled at the Portsea vestry (controlled by dockyard men until the post-Napoleonic war slump), and the satirical rate book published by Portsea tradesmen in 1817 highlights the problem.[62] Disappearance and reappearance of temporarily poor or favoured inhabitants, inconsistent recording (e.g. of the Temple brewery and many other businesses with work-shops as one property or several rateable parts), inclusion of land as well as houses, confusing nomenclature and boundaries and simple human error produce wild annual fluctuations.[63] Nor can a crude count of entries be used to compare Portsea's development with that of the rest of Portsea parish, since many of the latter assessments were not on buildings but on land, again listed in variable ways.

Writing c.1724, Defoe noted that 'a kind of suburb, or rather a new town has been built on the healthy ground adjoining the town, which is so well built, and seems to encrease so fast, that in time it threatens to outdo for numbers of inhabitants, and beauty of buildings, even the town itself . . .'.[64] Christopher Chalklin has traced this development, showing that the new town's layout was largely determined by the alignment of furlongs in West Dock Field. Landowners sold strips piecemeal to local tradesmen and craftsmen, who staked out a narrow roadway along the strip, dividing the rest into building plots. Streets were often initially built on one side only and known as 'Rows', completed later by similar development of an adjoining strip. Houses were mostly built in ones and twos by dockyard workers and building craftsmen acting singly or in small groups. Relatively low amounts of capital

(£300-400) were involved, local solicitors and businessmen often providing mortgages. The haphazard sequence of street-building depended on the willingness of landowners to sell, and inhabited areas were interspersed with arable strips, market gardens, ropewalks and deep gravel pits.[65] In this utilitarian development there were few early communal buildings except (predictably) public houses, already numbering 36 in 1715-16, apparently one in eight of the listed rateable properties, with 11 inns and brandy shops along Ship and Castle Row (later The Hard).[66] During the 1745 rebellion, fearing demolition of their homes to protect the dockyard, the Common's inhabitants claimed that it was 'a large and populous Town, containing One Thousand Houses, Ten Thousand Inhabitants and above Two thousand able Bodied Men well affected to his Majesty'. These suspiciously round figures represent worse than 19th-century overcrowding, but an accompanying map shows the characteristically piecemeal development.[67]

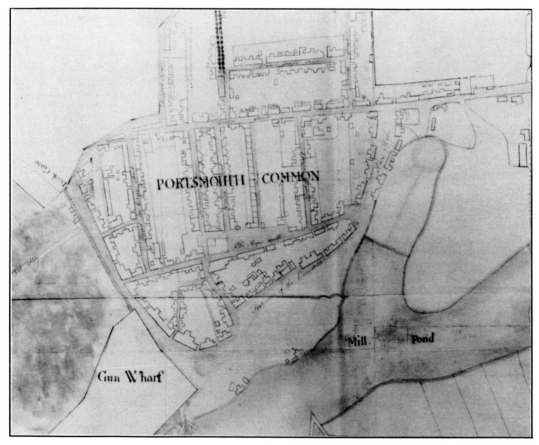

6.   Portsmouth Common (the town of Portsea), *c.*1745.

In 1764 the Common's first Paving Act provided for street maintenance and prevention of nuisances. Urban status was recognised by adopting the name 'Portsea', and the trustees forbade free-roaming animals and public slaughter by butchers. Main roads were spread with shingle from ships' ballast, nightsoil was to be thrown into the harbour near Flathouse, and Pudshole was rechristened St James's Street on the inhabitants' petition. A second Paving Act in 1792 achieved little more, and without sewers and hard paving little could be done to combat growing urban squalor.[68] By this time Portsea was enclosed in fortifications stretching from Flathouse to the Mill Pond, constructed in 1770-9 and separating the town from the rest of the island. Lion Gate gave access from Queen Street to Landport, and Unicorn Gate to the London Road via Flathouse. The 1775 Poor Rate Book lists 1,792 properties of which 1,543 were in the main streets, 166 in smaller lanes and rows, and 84 in alleys and courts behind the main frontages. Poor and prosperous lived side by side. Most houses and small shops were valued at £6-£11; only 104 properties were rated at £20 and above: 30 in Queen Street, 18 along The Hard and 13 inside the dockyard. Highest valued (£100) were Susanna Temple's house and brewery in St George's Row.[69]

Sadler's 1784 *Directory* reveals the extent to which Portsea had become not simply a dockyard dormitory but a busy retail centre supplying most of its inhabitants' needs. A total of 387 businesses are included, about a quarter of the currently listed rateable properties. Queen Street (twice the length of most streets) had 94 businesses and 17 inns; The Hard had 35 of which 13 were inns, including many familiar establishments like the *Keppel's Head*. St George's Square housed three attorneys, a surgeon and a navy-agent at one social level, and John Banks, bricklayer, and Mrs. Rands, rag-merchant, at another. The Old Rope-walk, and Butcher, Hanover, Union, Havant and Cross Streets each had between eleven and seventeen shops and inns listed, and the 32 streets with businesses formed a high proportion of the built-up area. Most shops sold daily necessities: 172 supplying food and drink including 80 victuallers and innkeepers, 27 butchers and 25 bakers, and 63 made or sold clothing and textiles, primarily boots and shoes but everything else also from hats to hose, with four slop-sellers for the sailors.[70] Sadly, little remains of 18th-century Portsea, although it clearly contained many substantial houses in the effortlessly elegant style of the period. Only a handful of these remain in Queen Street and St George's Square. Contemporary local writers presented the town's politer side, and echoes of ancient Rome are audible in R. H. Cumyns' 1799 description of a place 'sprung up almost by enchantment':

> ... where formerly harvests waved, and where the stillness and solitude of the scene was only interrupted by the lowings of the herds; or the hoarse voices of the laborious rustics; are now seen noble streets, splendid edifices, and magnificent gateways ... [71]

The wars of 1793-1815 brought boom conditions to Portsea Island, with high wages and long hours. Population overspilled into Landport and beyond, and packed tightly into Portsea, now confined to under one hundred and twenty acres and thronged with soldiers and sailors. As at Point, drink and women were in great demand and plentiful supply. Dr. George Pinckard found Point and Portsea particularly disgusting in 1795:

> ... hordes of profligate females are seen reeling in drunkenness, or plying upon the streets in open day ... poor Jack, with pockets full of prize money, or rich with the wages of a long and dangerous cruise, is, instantly, dragged ... to a bagnio, or some filthy pot-house, where he is kept drinking, smoking, singing, dancing, swearing and rioting, amidst one continual scene of debauchery ... until his every farthing is gone.[72]

Apart from the loss of their money the sailors probably enjoyed their stay more than Dr. Pinckard did. To meet increased wartime demands Richard Temple's brewery in St George's Square and Moses Miall's at the New Buildings were joined in 1807-9 by the Hawke Street Brewery and another in the Old Rope Walk.[73]

Population grew, but not to the heights claimed by most local historians and geographers from Gates onwards. Confusion between Portsea town and parish leads to the frequently repeated error that in 1801 the population of Portsea town was either 25,387 (enumerated population of Portsea parish, i.e. most of Portsea Island), or 24,327 (Portsea parish excluding the Guildable).[74] Before 1841 the census population of Portsea town was not separately recorded, and only after 1851 were estimated figures produced from the Portsea parish total. According to these, Portsea town may have mushroomed in just over a century to about 8,348 by 1801 and 13,919 by 1831, exceeding Portsmouth town (enumerated as 7,839 in 1801 and 8,083 in 1831) as Defoe had predicted.[75] The 1838 Poor Rate Book, the first to distinguish owners and occupiers, demonstrates the extent of infilling. Over 2,900 properties are listed, of which 600, almost a fifth, were in courts and alleys in groups of four to twelve, of the lowest rateable value (£3), and often named after their owners (Frett, Wigg, Grubb, Treadgold), except where these were prominent local men like Carter. Ownership was much fragmented with many absentees, and Portsea's people lived mainly in rented accommodation.[76] The 1841 census provided the first independent count of houses in Portsea: 2,693 inhabited, 272 uninhabited and four building, declining in 1881 to 2,670 with 10 per cent uninhabited.

Peace in 1815 meant unemployment and hopeless poverty for the dockyard towns, lasting almost to mid-century and affecting every trade in Portsea. Pleas were published for shopkeepers to buy goods (sacks, brushes, umbrellas, corks and many others) manufactured locally, and for jobs, however small, to be given to unemployed shoemakers and tailors.[77] Extremes of good and bad fortune in an overcrowded, poorly-drained site turned Portsea into an industrial slum. Following the 1849 cholera epidemic, Rawlinson's 1850 report revealed the details. In Narrow Court he found a pump with water unfit for cooking, a poulterer's chimney emitting suffocating smoke from burning feathers, and privies 'full of filth, so as not to be capable of use'. Even new streets were covered with 'foetid mud and water, green and rank, and most unwholesome'. Frederick Street, recently built after demolition of four hundred houses at the New Buildings, was already dirty, as were the new Lion Barracks, whose drainage went into the moats 'there to fester, or be washed into the harbour, as the case may be'.[78] All this demonstrated the failure of the Paving Commissioners, who continued inactive while clinging stubbornly to office. Not until 1863 did the Town Council as Local Board of Health take over their duties, and significant improvement began with the construction of effective sewers.

Portsea had its more fashionable areas, however, and by 1847, when the yard's fortunes were reviving, 57 addresses of gentry were listed in directories, mainly in Lion Terrace, built in 1835-40, and in Prince George's Street and St George's Square. Over a third were clergy and service officers, and another third were women. By 1855 directories were becoming more comprehensive, and 184 Portsea gentry included 30 senior officers living inside the dockyard and on the gunwharf.[79] Queen Street was the chief shopping centre, and although late 19th-century directories show little expansion in goods and services, some drapers and grocers were locally thought especially genteel. Innumerable other shops gave good value to those who could afford little. By 1861 Portsea's population peaked at about twenty thousand with males increasing since 1851 by almost two thousand five hundred to twelve thousand, mainly owing to yard activity and the larger garrison in barracks. Females decreased to 7,967: Portsea and Portsmouth towns reversed the normal civil population pattern of excess females.[80] Prostitution was a natural consequence, and notorious areas, some persisting well into the 20th century, were Bonfire Corner, Blossom Alley, 'Yorke's Drift', White's Row and Rosemary Lane. A connection between beerhouses and brothels was well-known, and neighbouring houses were often rented to groups of girls employed in the low-paid clothing industry. The 1861 census shows beershops and lodging-houses in Rosemary Lane containing 14 girls in their twenties listed as needlewomen, stay-stitchers and dressmakers, many born outside Portsea Island.[81] From mid-century began sporadic closure of lodging-houses: six in Rosemary Lane were refused registration in 1853, and in

1854 Nos. 19-24 White's Row were closed. It was no accident that the Rosemary Lane area was demolished and rebuilt in the 1890s, while in 1911 White's Row and Albion Street were replaced by Curzon Howe Road.[82] Although legislation endeavoured to curb drunkenness and vice, local residents' comments suggest that little essentially changed. Clearance of houses unfit for habitation continued intermittently until 1939, succeeded by heavy bombing in the 1940s and well-intentioned post-war demolition and rebuilding that effectively destroyed the old community. Its true spirit is most vividly recaptured by those who still remember making the best of life in dirty, rowdy, hard-working Portsea.[83]

Landport, the third of the four towns, was originally called Halfway Houses after an inn between Portsea and St Mary's church. By 1716 buildings had appeared around Spring Gardens; Ridge's brewhouse was on the corner of Edinburgh Road; and ribbon development along the edge of Town Field almost reached Lake Lane. By 1792-3 Hyde Park Corner, Spring and Fountain Streets, Charlotte and Conway Rows were all built, the Artificers' Barracks replacing Ridge's brewhouse. The area was still predominantly agricultural, however, with the pound and weighbridge at the end of Lake Lane.[84] Population expansion during the French wars, overspilling eastwards from Portsea, shows on the 1810 Ordnance Survey as the nucleus of a new town. Pigot's 1823-4 directory has 92 entries for Halfway Houses, and by 1855 many comfortable private residents inhabited Landport's detached villas and solid terraces. Behind these was a warren of slums. In 1849 the first fatal cholera case occurred in Fountain Street which, with Moore's Square, was 'from its enclosed situation, the miserable character of the houses, and the general poverty of the class of persons who inhabit them, peculiarly liable to disease'. Hyde Park Corner, Marylebone Street and Voller's Row suffered similarly, and Portsea Highways Board's chairman castigated speculative developers who bought field and garden strips and, 'without any plan of making watercourses or drains, commenced building streets, rows of houses and courts'. Many speculators realised 200-300 per cent on land, and the houses, cheaply built with old materials, produced 10-12 per cent to the investors, compared with three and a half per cent on more substantial properties. About five thousand of these tenements paid no rates and had no effective drainage: as roads became impassable and hovels fell into disrepair, the worst were deserted and building continued elsewhere.[85] The surprisingly high numbers of unoccupied houses in overcrowded areas represent this process, as do repeated listings of condemned premises in the M.O.H.'s returns.

The Landport of directories and maps is not the Landport of the census returns. Two census sub-districts divided along the Lake Lane-Fratton Road-Canal line, enumerating south Landport (built on Town Field) with Southsea, and north Landport (on Cherry Garden and Pesthouse Fields) with Kingston and the remainder of Portsea parish. In the 1881-2 diphtheria epidemic, the highest concentrations of cases occurred in mid-Portsea Island, infection being apparently checked by the railway line. Dr. Sykes noted the significant differences between the two parts of the Landport/Southsea sub-district, estimating the population of south Landport as 58,011 with a death-rate of 20.79, and Southsea as 9,909 with a death-rate of 14.73.[86] Conveniently sited outside the walled towns, Landport's function as a route-centre was temporarily enhanced by the canal terminus (1823) and then by the railway station (1847). The central spine and principal façade of the district was traffic-laden Commercial Road, lined with shops, offices and pubs, while week-end bargain-hunters thronged Charlotte Street's lively market. The Royal Hospital (begun 1849), Orphanages (1874-5) and the Union offices were joined by the Head Post Office (1881) and Water Company offices (1883). Demolition of the fortifications released much land for development after 1876, and following the building of the present Guildhall (1886-90) the Pearl and Prudential Buildings, Freemasons' Hall, Municipal College and Public Library clustered around the new commercial and administrative centre.

Southsea, the fourth town, spread c.1805-1911 across southern Portsea Island, separated from the sea by extensive commons and morasses preserved as open military ground but gradually adapted for recreation. The two earliest developments built c.1805-27 on Havencroft, Portsmouth's southernmost field, epitomised its mixed social character, with substantial dwellings backed by crowded artisan cottages. The five Regency terraces, gently angled to follow the outer boundary of Portsmouth's fortifications, faced westwards over open ground and grassy ramparts. Built piecemeal, King's and Jubilee Terraces honoured George III while Hampshire and Landport replaced a rope-walk. By 1847 the terraces, between the railway station and the sea, housed service officers, professional men and numerous lodging-houses: 13 of the 15 houses in Jubilee Terrace, six in King's and about half of Bellevue were lodging-houses. By 1890-1 many of the high-ranking officers and lodging-houses had moved farther eastwards into Southsea but solicitors had begun to appear, and fifty years later the three northern terraces had become a comfortably stylish business area, with solicitors, architects and accountants.[87] Behind them lay narrow streets, developed on Thomas Croxton's land during the Napoleonic boom, and very similar to Landport. East of these, Castle Road runs inland from the *Wheelbarrow*, forking at Fleming's Antiques into Great Southsea Street, still largely Georgian and early-Victorian, inhabited in the 1850s by skilled craftsmen, lodging-house keepers and dockyard employees. Castle Road's larger dwellings housed the upper-middle class, mainly on the eastern side outside the borough boundary which bisected the street north-east of Fleming's, and Elm Grove's big detached residences in their spacious gardens had a similar population.[88]

It was on the block of land between Castle and Victoria Roads, from Elm Grove to the Common, that Portsmouth's only area of high-quality housing was built, c.1835-60, on the enclosed lands of Fratton manor, free at last from constraints imposed by piecemeal development on narrow strips in the borough's open fields. It was fortunate for Southsea that Thomas Ellis Owen became an architect and developer when revived prosperity created a market for elegant houses near the sea. Born in Dublin, acquainted with Italy, son of a surveyor to Portsmouth's Royal Engineers' Department, Owen combined training, discrimination and business acumen. His work in Kent Road and Queen's, Sussex and Portland Terraces illustrate his interpretation of Regency and Italianate styles, while detached villas around Grove and Clarendon Roads and Dovercourt (Owen's own house) provide varied examples of Gothic Revival and the Picturesque.[89] Clifton, Netley and Richmond Terraces were probably the work of Henry Gauntlett who, with other local builders, similarly contributed to the stylish mid-century development of central Southsea. These properties appealed to active and retired service officers, independent, professional and business people and keepers of select boarding-houses and private schools. Some were purchased but more were rented by a mobile population mostly originating outside Hampshire, many born overseas.[90] East of Victoria Road in the early 1870s was New Southsea, where two other planned developments, Havelock Park and Nelsonville, failed to materialise. Pleasant terraces and villas were built in Campbell and Outram Roads, but as population increased Southsea's building reverted to Portsmouth's customary cramped monotony, with straight rows of large or small red-brick houses tailored to the occupants' income. Except in parts of Craneswater the variety and quality achieved by Owen and his contemporaries were never again repeated.

Infilling between Kent and Osborne Roads led to a high proportion (one-third to one-half) of boarding-houses, spreading to Western Parade by 1907. Owen's *Portland Hotel* was joined (1861-77) by six others overlooking the Common, beginning with the *Queen's*. Palmerston Road's fashionable shops and cafés, together with piers, esplanades, the Ladies' Mile and ornamental gardens, provided meeting places and promenades for residents and

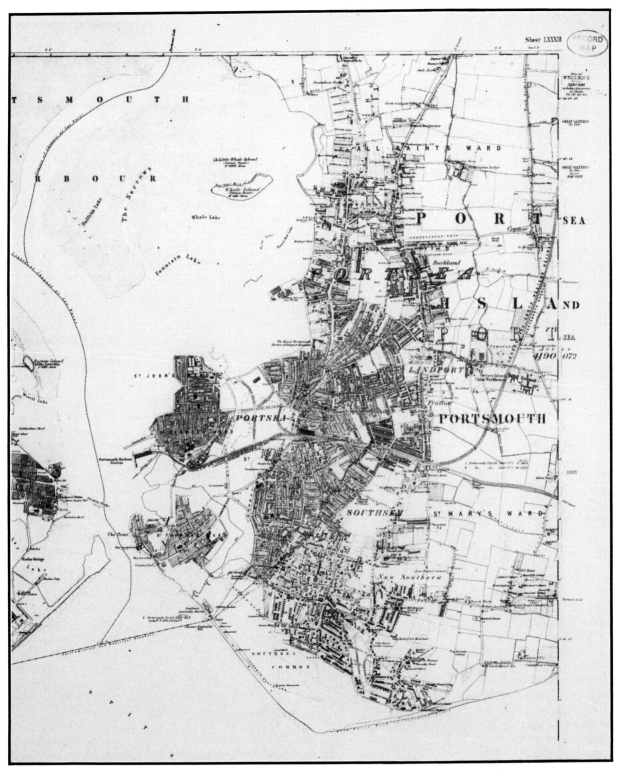

7. The western side of Portsea Island, from the 6″ O.S. map, revised 1873-4.

visitors alike. The British Association's 1911 Guide, however, lamented with many others who remembered

> that the Common was within the last 50 years a real common, on which furze and bracken grew, intersected by bogs and water-courses, on which hares and rabbits fed at night; that ponds, boglands and springs were numerous, that pleasant country walks might have been taken within the boundaries of the island, and that well-grown elm and other trees flourished where now miles of houses, tramways and other signs of man's handiwork exist.[91]

East Southsea's spread over the remaining farmlands, completed before 1914, resulted from another major dockyard and population expansion, providing few attractions for visitors and finally reaching the borders of Eastney and Milton.

A 1632 survey of Eastney and Milton showed Eastney manor 'of smale building, onely a farm house' with 200 acres of enclosed arable and pasture and 52 acres of furze and marsh. Five freeholders held 161 acres, while the copyholders shared 365 acres, many in multiples of the 30-acre yardland.[92] In the 18th century Eastney Farm and part of Milton belonged to the Whites of Southwick, passing to Ann Henderson, wife of Rear-Admiral Sir Philip Durham, Commander-in-Chief of Portsmouth, 1836-9. In 1858-60 the Henderson-Durhams sold 50 acres to the War Department and Eastney Barracks was built.[93] By 1871 Eastney was a Royal Marine suburb with 1,162 servicemen (306 living outside barracks) heavily outnumbering the civilian workers.[94] Milton remained agricultural until the early 20th century, largely owing to James Goldsmith's refusal to sell farmland for building. The six medieval fields (Eastfield, Westfield, Southtown, Domer, Crana and Sendram) were still partly open in the 17th century, 339 acres being enclosed in 1693.[95] Milton and Eastney Commons and Velder Heath, bordering Langstone Harbour, were partly brought into cultivation, 1716-50, the remainder (about two hundred and fifty acres) being enclosed in 1813 under an Act of 1810.[96] Lower Farm with around a hundred acres was on the Foster Hall site next to Milton House, whose old walled garden survives at the heart of the former College of Education. Domer Farm, opposite Velder Avenue, had lands stretching in 1750 across northern Milton, while Milton Park covers the site of the other two farmhouses. James Goldsmith had Upper Farm by 1872, his grandfather having bought Middle Farm (1808) with fields lying west of Hill Lane. In 1838 the family's holding was only 128 acres, but they acquired more property in 1858 and Lower Farm and Milton House in 1885.[97] Many arable fields grew rhubarb and vegetables, and smaller market gardens developed around the short-lived canal that bisected Milton from 1823. Farming, fishing, smuggling, shooting and netting birds were common occupations, with shotting (recovering practice shells for return to the Gunwharf) a profitable local speciality. The few shops were outnumbered by 10 public houses, the village acquiring a church (1841) and a school (1875), while other necessary institutions were established in this outlying area. The Union workhouse was built on north Domer Field in 1845; the Lunatic Asylum (St James's Hospital) on 75 acres north of Locksway Road in the 1870s; St Mary's and the Infectious Diseases Hospitals by the 1890s. The useless canal, filled with refuse, became Goldsmith Avenue in 1896, Milton's chief link with the advancing town.[98] James Goldsmith, bachelor and alcoholic, resisted change while the village decayed around him with 'old weather-beaten cottages, and, half-hidden by the trees of overgrown gardens, dilapidated plastered and thatched farm-buildings'.[99] When he died in 1911 change came rapidly. Middle and Upper Farms were demolished, only a barn surviving in a municipal park. Lower Farm and Milton House vanished under the Teachers' Training College, and Milton became another part of Portsmouth.

Fratton manor's eastern boundary marched with Eastney and Milton, approximately along Festing and Bath Roads, Fratton goods yard and the railway line. Fratton's land in central southern Portsea Island included East, West, St Andrew's, Hambrook, North and

South Breach Fields, with shared rights over Southsea Common and East Bere Forest.[100] The Domus Dei's houses, gardens and open-field strips in Portsmouth liberty, and various Portsea closes, remained with Fratton after the Dissolution, but subsequent changes included open-field enclosure by agreement (1600); conveyance to Nicholas Potbury of the lands north of Portsdown (1622); loss to Southsea Castle's captain (by lease or seizure) of the Common's fishing, fowling and rabbits; and enclosure and break-up of Fratton and Southsea Commons after 1785.[101] In 1801 Fratton was a rural retreat for prosperous townsfolk: 'Their residences are handsome and respectable, and in a situation where the *rus in urbe* is most completely realised'.[102] Edward Casher had Froddington House, and R. G. Temple's estate, broken up in 1832, included Fratton House, bought by Daniel Howard. Josiah Webb, farming Marmion and Wish Lane Farms, owned about a hundred and five acres in 1838 and doubled this by leasing from 11 other owners.[103] Market-gardeners, farmers and rural craftsmen lived in the village, drinking at the *Dog and Duck* and *Plough and Spade*, but by 1851 Fratton Road was colonised by active and retired servicemen and dockyard labourers, mostly immigrants. By 1915 it was a shopping street, backed by crowded houses.[104]

Copnor, at the junction of the tracks to Milton and Kingston, was surrounded by five open fields: Burfield, South, West, Garston and Breachfield; with Goslingscroft (by the Baffins track), Ketemarsh, Conyger Heath and 'Mydmuslemore' bordering Langstone Harbour.[105] Much of the land was enclosed by the 17th century, and some 18th-century farms can be identified. In 1738 John Moody leased to William Blake Baffins Farm (200 acres) and Copnor Woods (102 acres of arable). In 1798 Samuel Leeke owned 527 acres consisting of the Portsea mansion house and garden, Church, Copnor and Baffins Farms, Goslingscroft, and 10 acres at Fratton. All were occupied by tenants, and all the farms were divided: George Sheldon had Church farmhouse with 64 acres, 106 acres of Baffins and six acres in Burfields; William Poor had the rest of Church Farm (46 acres in four closes); George Smith had Baffins farmhouse and 120 acres; James Bartlett (70 acres) and Stephen Gauntlett (31 acres) shared Copnor Farm; while Henry Hill leased Goslingscroft and the Fratton closes. Previously the Smith, Bartlett and Gauntlett holdings (231 acres) were held by a single tenant.[106] This practice was locally common, two generations of a farming family seldom retaining identical holdings. On Leeke's death in 1806 part of the estate was sold. His widow, Sophia, received a life interest in the remainder, and in 1838 was living in Manor Cottage and leasing Manover Farm (71 acres) to Henry Hill and Baffins Farm (193 acres) to Andrew Nance. Stephen Gazelee, a London lawyer, owned Manor Farm (70 acres). Ann Stares inherited the Manor House and married Jonathan Rawson, a Manchester merchant, who battled from afar with badly-drained lands in 'a sad state of cultivation', a decrepit house, and difficulties created by the railway, which made his tenant's cows climb the embankment to and from their Burfields pasture four times daily. Two farmhouses became taverns, the *Harvest Home* and *Sportsman's Rest*, in competition with four others: progress in Copnor took the usual Portsea Island course. Andrew Nance employed 28 men at Baffins and rented another farm at Stamshaw. An energetic entrepreneur, director of the railway and Floating Bridge companies, he also had a Broad Street carrier's business. Copnor saltworks, partly drained, provided 38 acres of pasture still surviving east of Baffins Pond.[107] Late in the 19th century Copnor was still a village but housing was spreading eastwards along Powerscourt, Queen's and New Roads, part of Portsea manor's demesne had become Kingston Cemetery, and a brickworks occupied much of Burfield.

In 1292 Little Gatcombe, with 60 acres in Hilsea and Portsea, belonged to the d'Esturs, Lords of Gatcombe, Isle of Wight. By 1546 the estate had doubled in size and in the 18th century Gatcombe's co-heiress, Sarah Brady, married Sir John Curtis, Commander-in-Chief, Portsmouth, in 1809. The Board of Ordnance bought Gatcombe House and surrounding lands, incorporating it into Hilsea Barracks, while Sir Lucius Curtis inherited Little Gatcombe farm, sold as 'nearly ripe for building operations' in 1898.[108] Stamshaw, a carucate of land in the north of Portsmouth liberty, was valued at 100s. in 1292, and held of Edward I by Nicholas Malemeyns for one sparrowhawk and 35s. 4d. to Portsmouth's bailiffs. It was subsequently bought by two Portsmouth citizens, Richard Playfote, 1548, and Henry Bickley, 1659, and, in 1626, 50 acres of saltmarsh at Stampsey were included in the Wandesford Grant. By 1716 a line of enclosed fields was fringed by rough grazing and marshes, running out to Stampsey Point, later known as Tipner, where there were saltpans by 1773, powder magazines by 1797, and brick-kilns south of the truncated common, still part of the borough's waste.[109] By 1838 the Board of Ordnance owned Tipner, while the Admiralty had the surrounding mudlands, Samuel Twyford owned about eighty-three acres of arable and pasture, tenanted by Andrew Nance, and by the 1860s part of this was being broken up into small parcels for building. Stamshaw was unusual, however, in that a substantial block was bought and sold off in plots by the London-based United Land Company, who also developed part of North End. By 1898 most of the area was covered by rows of small terraced houses, with rifle ranges, signalling stations and a chemical works farther north.[110]

Stubbington Grange lay centrally between Stamshaw and Copnor, and had been given c.1164 by Baldwin of Portsea, together with St Mary's church and tithes, to Southwick Priory, its lands straddling the boundary between Buckland and Copnor. In 1268, 142 acres were cultivated, part of the produce being sent to Southwick and part providing food for visitors and workers, including 22 collectors gathering the Portsea tithes for five weeks after the harvest.[111] After the Dissolution Winchester College held Stubbington for nearly four hundred years, and most of the fields were enclosed before Thomas Carpenter's tenancy in the mid-16th century. By 1652 Stubbington was again connected with Southwick, leased first to Richard Norton and then to the Thistlethwaytes. Their most notable sub-tenant was Thomas Fitzherbert, a progressive farmer, who leased the 250 acres in 1780, and the Kents farmed there for about a hundred years.[112] Owned for centuries by two institutions, Stubbington presents an unusually compact appearance in estate and tithe maps, with fields in two consolidated blocks, one surrounding the farmhouse and another east of Stamshaw. Between them was a triangular area around North End junction: by 1898 development there drove a wedge of streets and houses between the two parts, with building steadily encroaching on the College lands.

Despite the overcrowded towns and spreading suburbs, Portsea Island remained largely rural until the 20th century. The 1838-9 tithe apportionment surveyed some 4,032 acres in Portsea parish, of which only 600 acres were classified as buildings, roads, canal and waste. The rest was still agricultural: arable, 1,305 acres; market garden, 814; common pasture, 13; glebe, 15; and tithe-free Stubbington land, two hundred and thirty-one. Government lands, fortifications and glacis amounted to 978 acres, including much open space used for grazing.[113] The population of Portsea parish increased from 25,387 in 1801 to 120,022 in 1881, while Portsmouth parish, 7,839 in 1801, reached 11,569 in 1871, falling to 7,661 20 years later. Portsea town's greatest intercensal increase, 21.9 per cent in 1851-61, brought its population to 19,967 in 1861, although it fell to 14,730 in 1891. Both of these areas had well-defined limits, however, and the first stages in transforming country into town accompanied the eight-fold increase, 1801-91, in the census districts of Landport with Southsea (10,130 in 1801; 80,306 in 1891) and Kingston (6,909 in 1801; 56,581 in 1891). Greatest intercensal increases in both areas occurred in 1841-51 (Landport 56.1 per cent, Kingston 45.6 per cent), both increasing continuously thereafter.[114] By 1898 the built-up area covered western Portsea Island northwards to Stamshaw and North End junction, still separated by fields from Stubbington and Copnor. Kingston and Fratton housing stopped at the railway, with Southsea just spreading beyond the curved Southsea branch line, and Eastney still a separate suburb. By 1910 there was some development in Copnor and more in Southsea, which expanded to meet Eastney. Building largely ceased in 1914-18, and post-war depression severely restricted slum clearance and rebuilding. Nevertheless, the city constructed 591 dwellings under the 1919 Act, mostly at Eastney, Milton and on Portsdown; and 951 under the 1924 Act, at Hilsea, Drayton, the Eastern Road, Cosham and Wymering. The 1929 clearance scheme rehoused Portsea slum-dwellers along Eastern Road and Gladys Avenue, and by the late 1930s the Wymering development, long advocated by Medical Officers of Health, was progressing well. Private housing, mostly semi-detached, spread rapidly over Copnor, North End, Hilsea and Cosham.[115] By 1938, following boundary extensions, Portsmouth borough's area had increased in 40 years from 4,486 to 9,217 acres, its population from 163,667 to 251,400, and its houses from 30,267 to 62,746.[116] By the outbreak of the Second World War the city of Portsmouth covered most of the island, only the eastern shores retaining any trace of the vanished open country.

Advertisement for a new library in Portsea, 1813.

Chapter Three

Wooden Walls and Ironclads

The combination of a sheltered harbour rimmed by easily converted mudland with an eminently defensible entrance, a position on the English Channel opposite France the traditional enemy, coupled with reasonable access to supplies of timber in the Forest of Bere and elsewhere, provide sound *prima facie* reasons for the selection of Portsmouth as a naval dockyard. Yet without reducing the weight of these advantages, the vicissitudes experienced by the dockyard can only be fully explained by reference to political and military strategies adopted by monarchs and governments in their efforts to appropriate foreign territories, to retain them, and to ward off unfriendly incursions upon British soil. Although very different in scale, the first rudimentary repairing facility established in the late 12th century and the contraction instigated by the Defence Review of 1981 have in common a strategic origin. Small wonder that Portsmouth has been a hostage to the press of naval activity rather than to the market forces that drive most towns. This chapter traces the interrelationship between policy and its implementation in both physical and organisational terms within the dockyard, considers working conditions, and comments briefly on the yard's economic impact upon the town.

Portsmouth was employed as a point of departure and arrival by feudal lords travelling between England and France as a consequence of the Norman Conquest, and doubtless this was a cause of the decision to use the site for the servicing of ships. In all probability this was no more than a hauling-up facility for vessels which were beached at high tide and dragged a short distance up the shore, enabling repairs to be undertaken. Sited on the creek to the north of the original settlement of Portsmouth, in the vicinity of the present-day entrance to H.M.S. *Vernon*, the facility was later improved in the wake of the loss of Normandy in 1204 by the construction of a wall, King John writing to the Sheriff of Southampton on 20 May 1212 requesting 'our dock at Portsmouth to be enclosed with a good and strong wall . . . for the preservation of our Ships and Galleys', together with the erection of 'penthouses' for the storage of tackle.[1] That the wall had collapsed by 1224, not to be rebuilt, is an indication of the perceived value of the site, given that troop movements came to be effected by merchant vessels leased to the crown, in particular from the flourishing Cinque Ports, rendering the maintenance of a navy less than imperative. The reversal of this policy by Henry V, who had built up a fleet of about 34 vessels by his death in 1422, failed to revive Portsmouth's fortunes, in part because of the selection of Southampton as a collecting point for ships, and it was not until Henry VII's time that Portsmouth's strategic advantages were once more recognised.

Since a distinction between warships and commercial vessels had not yet been made, Henry planned to use his ships to encourage trade in peacetime and to protect commercial vessels in war, and to further this goal, and because some ships were now too large to be beached, he ordered a dry dock for bottom cleaning and repair work. Possibly because access was required to deeper water than was available at the earlier site, the dock, which was constructed between 1495 and 1496, was sited about half a mile north of its predecessor, a few yards astern of the *Victory* as she presently lies in No. 2 dock.[2] It was entirely appropriate that Robert Brygandine, the Clerk of the King's Ships, should have had charge of the works, for they constituted the first dry dock in a royal dockyard, and probably anywhere in this country.[3] The dock gates were of an innovatory design developed by Sir Reginald Bray, chief architect to the king. Fearing that water pressure from the harbour would be too great for a single gate when the dock was empty, and in an attempt to achieve watertightness, Bray provided two gates and filled the space with clay and shingle; pumping was by means of a bucket-chain driven by a horse engine. The dock, its wooden walls bolted together and powerfully backed with stone, proved as strong as its gates, even if it took 20 men some 29 days to remove the clay and shingle to undock a ship.[4] Associated with the dock on the eight-and-a-half acre plot – the first royal dockyard – were a storehouse, forge and smithy; since the 80 bm *Sweepstake* is known to have been launched in 1497, and since it is possible that other ships may have been built and hired by the king at an earlier date, it is safe to assume that a building slip also existed.[5]

Henry VII's view of Portsmouth as a building yard was initially echoed by Henry VIII, who was determined to keep his navy abreast of that of the French. The upshot of this policy was the construction in 1509 of arguably the port's most famous warship, the 500 bm *Mary Rose*, her fort-like fo'c'sle and poop unfortunately creating a high centre of gravity, a design characteristic which contributed to her capsize when moving to engage the French on 19 July 1545. The slightly smaller 450 bm *Peter Pomegranate* left the slip in 1510, but apart from the 180 bm *Jennet*, launched in 1539, building subsequently played a secondary role to repair work, hardly a surprising strategy since Portsmouth possessed the navy's only dry dock.[6] The latter was enlarged in 1523 to accommodate Henry's flagship the *Henri Grace à Dieu*.[7] The problems of communicating with a yard so far from London and from the Tower where the ordnance was stored ensured the establishment in 1513 of two other royal dockyards on the Thames, at Woolwich and Deptford, but there could be no gainsaying Portsmouth's seniority.

Notwithstanding Henry's early support for Portsmouth, towards the end of his reign the local shortage of skilled men, which could never adequately be overcome by impressment, the paucity of a merchant class rendering victualling problematic, supplies more often than not coming from Southampton or London, and the ease with which the French could approach, as they did in 1545, all militated against further investment in the yard. Thus in 1547 expenditure on Deptford totalled £18,824, compared with a mere £1,211 for Portsmouth. The pattern continued under Elizabeth I, and between 1559 and 1570 £73,305 was injected into Deptford, Portsmouth having to make do with £6,641.[8] Now the enemy was Spain and the Thames yards were more conveniently placed for operations against the Spanish Netherlands.

During the reign of James I, who was not of a warlike persuasion, the dockyard regressed to pre-1490 conditions, for in 1623 the dry dock was filled in 'to protect the Dockyard from encroachments by the sea'[9] on the orders of the Duke of Buckingham, and its intended replacement was not built since in 1628 he was assassinated by John Felton.[10] Perhaps fortunately plans dated 1628 for a dock, wharves and storehouses at Portchester Castle did not bear fruit, but the widespread acceptance of the rumour that the harbour was infested with the boring worm *teredo navalis* certainly assisted the arguments of vested interests behind the Thames yards.[11] Even though the two La Rochelle expeditions of 1626-8 were victualled and fitted out by the dockyard, the absence of a dry dock was a severe handicap to the amount of work undertaken, contributing to Sir George Blundell's observation in 1627 that the town was 'a poor beggarly place, where is neither money, lodging nor meat'.[12] A nadir it might have been, but the use of Portsmouth for fitting out part of Charles I's ship-money fleet between 1634 and 1639, followed by a dramatic change in the national political scene, was to place Portsmouth's star in the ascendant.

The Civil War, in which Portsmouth was taken by the parliamentarians in 1642, the defeat of Charles I in 1645 and his execution in 1649, ushered in the Commonwealth era during which the yard was finally and firmly established. A Commissioner, Colonel William Willoughby, was appointed in 1649 with a brief to mount a shipbuilding programme designed to clear the Channel of pirates and royalist ships. Moreover the first Dutch War of 1652-4 confirmed the importance of Portsmouth since the Channel was extensively used by Dutch colonial traffic. A building slip was immediately laid out in 1649,[13] and the following year the appropriately named 422 bm *Portsmouth* was launched. Built by Thomas Eastwood,[14] the *Portsmouth* was not only the first vessel to be constructed in the yard since the *Jennet* more than a century earlier, but also the first to be classified according to the number of guns carried; with 38 guns she was designated as fourth rate.[15] Some seven warships, a ketch and a hoy had been launched by the accession of Charles II in 1660, three of which, the 764 bm *Lyme*, the 600 bm *Sussex*, and the 532 bm *Bristol*, although fourth rates were nevertheless larger than the *Mary Rose*.[16]

It was to be expected, however, that the largest ships were built at Deptford and Woolwich after they had been so many decades in the van. Without a dry dock, repairs at Portsmouth had to be effected by the ancient practice of hauling-up, which was both labour intensive and failed to provide shipwrights with good access to the hull. Francis Willoughby, William's son, who became Commissioner in 1652 and whose achievements give him a good case for being regarded as the father of the dockyard, strongly argued for a dry dock.[17] His persistence was rewarded in 1656 when a double dock to receive a third and fourth rate in line was authorised. That the magistrates and burghers of the town should have offered £500, about one-sixth of the cost, is an indication of supply contracts they felt they could anticipate,[18] despite the dock's inability to accommodate the largest vessels, about which the dockyard officers were immediately rueful.[19] Willoughby was also instrumental in the addition of a mast wharf in 1655 and a tar-house in 1657; in 1658 he leased a small one-and-a-half acre plot to the east of the yard (*see* map opposite) to serve as a rope-yard. Yet all these facilities were manned by a relatively small workforce, the establishment being set at one hundred and eighty.[20]

The restoration of the monarchy in 1660 emphasised the expansionary trend begun under the Commonwealth. The Second and Third Dutch Wars of 1665-7 and 1672-4 respectively saw no reduction in the value of Portsmouth's strategic location, while timber shortages began to assail the Thames yards. Moreover, Portsmouth had the support of the influential Samuel Pepys, Secretary of the Navy Board and later of the Admiralty. Money for a second dry dock was voted in 1662, although it was not in fact completed until 1685, and an eight-acre strip of land, on which an enormous thousand-foot-long wooden rope-house was constructed, was added to the south of the yard in 1663. On De Gomme's advice the yard was enclosed by an earthen rampart topped by a wooden palisade, the line of the fortification including an east-facing and a south-facing bastion; sandwiched between the ramparts and the yard itself were the strips of land constituting Dock, Chillmarsh and Catcliffe Furlongs, which continued to be cultivated.[21] Outside the yard, to the south, a mast pond, where stored spars were more readily accessible than when floating in the harbour, was begun in 1664 and completed two years later. Then in 1677 the whole of Dock Furlong, some nine acres, was taken into the dockyard; since 1658 the yard had trebled in size.

Concomitant with these developments, Portsmouth became a leading building yard. Between 1660 and the end of the Third Dutch War in 1674 no less than 18 vessels were launched, among them two second rates and two first rates: the 100 gun, 1,426 bm *Royal James* launched in 1671, and the 100 gun, 1,443 bm *Royal Charles*, launched in 1673. Not only was Portsmouth in full competition with the Thames yards, but also it was the scene of technological innovation, for the *Phoenix*, a fifth rate of 368 bm launched in 1671, was the first ship to have its bottom sheathed with lead as a protection against the *teredo navalis*.[22]

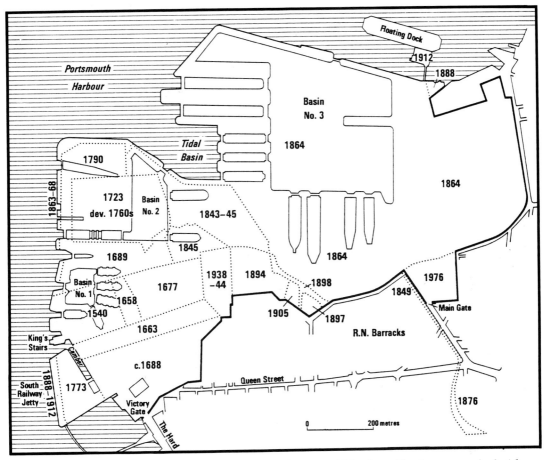

Portsmouth
Harbour

Floating Dock
1912
1888

Basin
No. 3

1864

1790
1863-68

Tidal
Basin

1723
dev. 1760s

Basin
No. 2

1864

1843-45

1864

1845

1689

1938
-44

1894

1898

1976

Basin
No. 1

1677

1849

Main Gate

1658

1905

1897

1540

1663

R.N. Barracks

King's
Stairs

c.1688

Camber

South
Railway
Jetty

1773

1888-1912

Queen Street

Victory
Gate

1876

The Hard

0   200 metres

8. The growth of Portsmouth Dockyard showing dates at which plots of land were acquired. *After* Morgan, L. V., 'An Historical Review of Portsmouth Dockyard in Relation to our Naval Policy', *Transactions of the Institution of Naval Architects*, vol. 90 (1948).

Inevitably the end of the war witnessed retrenchment, and on 11 April 1674 the Navy Board directed that the workforce be cut to two hundred and twenty.[23]

The deposition of the Catholic James II in the 1688 revolution proved to be yet another political change which had repercussions on Portsmouth. The crown was offered to William of Orange, a Protestant Dutchman who was an outstanding francophobe and for whom a base opposite France was a crucial part of foreign policy. By the end of the 17th century Portsmouth had emerged as the country's leading naval dockyard, consequent upon the inauguration in 1689 of a dock building programme under the supervision of Edmund Dummer, Surveyor to the Navy Board. This programme saw the creation by 1698 of the first naval stone dock behind an enclosed basin, where ships could be more effectively refitted than in the harbour, together with a small wooden dock.[24] In a report on the completion of the stone dock, Richard Haddock and Edmund Dummer claimed that it would reduce 'overtime and materials lost or embezzled in transport; it is better to bring the ships to the men . . . [since this] saves one third of expense and time. There is no such work in the world that can clear and refit two-thirds of the Navy in a season'.[25] Quite apart from the ingenious system of pumping introduced to drain the docks and basin, the very reclamation of the land itself from the harbour was a notable enterprise. A second rope-house of equal proportion to the first and the Great Long Storehouse adjacent to it were also added. The mast pond and mast house of 1685 were enclosed behind realigned ramparts so that with the Dummer works the yard increased its area by 28 acres, doubling its former extent.[26] Shortly afterwards, in 1703, another dock known as South Dock was completed.

Twenty-one vessels were launched during the reign of William III, and their nature illustrates Portsmouth's function as a leading building yard, but even more importantly as a repairing and refitting yard. Thus not a single first rate and only three second rates, the largest of which was the 1,459 bm *Association* launched in 1697, left the slips while no less than six of the vessels built were hoys and advice boats used for communications between warships. William's policies occasioned a signal increase in the numbers employed: prior to his accession, in 1687, some 294 men were on the dockyard's strength, but by 1697 no less than 1,271 were employed. By 1711 the workforce exceeded two thousand, and even though the end of hostilities in 1713 witnessed a contraction to 1,200, the dockyard was possibly the largest manufacturing enterprise in the country; at this stage of commercial evolution only public capital could have underpinned such an investment.[27] Even as late as the 1840s firms in the leading commercial industry, cotton textiles, had not attained such a size, only five in Manchester employing more than one thousand workers, and even then often located in separate mills in different parts of the town.[28] Defoe was certainly impressed by what he saw in the early 1720s: 'since the encrease of business at this place, by the long continuance of the war, the confluence of the people has been so great . . . that a kind of suburb [i.e. Portsea] . . . has been built'.[29]

The acquisition in 1723 of 27 acres of mudland to the north of Dummer's docks and basin, although it proved invaluable for the construction of building slips in the 1760s and afterwards,[30] was at the time a somewhat curious decision, for the years prior to the War of the Austrian Succession (1741-8) were quiet ones for the dockyard, only three warships being completed between 1713 and 1737. Ironically one of these was the *Victory*, a first rate of 1,921 bm, making it the largest warship to be launched at Portsmouth.[31] Four ships were completed in the 1740s, but spurred on by the Seven Years War, 1756-63, production took a notable upturn in the 1750s and 1760s when 14 ships were built, the *Britannia*, a first rate of 2,116 bm completed in 1762, assuming the mantle formerly held by the *Victory*.

Deficiencies in the organisational layout of the dockyard laid bare by a Navy Board visitation – for example, the folly of having building slips issuing into the basin where ships were being fitted out, rather than discharging new vessels directly into the harbour – gave rise to the dockyard plan of 1760.[32] Building slips were set out on ground obtained in 1723, a second stone dock giving into the basin was finished in 1772, and taking cognisance of the fire risk inherent in wooden buildings, provision was made for a number of new brick storehouses. This also went for the new double rope-house[33] built in 1770 (rebuilt after a fire in 1776[34]) on the site of the two former rope-houses, for the adjacent tarring house of 1771 and for the hatchelling house where the hemp fibres were carded, also of 1771. Providentially, almost all these fine Georgian structures were in place in good time for the War of American Independence, 1775-83;[35] they have in large part survived, despite damage in the Second World War, and form the kernel of the present day Heritage Area.[36] Commensurate with these new facilities and the amount of refitting generated by war, the numbers employed exhibited a long-run tendency to rise.[37] Some two thousand were in post during the Seven Years War, which was followed by a slight decrease, but from 1771 onwards more than two thousand worked in the yard. The American war prompted a total

9. The launch of the *Prince of Wales* before their Majesties at Portsmouth, 1794.

of 2,471 in 1783, while the war against France caused almost three thousand to be recorded in 1800, rising to 3,878 by 1814.[38]

Against the background of such a substantial increase in the number of workers, shipbuilding was surprisingly muted. In the 1780s only four launchings occurred: one of a sloop, two of sixth rates, one of a second rate, the *St George*. The following decade produced an even more attenuated pattern, for only two sloops and the second rate *Prince of Wales* were completed. The first decade and a half of the new century witnessed a more predictable volume of completions, some sixteen in all, but six of these were sloops and only two were second rates, the *Dreadnought* of 2,110 bm and the *Boyne* of 2,155 bm. One reason for the phenomenon was the decision by the Navy Board to put out a good number of hulls to private builders at, for instance, Bursledon, Beaulieu and Cowes, leaving the arguably more intricate task of fitting out to be undertaken at Portsmouth. During the 1770s alone some fifteen vessels built on the Beaulieu river were fitted out in the yard, and between 1773 and 1814 a total of 46 ships came into service in this manner.[39]

Repair work was another important aspect of shipwrights' work, a task which was clearly exacerbated in wartime. Thus in 1702, 98 ships were repaired and cleaned in the docks, quite apart from those careened and graved in the harbour.[40] In 1810 some eighteen times more man-days were expended on repair work than on construction, while in 1812 no fewer than 79 ships were docked for repairs and 165 were worked upon at Spithead and in the harbour.[41] From time to time the dockyard was exercised in the repair of foreign vessels, as occurred in December 1769 on the arrival of a squadron of Russian men-of-war.[42] The decommissioning of vessels and fitting them out for 'the Ordinary', that is, the reserve fleet, by the removal of masts and rigging, engaged much labour at the cessation of hostilities; there was mooring accommodation for 53 ships in the harbour in 1703.[43] The truce with America and France in January 1783, and with Spain and Holland the following September, saw more than fifty ships paid off into the Ordinary at Portsmouth, and not until June 1784 had the bottleneck been removed and ships got to their moorings.[44] A further element of a shipwright's job was the breaking up of ships declared surplus to requirements. In short, launchings may have been the most ceremonial of occasions, but they were only one element of dockyard activity.

Although two land-reclamation projects were undertaken during the latter part of the 18th century, namely the absorption of Watering Island, an offshore mudbank, and a further northern extension beyond the building slips (Plate 8), the major changes associated with the Napoleonic Wars were effected in the oldest part of the dockyard. Mindful of the shortfall in repair and refit capacity, the Navy Board in 1795 invited Samuel Bentham to submit proposals for the improvement of work practices. Noting that an excessive amount of time was spent by shipwrights gaining access to ships in the harbour, termed 'afloat time', he argued that the basin be greatly increased in size, that two further dry docks be constructed giving into the extended basin, that the double dock and South Dock be removed to make way for the new structures, and that a further dock with direct access to the harbour be introduced. His proposals were accepted and as Inspector-General of Naval Works he supervised the operation, which was completed in 1803, incorporating a pontoon or caisson for use as a roadway, in place of the standard gates, at the entrance to the basin. Not only did Bentham use Dummer's reservoir to drain the new docks, but also he introduced a steam engine to pump the water out of the reservoir in place of the traditional horse power. It was the first use of steam power in a royal dockyard and it began that process which was to transform the yards by the mid-19th century.[45] Ever eager to encourage efficiency, Bentham recognised the potential savings to be derived from Marc Brunel's pulley-block making machinery and persuaded the Navy Board to have the intricate machines made by Henry Maudslay, thereby making the Navy independent of the private contractors, the Taylor family, at Southampton. The block mills, built over the reservoir to economise on space, were the first steam-powered factory in a British naval yard, and the 45 machines constituted the world's first example of the use of metal machines for mass production. By ensuring that there was no imbalance in the flow of blocks between each machine, Bentham and Brunel demonstrated their flair in production as well as mechanical engineering.[46] Among other innovations by the remarkable Bentham was the provision of a water tank as a fire-fighting precaution in the roof of the block mills, the construction of a water tower near the rope-house for similar purposes, and the building of a steam dredger for clearing the basin.

The sequel to Waterloo was a familiar contraction in the establishment to some 3,159 in 1820,[47] followed by a slower but substantial decline to 2,079 by 1830.[48] Although twice the number of vessels left the slips between 1816 and 1830 than did between 1800 and 1815, examination of their size reveals that 24 of the 37 were cutters and sloops, eight were fifth and sixth rates, and only one, the 2,443 bm *Princess Charlotte*, was a first rate. The 1830s, on the other hand, were characterised by an impetus quite new to the dockyard, the advent of a wholly novel form of propulsion, the coal-fired steam engine. Although no major war was in the offing, the introduction of such technology became necessary if for no other reason than navies elsewhere would be certain to utilise it. By the early 1830s the Admiralty[49] was considering Portsmouth as suitable for steamship construction,[50] the outcome being the launching of the steamships *Neptune* of 2,694 bm in 1832, and the *Queen* of 3,104 bm in 1839, which were the largest vessels to have been built in the yard. The realisation in 1840 of the advantages of the screw propeller over the paddle both in terms of its power efficiency and

10. The *Boyne*, formerly a 98-gun ship, moored off the south-western tip of the dockyard. Drawn by Henry Moses in 1826.

11. View of Portsmouth Harbour with the dockyard on the right. Drawn by Henry Moses in 1825.

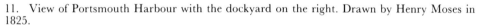

its lack of interference with the number of guns carried, caused a wholehearted switch to steam; of the 36 ships launched in the 1830s and 1840s, no less than 15 were steamers. The workforce rose once more, reaching 2,246 in 1845, rising to 3,383 in 1848.[51] A good proportion of the trades were new to the yard, engineers, fitters, boiler-makers and foundrymen rubbing shoulders with the traditional artisans and announcing that at last the Industrial Revolution was in full flood.

The increasing size of ship called for new docks and the new technology required new premises; the 1843 plan gave approval to both. On land already reclaimed, and on 17 acres freshly won from the sea, a team of Royal Engineer officers – Lt.-Col. Brandreth and Captains William Denison, Henry James and. R. I. Beatson – set out a seven-acre steam basin, completed in 1848, two dry docks, an outstandingly elegant steam factory, a smithery, a boathouse, cast-iron roofs for two of the slips, a brass and an iron foundry and a dock pump house, structures of such proportions that they dwarfed all but the rope-house in the older areas of the yard.[52] The age of steam and iron was emphasised by the opening in 1849 of a branch railway line into the dockyard, steam locomotives sharing the work of haulage with horses and convicts.

Having girded themselves to fight with the most up-to-date warships, the Admiralty was not kept waiting too long to test them, for the Crimean War broke out in 1853. The spate of launchings initiated by the war continued after the Treaty of Paris in 1856 because of the perceived threat of war with France. In the nine years from 1853, 12 warships were constructed as part of a sustained programme designed to increase the Navy's strength through the provision of large vessels. If the *Queen* is discounted, eight of the 12 were larger than anything produced hitherto, while seven were bigger than the *Queen*; appropriately the largest was the 121-gun, 4,127 bm *Victoria*, completed in 1859. These wooden-hulled, sail and steam driven vessels combined both old and new technologies, and not surprisingly their construction required a substantial workforce, which reached 4,633 in 1860.[53] Yet such was the speed of change that a new breed of warship, of which the *Warrior* was one, emerged in response to the advances epitomised by the French *La Gloire*, and the extensions of the 1840s were found to be inadequate. Therefore parliamentary approval was obtained in 1864 for further work which was so extensive that it trebled the area of the dockyard from 99.to 261 acres, half of the land being reclaimed from the harbour and the rest largely deriving from land made available by the removal of the Portsea fortifications.[54] The overall scheme was drawn up by Colonel Sir Andrew Clarke and the work was superintended by three civil engineers on the Admiralty staff: H. Wood, J. Macdonnell and Charles Colson.[55] The central feature was the three interconnected basins with a combined area of 52 acres, together with five docks and a range of linked workshops far removed in scale and function from those in the Georgian yard. Work on this, the Great Extension, began in 1867 and was completed in 1881, long after the threat of war from France had passed. With further modifications to basins and docks in the 1890s and early 20th century, Colonel Clarke's plan proved capable of accommodating the leviathans generated by the rearmament programme and the escalation of naval power prior to 1914.

The pattern of shipbuilding from the 1860s down to 1914, as the graph opposite illustrates, was one of the production of a modest number of warships whose average size and, therefore, firepower rose dramatically. In *Devastation*, of 4,406 bm/9,380 tons, launched in 1871, the Navy received her first ship whose masts were used only for signalling and whose construction was of metal; in *Inflexible*, of 11,880 tons, her armament including four 16-inch guns, the dockyard christened her mightiest product in 1876. If the 1880s saw a sprinkling of large warships amid the total of 12 launched, the final decade of the century was devoted to the manufacture of truly large men-of-war, four of the 11 completed – *Royal Sovereign*, *Majestic*, *Prince George* and *Caesar* – displacing a tonnage significantly above that of *Inflexible*.[56] The most tangible and jingoistic outcome of the race to produce ships capable of outgunning any other afloat was *Dreadnought*, 17,900 tons, launched in 1906, even though all eight ships launched after her until 1917 were larger, in some cases substantially so. The *Iron Duke*, christened in 1914, displaced 25,000 tons, while the *Queen Elizabeth* in 1916, displacing no less than 27,500 tons, represented the highest peak of the yard's endeavour. It was Admiralty policy for the first vessel in each of the *Dreadnought* classes to be built in a naval dockyard,[57]

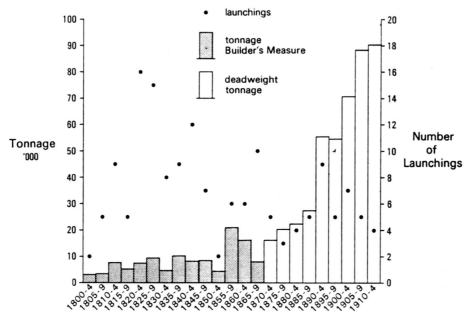

12. The number of ships and tonnages launched at Portsmouth dockyard 1800-1914.
Source: Morgan, *loc. cit.*

and it said much for Portsmouth's reputation that it was selected to execute all the work involved. Despite the panoply of sheer-legs, floating cranes, and above all the gargantuan 240-ton capacity cantilever crane that dominated and indeed symbolised the dockyard until its demolition in 1984, late Victorian and Edwardian shipbuilding was a labour intensive process. Ships' plates were manoeuvred into position largely by human effort, slipway cranes were nothing more than simple derricks, and the system of riveting plates together was nothing if not laborious; some 655 riveters and drillers were on the strength in 1914.[58] That the *Dreadnought* could be launched just 366 days after her keel was laid down was the result of work practices that depended at least as much on the numbers employed as on building technology. Added to this was the introduction of yet another novel form of naval craft, the submarine, five of which were launched between 1916 and 1917. Small wonder, then, that the workforce crept up from 6,300 in 1881 to 7,976 in 1901, attaining 10,439 in 1911[59] and 15,000 by 1914.[60]

The *Royal Sovereign*, which left the stocks in 1917, proved to be the last capital ship to be launched by the dockyard, in part because of the physical limitations imposed by the size of the principal building slip, in part because of the urgent need to fit warships with anti-torpedo bulges and with improved armour plating following the deficiencies exposed at the Battle of Jutland in 1916,[61] and in part as a result of the disarmament agreements signed in Washington in 1922 and then in London in 1930 and 1936. After 1917 no ship of any description was launched until 1922 when the oiler *Murex* was completed, and although production did rise between 1925 and 1930 when the cruisers *Effingham, Suffolk, London* and *Dorsetshire* were finished, by 1931 the numbers employed in building were reduced to two-thirds of the 1914 figure.[62] During the later 1930s much of the dockyard's efforts was expended on extensive reconstruction of existing battleships such as the *Repulse, Warspite,*

13. One of the Royal Navy's first aircraft-carriers, H.M.S. *Furious*, launched as a cruiser in 1916 and re-built as a carrier in 1918, tied up at Portsmouth dockyard *c*.1930.

Renown and *Queen Elizabeth*, the maintenance of the newly introduced aircraft-carriers, and the conversion of light cruisers to anti-aircraft ships and of 'W' class destroyers to anti-submarine escorts. Some building was undertaken, three cruisers being launched between 1934 and 1937, but it was the repair and refit work that was instrumental in raising the dockyard strength to 1914 levels once more by 1938.

During the Second World War recruitment rose even further, reaching 22,000 by the end of hostilities. One vessel was launched during the war, the cruiser *Sirius*, but she had been laid down before September 1939, and unquestionably the emphasis of the 1930s was underlined, especially since proximity to France was now a distinct liability, rendering the yard vulnerable to German air attack, ensuring that the larger fleets seldom visited. Preparations for the Normandy landings of 1944, both in respect of vessels and of the Mulberry harbour system, constituted an important element of work from 1943 onwards. Two submarines, the *Tireless* and the *Token*, were launched in 1945, but it was not the beginning of an upsurge in shipbuilding, for in the next 22 years only a handful of frigates – the *Leopard* (1951), *Rhyl* (1959), *Nubian* (1960), *Sirius* (1964), and last of all the *Andromeda*

(1967) – were constructed on the slips whose pedigree extended some four and a half centuries. Ballistic missiles, rocketry and nuclear submarines with awesome weaponry came to reduce the role of the Navy, and in 1981 the government accepted recommendations that only two main bases were sufficient for the country's needs. Plymouth and Rosyth were selected; Chatham, the old rival, was ignominiously closed, and Portsmouth itself was relegated to a secondary maintenance and repair role. At the same time it lost its title of 'Dockyard' and became H.M. Naval Base Portsmouth. The Falklands War broke out in the spring of 1982, by a remarkable stroke of good fortune before the Defence Review proposals could be implemented. Overnight the yard became frenetically active preparing vessels for operations in the South Atlantic, yet the workers knew that wholesale redundancies would occur once hostilities ceased. And so it proved to be. The workforce, which had stood at 8,000 in 1981, was reduced to proportions exceeded during Napoleonic Wars, that is, some 2,800, while much of the Georgian dockyard was declared superfluous, its buildings being placed in the charge of the Naval Base Property Trust and its new tourist function managed by the Portsmouth Naval Heritage Trust.[63]

It is understandable that the management structure of this huge enterprise should effectively date from the Commonwealth period when the dockyard began the definitive growth which was to continue for three centuries. From 1630 a Master Shipwright had been in charge of the yard,[64] but in 1649 a Resident Commissioner[65] was appointed – the first was William Willoughby as we have seen – under whom there were a number of theoretically-equal principal officers. In practice the most senior was the Master Shipwright, known as the Builder,[66] who was in control of all the work connected with the building and refitting of ships, and who might design a vessel himself, as did John Tippetts in the 1650s.[67] The Master Attendant was responsible for the movement of vessels, for the supervision of riggers and sailmakers, and for the Ordinary. The Clerk of the Cheque was concerned with finance, the payment of wages and mustering. The reception and handling of stores was the task of the Clerk of the Survey, and the storage and issue of materials was the domain of the Storekeeper. The Boatswain of the Yard had control of the labourers. The master workmen were those in charge of particular trades such as ropemaking and sailmaking, although many of the master workmen such as the Master Mast Maker, the Master Joyner, the Master Boat Builder, the Master House Carpenter, the Master Smith and the Master Bricklayer were actually on the staff of the Master Shipwright.[68] Below the principal officers were the inferior officers whose job it was to carry out checks on work undertaken.

Curiously enough the principal officers were not responsible to the Navy Board, of which the Commissioner was a member, but to the Admiralty, to whom in turn the Navy Board was also responsible. Commissioner Middleton complained in 1774 following an investigation into the cause of the subsidence of the basin that the principal officers were 'as independent of us as if we were unconnected with them'.[69] Moreover recommendations for promotion made by the Navy Board could be, and were, sometimes overruled by the Admiralty. The principal officers received incomes at least as high as those received by senior management in commerce. In the early-Victorian period the Master Shipwright was paid £650 a year, the Storekeeper, Engineer and Clerk of the Cheque only slightly less, while the Assistant Master Shipwrights received £400. It has been estimated that in the early 19th century the very highest managers received £500-£2,000, 'typical managers' being paid £100-£250.[70]

Concomitant with their sizeable incomes the officers were provided with houses and gardens within the yard, although until the Commissioner's house was built in 1666 he had to reside with the Mayor. 'Wheare I am now', complained Commissioner Thomas Middleton to Pepys in 1665, 'wee are forsced to packe nyne people in a room to sleepe in, not above 16 foote one way and 12 foot the other. We are 26 in family in Mr Mayour's house, 9 of which are small children'.[71] Houses had been provided for the Master Attendant, First Assistant, Master Caulker, Storekeeper and the Surgeon by 1665, and by 1700 there were 15 officers' houses scattered about the yard.[72] In order to provide more space for timber stacking and to ease movement through the yard, a formal urban terrace known as Long Row, latterly the Parade, backing on to the dockyard wall, was completed in 1717, for nine of the officers. At the foot of their gardens a horse pond was stocked with fish for culinary convenience. Long Row was followed much later by Thomas Telford's Short Row of 1787, allowing the remaining houses to be taken down. The Commissioner's house, whose garden had by 1774 come to achieve a length of 200 yards, was replaced in 1786 by Admiralty House, designed by Samuel Wyatt, in a less obstructive location in the south-east of the yard.

Admiralty House was built on the site of the dockyard chapel constructed in 1704 from a voluntary subscription of 2d. a month by dockyard-men, and as a consequence a new place of worship, St Ann's, was erected in 1785 to the design of John Marquand and Thomas Telford.[73] The church provided a spiritual focus for the officers of the yard, their families and servants, and for the staff and scholars of the Naval Academy which opened in 1733 in architecturally-outstanding premises, now used as the staff officers' mess. Some forty young gentlemen between the ages of 13 and 16 were registered to receive an education and training as naval officers, the rationale being that these twin aims could be carried out more effectively ashore than at sea. It was also a means by which the Admiralty hoped to provide a mode of entry for its own nominees as an alternative to the method favoured by naval officers, who simply sponsored their own protégés.[74] Unfortunately the scheme never found favour since the naval establishment 'looked upon scientific attainment not so much as a waste of time, but as injurious to the acquisition of seamanship and the details of routine'.[75] The Academy was later reconstituted as the Royal Naval College and as such was the precursor of the colleges at Dartmouth and Greenwich. The first, but short-lived, School of Naval Architecture was opened in 1811 almost opposite the Academy, with which it was combined in 1816, the architect of this sombre building being Edmund Hall. The yard officers and their dependants, the academics and scholars, who collectively totalled 253 souls at the 1851 census, constituted something of an élite community in what was essentially a working environment.

However important the officers of the yard may have been, the great majority of those employed belonged to the lower grades in the hierarchy. As might be expected there was a wide range of skills to be found in a naval dockyard, 28 being listed for Portsmouth in 1739.[76] The shipwrights were the most numerous, followed in the era of the wooden ship by the house carpenters, caulkers, scavelmen who were responsible for cleaning and pumping out the docks, the ropeyard spinners and the sawyers. Of these trades the shipwrights, who worked in gangs of 15 in the charge of a quarterman, were the most senior, a position reflected in their rates of pay, which remained unchanged for all dockyard-men from the 1690s until 1788.[77] Shipwrights received 2s. 1d. a day, as did caulkers, joiners received 2s., house carpenters and sail makers were paid 1s. 10d., hammermen in the smithy were paid 1s. 8d., riggers got 1s. 6d., scavelmen between 1s. 3d. and 1s. 6d., and labourers between 1s. 1d. and 1s. 2d. a day. A lodging allowance of $2\frac{1}{2}$d. a week was made to shipwrights, caulkers, joiners, house carpenters, sailmakers and smiths, a practice dating from the early 17th century when short-term employment was the rule, but which remained in force after permanent employment was established. From 1801 until 1830 shipwrights received 6d. a day and labourers 3d. a day as 'chip money' in lieu of the right to remove from the yard pieces of wood less than three feet in length. The concession was systematically abused and wood was routinely cut to lengths of 2 ft. $11\frac{1}{2}$ in., powerfully influencing Portsea's domestic architecture, since stairs, doors, shutters and cupboards were invariably made from wood of this measurement.[78] One in five shipwrights was entitled to an allowance of 1s. 2d. to 1s. 10d. as reward for supervising an apprentice, and all grades were paid overtime in multiples of 'tides' of 1½ hours, which equated with one-third of a day's pay; during the 18th-century wars two 'tides' were regularly worked.[79] Plain-time rates were gradually abolished from 1775 and the task and job system introduced in its place,[80] while in 1834 merit payments were made. Three categories were recognised: the industrious, accounting for one-fifth of the workforce, the mediocre, and the ill-behaved and idle; the system lingered on until the 1890s.[81] Until 1814 wages were paid quarterly and in arrears, requiring a man to work for six months before receiving any wage at all. As a consequence the role of credit, epitomised in the 'ticket' system, was important to the town, since workers often lived for long periods on credit from local 'ticket' dealers who drew the men's tickets for pay from the Navy Office. The system certainly helped to tie workers to dockyard service, and moreover it has been estimated that a shipwright forfeited 40s. a year in interest payments incurred.[82]

Because of the lack of effective artificial lighting until the use of gas in the 19th century, dockyard hours were very much determined by the season. Between March and October a 12-hour working day from 6 a.m. to 6 p.m., with half an hour for breakfast and one and a half hours for dinner, was the rule. In winter the hours were from dawn to dusk with no allowance for breakfast and one hour for dinner.[83] From 1861 work on a Saturday finished at 4 p.m. Official time was sounded by the bell of the dockyard clock, which after 1780 was located in the cupola above the Middle Store.[84] The 19th-century dockyard-man was granted regular paid holidays: the occasion of the royal birthday, coronation day, Easter day and Christmas day. Launch days and election days were similarly treated, while four days were granted for the purpose of visiting the Great Exhibition in 1851, and three days were offered for the enjoyment of the Crystal Palace exhibition in 1862.[85] The seasons impinged upon the life of a dockyard-man from a second direction, for marked peaks in the numbers employed were exhibited in the winter in wartime since naval campaigns were normally mounted in the summer when the weather was more clement. In the summer of 1693, for instance, some eight hundred men were on the strength, but during the following winter the total climbed to no less than fifteen hundred.[86] From 1774, however, these seasonal peaks disappeared as naval warfare became an all year round activity. What did not disappear was the marked contraction of the workforce immediately on the cessation of hostilities, noted above, although by the second half of the 19th century a rather more humane view prevailed. While on the one hand Gladstone could see no justification for the maintenance of the 5,358 employed in 1866, pruning the establishment to 4,004 by 1870,[87] on the other at least troopships were provided to facilitate the emigration of the unemployed to Canada in 1860 and 1870.[88]

The apparent ease with which the Navy Board was able to dismiss workmen owed much to the practice of recruiting hired labour, which for instance comprised 15 per cent of the total in 1841, but 40 per cent in 1860, and whose services could readily be dispensed with.[89] Men with unsatisfactory records were regarded as prime candidates for dismissal, and those who had lost more than 70 days work during 1815 were the first to lose their jobs in March 1816.[90] The presence of hired labour was advantageous to the Navy Board in another sense, for although the hired men received a better wage than established men, the relative security enjoyed by the latter caused the hired men to seek selection for permanent status, thereby reducing pressure for wage claims, and indeed militancy. Working in the same direction was the practice of shoaling, by which shipwrights were dismissed once a year and re-employed the same day through selection by Quartermen in the latter's order of seniority.[91] Shoaling was later modified so that a chargeman kept some of his men, but it was still divisive and was not abolished until the early 1950s.[92] The employment of ex-naval ratings accustomed to discipline also helped to damp down on pressure for improved pay and conditions. Another source of docile labour was convicts, conveniently if miserably housed in hulks moored in the harbour. When, in 1828, 100 labourers were dismissed and the horse contract cancelled, convicts replaced both men and the horses which were used on the dockyard tramway.[93] Some six hundred and fifty convicts were working in the yard in the 1830s,[94] the construction of the steam basin in the 1840s involved twelve hundred,[95] and during the Great Extension they manned the on-site brickworks in addition to carrying out labouring tasks. In the light of these influences trade union membership did not become general until the 1860s and 1870s,[96] but even then the Admiralty insisted that the traditional yard procedures of annual petitions and deputations be followed, thus reducing union power.[97]

Yet strikes were far from unknown in the yard. During the 17th century the government was consistently slow in paying wages, sometimes as much as a year's pay being owed,[98] causing the shipwrights in 1652 to refuse to work until they were paid.[99] Matters did not improve and in 1664 workmen were being 'turned out of doors by their landlords and perishing more like dogs than men'.[100] Writing to Pepys on 29 June 1665, Commissioner Middleton remarked that 'the ropemakers have discharged themselves for want of money and are gone out into the country to make hay'.[101] Even the drastic strategy of a payment of 10s. to each man by Middleton from his own pocket in October 1665 failed to conclude the strife, although it had petered out by November.[102] Poor pay, dismissals and above all the attempt to introduce the task-and-job system led to the strike of 14 June 1775. An appeal was made 'To the gentlemen, tradesmen and inhabitants of Gosport, Portsmouth and Portsmouth Common' on 7 July, and most of the men held out until mid-August;[103] at least task-and-job was not immediately brought into force. August 1795 saw the ropemakers on strike; as a group they seem to have been particularly sensitive to mismanagement, a Company of Ropemakers having been formed in the dockyards in the late 17th century.[104] They certainly had real standing in Portsmouth for in 1828 it was reported that on the king's visits to the town they would precede the royal carriage from the borough boundary, uniformly dressed with blue sashes across the shoulder, bearing white staves and the national flag.[105] The dockyard-men were involved in one of the earliest attempts at labour co-operation, for arising from the need to buy cheap flour and bread in the war, on 10 May 1796 they formed the Union Society and built a windmill on the shoreline to the east of the Portsea fortifications. Undeterred by the acquisition of the site in 1816 by the Board of Ordnance, and reconstituting themselves as the Dock Mill Society, they constructed a second mill in 1817 in what is now Napier Road, Southsea.[106]

Self-help, albeit of a less legitimate kind, had long been a feature of naval dockyards, and Portsmouth was no exception. The pilfering of government stores was the principal reason for the De Gomme palisade and its brick successor built between 1704 and 1711. For the same reason stores were stamped with an arrowhead to assist their identification, and heavy penalties were meted out to those caught removing goods. In 1813 John Griffin, for example, was arrested in possession of 75 lbs of copper and lead and was sentenced to death, although this was later commuted to transportation for seven years.[107] Pilfering was relatively easy for sailors bringing contractors' stores, and on one occasion in 1782 cordage to the value of more than £50 was found on a Sunderland coal brig.[108]

The very presence of the dockyard police acted as a deterrent to workmen's enterprise, although not with complete success: it was the police who first noticed the apparently eccentric habit of one dockyard-man who used to take his wheelbarrow home to lunch with him every day, some time elapsing before it was realised that he never returned with it after the break. The early dockyard police were termed watchmen and worked only at night; they were controlled by the Porter, whose lodge at the Victory Gate is the oldest building in the yard, dating from 1708.[109] During the 19th century the police were in fact members of the Metropolitan Police on detachment, 49 being enumerated in 1851 of whom one was a superintendent, seven were sergeants and the remainder constables. A fire brigade came to be an integral part of dockyard life, for many years the space beneath Bentham's water tower being used as the fire station. In similar military vein, dockyard-men were themselves used as a fighting force, 1,204 taking oaths of allegiance in 1715 during the anti-Jacobite campaign, two months after which a dockyard foot regiment was raised under Commissioner Townshend.[110]. Predictably the other senior ranks reflected the yard hierarchy, the Master Shipwright becoming a lieutenant-colonel, the Clerk of the Cheque a major, and the other officers captains and lieutenants.[111] A Dockyard Battalion was formed in 1847, comprising 12 infantry and 10 artillery companies; the men were resplendently dressed in blue coats, dark trousers with a red stripe and an Albert cap.[112]

The scale, variety and technological excellence of the dockyard were sources of fascination to contemporary topographers and to the public alike. The block mills, the smithery where 'the scene can only be compared to the classic description of the Vulcanian forge, while the Herculean forms of the artificers afford the finest possible models of human strength',[113] and the convict hulks were especially popular with visitors, who were able to undertake tours of inspection in the 1820s during the hours of 10 a.m. to 3 p.m. in summer and 10 a.m. to 2 p.m. in winter.[114] More importantly, the dockyard was the workplace for very large numbers of Portsmouth men, between three-fifths and two-thirds of those working in manufacturing passing through the dockyard gates between 1841 and 1901.[115] Measom could justifiably remark of Portsmouth that 'Everything looks, breathes and smells of soldiers, sailors and dockmen, the three classes who rule the state of society here'.[116]

Given the voracious appetite of the yard for materials, it is not unreasonable to have anticipated the emergence in the town of a range of manufacturing firms relying on dockyard contracts. For reasons of economy and quality control, however, the Navy Board pursued a policy of self-sufficiency, providing the yard with its own ropehouse, foundry, smithery, copper mill, saw mill, sail loft and eventually a pulley-block mill. Those local firms that did supply the yard were all small undertakings. This certainly applied in the 1650s to William Smith and John Timbrell, respectively makers of pulley blocks and anchors,[117] in the 1770s to Geo. Poate, Tho. Bartlett and Jos. Feltham, respectively makers of candles, founder's wares and bricks,[118] and in the 1860s to J. A. Baldy, ironfounders.[119] The enormous quantities of timber supplied undoubtedly added to the wealth of some local landowners such as Richard Norton at Southwick in the 1660s,[120] and to many local merchants who handled imports of this and many other commodities such as coal, hemp and iron, but their transformation was achieved behind the dockyard wall. Even then the potential for local merchants was limited since most supplies were delivered direct to the yard, local representatives not being used.[121] Further, the contractors employed on the successive extensions were in the main not local. The London firm of Templar and Parlby was responsible for much of the Georgian dockyard, Leather Smith & Co. of London built the Great Extension, and the Glasgow firm of Morrison and Mason were the contractors for the Edwardian modifications.[122] Only Benjamin Bramble, who was mayor in 1850, 1851 and 1852, broke this monopoly; he constructed building slips in the 1830s and, with the London contractor Peter Rolt, he won the steam basin contract in the 1840s.[123]

If the dockyard provided little other than wages for a large labour force, in an indirect fashion it was responsible for the emergence of the clothing industry as the 19th- and early 20th-century civilian counterpoint to naval shipbuilding. Between 1841 and 1911 the production of clothing occupied between 38 and 45 per cent of the manufacturing work force, while, as late as 1961, 11 per cent was still so employed, representing the second most important manufacturing activity. The importance of naval tailoring was one reason, but more crucial was the availability of female labour, following the absence of husbands serving abroad in both the Navy and the Army, the presence of so many widows consequent upon naval disasters, and the draconian dockyard dismissals in 1816, 1857, 1868-9 and 1887.[124] Portsmouth wages were much lower than those in London, and in respect of the town's specialisation, corsets,[125] one of Mayhew's correspondents remarked in 1849 that 'They are mostly stitched at Portsmouth now. They can get it done cheaper there . . . owing to the sailors' wives round there I suppose'.[126] By 1911 no less than 2,896 Portmuthians, almost all women, were employed in the manufacture of corsets, the leading firms being those of the Leethem and Reynolds families.

To the dockyard may be ascribed a number of other idiosyncratic elements of Portsmouth's economy. The corporation was consistently refused permission by the Board of Ordnance to develop the Camber in Old Portsmouth, whither the railway company was never able to build a line, and schemes for the construction of docks on the site of the mill pond between Portsea and Old Portsmouth, and in Langstone Harbour,[127] were vetoed. The paucity of Portsmouth's commercial shipbuilding industry in the 19th century and after must owe something to the reluctance of the Admiralty to allow activities which might interfere with naval movements in the harbour.[128] The great institution that was the dockyard, to which arguably Portsmouth owed its existence and to which the nation owed so much, inevitably shaped Portsmouth to its image, and only in the fourth quarter of the 20th century is its impact beginning to wane.

A convict hulk.

Chapter Four

Stone Towers: The Fortifications of Portsmouth

By the end of Henry VII's reign, the town of Portsmouth, in the south-west corner of Portsea Island, was one of the most heavily defended areas in Northern Europe. It was its importance as a naval port with shipbuilding and repair facilities as well as victualling resources that had persuaded successive monarchs from the late 14th century to fortify the harbour entrance and defend the town. The Earl of Surrey, writing in 1513 to the Privy Council, was confident that the French would not dare enter Portsmouth Harbour if they knew how well it was thus defended 'which is the most best fortified thing with bulwarks, trenches and great pieces of artillery thick in them that ever I saw or heard of . . . '.[1] And, a generation later, Marillac,[2] writing to his master, the King of France, Francis I, reported that work still continued apace, ramparts and fortifications being well advanced.[3] However, he noted further, to Montmorency,[4] in another letter, that the fortifications although almost finished 'and of very great extent, sufficient to make good defence of that coast . . .', were 'not very durable, being made of stakes filled with earth, as if made in a hurry . . .'.[5] It was a familiar story. The Bishop of Winchester, Richard Fox, wrote in a letter to Wolsey in February 1518 that: 'If war be intended against England, the Isle of Wight and Portsmouth are too feeble for defence. Our manner is never to prepare for war to our enemies be light at our doors'.[6] The trouble was that although Portsmouth was indeed heavily defended by the end of Henry VII's reign, there was no continuity of building over the years and little maintenance of the fortifications. They were 'summoned to life' by the renewal of warfare, usually with France and, when hostilities ended, they returned to disuse and disrepair. Portsmouth's strategic importance ensured that when conflict threatened, however, the town played a key part in any schemes for the nation's defences, and this situation obtained until the mid-19th century.

The fortifying of Portsmouth began in the late 14th century, as a direct result of the Hundred Years War. The town was attacked and burnt twice by French raiding parties during the reign of Edward III. It was also becoming an increasingly important port of embarkation for continental expeditions. Therefore in 1386 a commission was appointed to survey the town and take appropriate steps to improve its defences. It is probable that at this time a simple earthwork was put up round the town. The Round Tower at the harbour entrance was under construction *c.*1416-22, the building being supervised first by Robert Rodyngton, who was appointed 'surveyor of certain works to be done with all good speed at the entrance of the port of Portsmouth' in December 1416, and secondly by Robert Barbot, who was clerk of the works at Portsmouth 1420-22. Barbot spent £1,069 9s. 8½d. building the Round Tower during this time and erecting a wharf at 'Childrode', on the Gosport side of the harbour, as a prelude to building a second tower in order to stretch an iron chain across the harbour mouth between the two towers. This second tower does not seem ever to have been completed, however. The Round Tower still stands at the entrance to the harbour though. It was recorded in Elizabeth's reign, in the Articles of Complaint against Sir Adrian Poynings, Captain of the Town, that

> by the orders and aunciente constitucions of this Towne of Portesmouthe ordayned by the wyse and discreat governors thereof, whiche hathe contynued the space of ii hundrethe yeares and over that all the passag botes that sayle usithe betwene the yle of wighte and Portesmouthe should brynge everye of them once in the yeare one bote lode of rocke stones and laye them within the pyles of the

14. The Round Tower, under construction c.1416-22.

rounde Tower near to the havens mouthe by the maiors appointment and order, Or else to paye unto the Towne iis a peace for everye suche defaulte whiche was and is for the better preservacion of the sayd Tower.[7]

Stephen Lote, the king's Master Mason, was in charge of the works when they began. He died soon afterwards, when his place was taken by William Colchester and, two years later, by Thomas Mapillon.

In 1494 work began on the Square Tower and a bulwark to protect the town on the seaward side. According to Sir Frederic Madden the architect employed on the Square Tower was Richard Shirborne, at the command of Henry VII.[8] In 1495-6 Henry VII built a dry dock on a site some fourteen hundred yards north-north-west of the town, near to where H.M.S. *Victory* is today. There is evidence that buildings already existed on this site: the offices of the clerk of the king's ships, a storehouse and a forge. It seems also that the dock itself was not new but rather was being repaired or reconstructed. The date 1495-6 is usually regarded as the birth date of the dockyard, however, and therefore of fundamental importance to the growth of Portsmouth.

The victualling base was established in the town itself, the first beerhouse, brewery or brewhouse, as it was more commonly called, being built in about 1492. Improved brewing and baking facilities were provided in 1512-13 and a great storehouse in 1514. Indeed, it has been suggested that the principal reason for the building and subsequent improvement of the town's defences was the security of these breweries, bakeries and storehouses, not the safety of the town itself.[9]

Little of a major and lasting nature was done to improve existing defences before the invasion crisis of 1538-9. Between Autumn 1522 and Spring 1524 it would seem that there was built an earthwork line of bank and ditch possibly with some timberwork in the revetting or parapet, strengthened by a series of bulwarks, also of earth. By 1526, however, the town and its new defences were reported to be 'in sore ruin and decay'.[10] The period 1522-4 probably saw also the construction of some of the outlying bulwarks including Palshed's Bulwark, also known as the Windmill Bulwark, to the west of the present South Parade Pier and to the east of Ketes Point where Southsea Castle was later built. These bulwarks also were allowed to fall swiftly into decay. But in the spring of 1539, there was a furious burst of renewed activity in the face of the threat of a combined invasion of these shores by France and Spain. Defences of earth, stone and turf were rushed up round Portsmouth and the defences to the east of the town along the shore were consolidated with two new bulwarks being built, one in the Clarence Pier area and another, Chatterton's Bulwark, much farther east in the area of Lump's Fort. John Leland has left an account of these defences:

> The toune . . . is murid[11] from the est tour[12] a forowgh[13] lenght with a mudde waulle armid with tymbre, wher on be great peaces both of yren and brasen ordinauns, and this peace of the waulle having diche without it rennith so far flat south south est, and is the place most apte to defend the town ther open on the haven.
>
> Then rennith a diche almost flat est for a space: and withyn it is a waulle of mudde lyke to the other: and so thens goith round aboute the town to the circuite of a myle.
>
> There is a gate of tymbre at the north est ende of the town: and by it is cast up an hille of erth dichid; wherein be gunnes to defende entre into the town by land.[14]

On the seaward side of the town the defences ran now in a line over a thousand yards long from the Round Tower, encompassing the Square Tower, the Platform alongside, the bulwark in between, known as the Green Bulwark, and the New Bulwark, on the site of Clarence Pier. Thus, an enemy ship attempting to enter the harbour would be fired on and any hostile force attempting to land farther along the coast and threaten the victualling base in the town and the undefended docks would come under fire from Palshed's Bulwark and Chatterton's Bulwark. A bulwark at 'Portswaye', i.e. at Portsbridge, was built at this time too to defend the northern approaches to the town. This was the beginning of attempts to defend the whole of Portsea Island although the defences were still medieval in character. In the works which continued in Portsmouth in the following years, however, and in the schemes projected for the town but not completed, a growing awareness now of new ideas in defensive warfare may be seen.

Southsea Castle, which was begun in 1544, represents a major shift in ideas relating to military engineering, being a stage in the move from rounded to angled bastions. The works projected in the plans of new defences for Portsmouth produced following Henry VIII's visit to the town in 1545 and the encounter with the French off Portsmouth when the *Mary Rose* sank, indicate a complete grasp now of these new notions. Briefly, the gun had now taken the place in warfare of the missile-throwing devices of the Middle Ages, and medieval rounded towers and bastions represented too great a target for cannon and provided too little flanking cover. An angled bastion gave minimum target to the front and it was possible to site guns in the flanks of adjacent bastions to give all-round cover. It was a style of military architecture which was developed first in Italy and the Eastern Mediterranean and

15.   Southsea Castle, begun 1544, from the air. The D-Day Museum, 1984, can be seen in the background.

only slowly became accepted in the west. However it was to remain the dominant feature of defensive works for some three hundred years.

It has been suggested that the first true angle bastion in this country was in fact built in Portsmouth, as part of the planned new defences for the town which included a new line of bastions and curtains to be constructed, initially of earth, incorporating angle bastions with batteries in their recessed flanks. These bastions can be seen on a contemporary map.[15] The full extent of the works contemplated is contained in a document now at Hatfield House amongst the archives of the Marquis of Salisbury.[16] The project was never seen through. The crisis receded, money was in short supply and disease took its toll of the labour force. Of work done, however, a 'bastylian' was erected between the Round Tower and Point Gate, a similar 'bastylian' was erected by the town gate and another, known later as

Guy's Bulwark, was built 'towardes Kingeston'.[17] The four brewhouses were further protected by a new 'mounte' and another bulwark built at the extreme north-west corner of the town, later known as the Square or Dock Bulwark. Work was also done at this time to strengthen the defences on the southern shores of Portsea Island.

Inevitably, though, these works soon fell into a state of disrepair. The young King Edward VI, visiting the town in August 1552 while on a tour of the south coast, was not impressed by what he saw:

> we find the Bulwarkes chargeable, massie, well rampared, but il facioned, il flanked, and set in unmete places, the toune weake in comparison of that it ought to be, though great (for within the walls ar faire and large closis and much vacant rome) the haven notable great and standing by Nature easy to be fortefied . . .[18]

He 'devised tow fortes to be made upon the entry of the haven'.[19] Nothing was done, however, until 1556, when relations with France deteriorated once again. A warrant was issued for repairs to be carried out to the docks and defences but it was only tinkering with the problem and little was done. Matters dragged on throughout the period 1557-60 and it was not until 1560 that serious work got under way. Masonry revetements were probably added to the existing earthworks, the four brewhouses, storehouses and other buildings repaired and a new stone quay or wharf constructed with three cranes. This work continued between 1560 and 1563. Between 1568 and 1572 a new gun platform was built and works carried out at the Round Tower. Surveyor of these works was Richard Popinjay, who had first been appointed to oversee work on the town's defences in 1560 as 'overseer' in succession to the then surveyor, William Ridgeway. He was not in fact styled 'surveyor' as such until 1562.

A new programme of works to protect the town began in 1584 as invasion of the country was feared either directly from Spain or from the Spanish Netherlands. Between 1585 and 1594 the old walls and earthworks were remodelled on Italian lines. This included repairing the earthworks from the Green Bulwark to the Dock Bulwark and wharf on the west, building a stone wall along the east side of the Camber connecting the wharf with the seawall near the Round Tower, modifying the long curtain between the Green Bulwark and the East Bulwark which was so long that its middle part, near where the brewhouses stood, was unprotected by cannon-fire, making two small flankers near the brewhouses and, finally, constructing a full-size bulwark at the brewhouses (the Four Houses Bulwark), making alterations to the ditches and rebuilding the storehouse. The works on the north side of the town included also building a bridge across the ditch at the nothern entry into the town. It was quite an elaborate structure in two sections which crossed the ditch by way of a small ravelin and entered the town through the Gate Bastion. There were stone gatehouses at both ends and a drawbridge which was operable from the outer gate. The inner gate was the gate-keeper's lodge. It is significant that, apart from Berwick, Portsmouth was the only English town where an up-to-date bastioned system of defences was built during Elizabeth's reign.

There were no further major alterations or additions made to the town's defences until after the Restoration. In fact no new forts were built in England between Elizabeth's reign and the outbreak of the Civil War. Shortly after his return, however, Charles II put in hand a thorough-going review of the nation's defences and over the next twenty years or so the defences of the more important naval ports and dockyards opposite the coasts of France and the United Provinces were brought up-to-date in accordance with the latest theories of military engineering. Work began in Portsmouth in 1665 to the designs of Sir Bernard de Gomme, the king's chief engineer. De Gomme was a Netherlander who had served with some distinction on the royalist side during the Civil War. He was clearly familiar with the advances which had been made in the theory of fortification during the 17th century not only in his own country but in France where engineers were moving the main emphasis of defence from the curtain walls of their strongholds outwards, beyond the original moat, by means of additional moats or water barriers and outworks.

In Portsmouth, de Gomme retained the original line of the fortifications round the town but the ramparts themselves and the bastions were remodelled, the flanks being, eventually, perpendicular to the line of defence, not the curtain, and thus capable of achieving direct fire over the face of the adjacent bastion. The moat was widened and a second moat was dug outside the first, being separated from it by a covered way with bastions opposite two of the main salients: Pembroke Bastion and Town Bastion, and redans, outworks consisting of two faces forming a salient angle, opposite the curtains. There was also a glacis built on the counterscarp of both moats, i.e. a continuous earthwork pitched on the outside face at an angle to the ramparts. Spur Redoubt was built on the seafront on Long Curtain, which

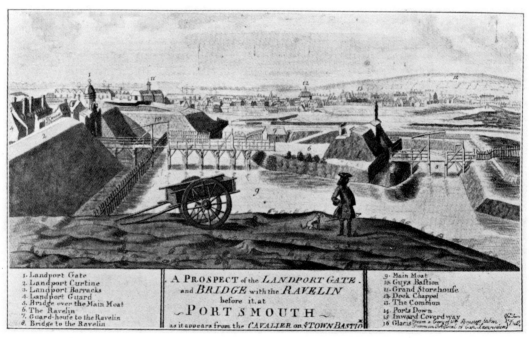

1. Landport Gate
2. Landport Curtine
3. Landport Barracks
4. Landport Guard
5. Bridge over the Main Moat
6. The Ravelin
7. Guard-house to the Ravelin
8. Bridge to the Ravelin

A PROSPECT of the *LANDPORT GATE* . and *BRIDGE* with the *RAVELIN* before it, at
~ P O R T S M O U T H ~
as it appears from the *CAVALIER on TOWN BASTION*

9. Main Moat
10. Guys Bastion
11. Grand Storehouse
12. Dock Chappel
13. The Common
14. Ports Down
15. Inward Coverd way
16. Glacis

16.   Landport Gate, *c*.1717.

may still be seen, and at Landport a ravelin, a detached bastion, was built in the moat between Town Mount and Guy's Bastion, making it necessary now to cross three separate bridges to gain entrance to the town: one over the outer moat, another across the inner moat to the ravelin and, finally, a last bridge from the ravelin into the town. This was the first of four ravelins to be built on the land between the two moats between now and the middle of the next century. Other work included building a great, casemated battery, 'Eighteen-Gun' or 'Sally Port' Battery, beside the Round Tower and another to match across the harbour at Blockhouse Point, and a bastion, Camber Bastion, to protect further this part of the town. The dockyard was also enclosed within a very simple earthwork. At Southsea Castle the defences were strengthened with a dry moat, glacis and covered way. Gosport's increasing importance was reflected in the scheme of defensive works put in hand there in

1678. A rampart and moat were constructed to protect the town on the landward side and two small forts were built to strengthen the defences at the entrance to the harbour: Fort Charles to the north of Gosport Hard and Fort James on Rat Island, in the harbour.

An interesting insight into what building these new works meant for the owners of the land required for these schemes is contained in the Schedule to the Act of 1671 which compensated them.[20] Some fifty-nine acres of land in the various common fields surrounding the town of Portsmouth, with an annual value of approximately £60, were purchased by the crown. The sum offered by way of compensation was £1,390 and an agreement was entered into between the Treasury and Richard Norton of Southwick,[21] acting on behalf of all the owners, being one of the principal landholders himself, for the money to be paid over to him for distribution to the other owners. Twenty-four separate individuals received sums varying between the £5 paid to Mrs. Beeston and £5 7s. to Richard Norton himself, and the 5s. paid to Mrs. Pickers and 4s. 6d. to Mr. Moody.

Britain was at war for a good part of the 18th century, chiefly against France, and Portsmouth's strategic importance was reflected in the fact that it was the only place in England where fortifications were built on any large scale. The main aim of the works now, however, was not so much to protect the town and dockyard but to extend the fortified area to embrace the whole of Portsea Island – a trend first discernible almost two hundred years before. Briefly, cannon for use in the field had now become sufficiently mobile to make it practicable for an enemy force to land at some nearby spot on the south coast, march inland and capture Portsmouth from the rear, to the north. Works were therefore put in hand at Portsbridge, where a simple fortification had existed since the 16th century but was now, according to a newly-discovered document lodged recently in the Portsmouth City Records Office entitled 'State of the Government of Portsmouth 1745', 'ruinous and the drawbridge rotten and gon, and the ditch fill'd up . . .'.[22] A continuous rampart with moat was built 1746-7 across the northern edge of Portsea Island linking Langstone Harbour and Portsmouth Harbour, and the redoubt at Portsbridge itself was rebuilt. Work also began on the first Fort Cumberland, in the south-eastern corner of Portsea Island at the entrance to Langstone Harbour, which with its two supporting batteries built at Lumps and Eastney would protect the entrance to the harbour where, as the anonymous author of the 'State of the Government' noted, was 'a convenient landing place by deep water, and the only landing place in the island of Portsea between that harbour [Langstone] and the harbour of Portsmouth'.[23]

Aside from these new works, alterations were made to the fortifications of the old town under the direction of John Peter Desmaretz. Between 1745 and 1756, the double moat built by de Gomme disappeared and the two covered ways were made into one. Thus the fortifications acquired the shape they were to retain until the end of their useful existence a hundred years later, with the curtain between the various bastions protected by single large ravelins and the whole encircled by the glacis and the one covered way. Desmaretz, who was living in Warblington Street in 1758, was in fact buried at Portsmouth in the Garrison Church. A plaque erected there to his memory by his daughter recorded that he died on 16 September 1768, aged 82, and that

> Though born a foreigner, he early adopted every generous sentiment of civil and religious liberty, and exerted his active abilities for the service of this nation, in quality of an engineer. An indefatigable zeal and unshaken integrity in the execution of several important works committed to his charge deservedly entitled him to the approbation of his superiors and the esteem of the public . . .[24]

It has been suggested that this reorganisation of the town's defences made it possible to reduce the size of the garrison and made the whole business of guarding the town easier.[25] There is a description of the garrison in the 'State of the Government'. Apparently it consisted at this time of a governor, lieutenant-governor, town adjutant, surgeon, marshal, town porter, master gunner and 15 gunners. On the five bastions, two demi-bastions and other works some 133 guns were mounted. The author does not mention the number of men. Stephen Martin-Leake writing in January 1728-9 indicated, however, that the garrison in war was composed normally of two regiments of foot but in peace of eight companies of invalids, making 400 men.[26] He gives a glimpse of what life was like in a garrison town, too. The same order was observed, he said, as in other such towns:

> As soon as it is dusk a gun is fired from the platform, as a warning it is time to shut the Land Gate, whereupon the tattoo is beat round the town and in a moderate time after the Land Gate is shut; but the Water Gate is not shut till ten o'clock, and the Point Gate not till eleven, when notice is given by ringing a bell of the church.[27]

Daniel Defoe, writing a few years before in 1724 reported that few inhabitants complained of 'such things as are the consequence of a garrison town, such as being examin'd at the gates, such as being obliged to keep garrison hours, and not be let out, or let in after nine a clock at night, and the like'. These are things, he continued, that 'no people will count a burthen, where they get their bread by the very situation of the place, as is the case here'.[28] Thus Defoe put his finger on a fact which was as applicable then as it had been in the 15th century, a fact which continued to be applicable until comparatively recently, which was that Portsmouth's whole economy was geared to being the home of the dockyard. Leland sensed this almost two hundred years earlier when he wrote that 'the town of Portesmouth is bare and litle occupied in time of pece'.[29]

Work on the fortifications continued in the second half of the 18th century and into the 19th century. In 1770 the fortification of the dockyard and its satellite town of Portsea started and in 1794 work began which was to continue until 1820 on the second Fort Cumberland. It was a bastioned fort of irregular pentagonal shape. A new departure was the use made of casemates below the ramparts, primarily for barrack accommodation. This was to be an important trend in mid-19th-century military engineering and interestingly Fort Cumberland with Fort Monckton, which was built a little while before on the Gosport shore to prevent attack on the dockyard from that quarter, were two of the last bastioned forts to be built in England, for new ideas in military engineering were gaining currency. The old bastion system was now acknowledged as inadequate. Chief among the problems was the difficulty experienced in providing good frontal fire and concentrating fire from the different faces in the directions required. It was also easy for the enemy to rake the bastions with their guns. Finally, the very complexity of defensive schemes such as de Gomme's dispersed a possibly stretched, beleaguered garrison.

As in the past, the new ideas came from Europe, this time not only from France but from Germany, too. Active rather than passive defence was now the order of the day. Basically, ramparts were to be designed to hold as many guns as possible – to overwhelm the enemy fire. The faces of the forts were to be made up of straight lines of parapets with deep ditches flanked by caponiers, or bomb-proof galleries, projecting into them. This was the 'polygonal' system of fortification. As artillery improved, a further refinement of the polygonal system was the 'Prussian' system: a series of mutually supporting detached forts in place of a continuous line. Forts Elson and Gomer to the west of Gosport, begun in 1852, were the first forts to be built in this part of the world on polygonal lines with caponiers protecting the ditches and, with Forts Grange, Rowner and Brockhurst built in between, they were the first polygonal forts to be built in England. The same thinking which had led to the building of Fort Monckton some sixty years before determined the building now of the Gosport forts: the need to protect Portsmouth Harbour and the dockyard from a landing in the west.

Complete reorganisation of Portsmouth's coastal defences took place a few years later. A combination of events dictated military thinking. Recent dramatic improvements in the range and effectiveness of artillery indicated that the enemy had now to be kept at a distance of at least 8,000 yards, which meant pushing the defensible area round the dockyard out at least as far as the Needles Passage and Portsdown Hill. At the same time, the activities of our traditional enemy, France, were causing considerable unease. It was not just her activities in Italy.[30] It was the building of ironclad battleships, the first of which was *La Gloire*, and the stockpiling of weapons, the strengthening of the arsenal at Cherbourg and the rumoured concentration of troops there. Invasion seemed imminent. Misgivings about the general adequacy of the nation's defences prompted the government led by Lord Palmerston to appoint the Royal Commission on the Defences of the United Kingdom, which began work in 1859. The Commissioners dealt with their task with some expedition, reporting to parliament in July 1860, within a year of their appointment. There was considerable opposition in parliament to the proposals, chiefly on the grounds of expense. It was during the furious dispute behind the scenes between the Prime Minister, Lord Palmerston, and his Chancellor of the Exchequer, Mr. Gladstone, who did not believe that France posed any danger to the nation's security and was threatening therefore to resign, that Palmerston made his famous remark that if it came to a choice, it would be better to lose Mr. Gladstone than to lose Portsmouth.[31]

The Commissioners acknowledged the need to protect both the dockyard, which was by now the most important in the British Isles, and the anchorage at Spithead. To this end, it was therefore deemed necessary to protect the harbour entrance, to prevent an enemy landing on any part of the shore between Browndown and Fort Cumberland, to protect the Spithead anchorage and the dockyard against bombardment from that same anchorage, to defend the Needles Passage and to prevent a landing on the Isle of Wight. It was felt that the defences at the harbour entrance and those between Browndown and Fort Cumberland were probably adequate, but massive earthwork wing batteries with 32 guns were built at Southsea Castle, and Lumps Fort and Eastney Batteries were completed. The existing defences were not sufficient, however, to protect either the dockyard or Spithead against a modern bombardment. To defend them, the sea forts were built – of iron and granite – on shoals at Spitbank, Horse Sand, No Man's Land and St Helen's. The defence of the dockyard and harbour against attack by a force which had landed elsewhere led to the strengthening of the lines at Gosport and Stokes Bay with the building of a large fort at Gilkicker Point and the construction of a line of six fortresses along the length of Portsdown Hill: Forts Wallington, Nelson, Southwick, Widley, Purbrook and Farlington. Facing north, they made a formidable defensive line. They were detached but mutually-supporting and developed out of the polygonal forts of the Gosport lines. Large, brick-built, barrack accommodation was provided at the rear of the forts, on the south-facing side. Fort Fareham was the link between the Gosport defences and Portsdown. On the Isle of Wight, new batteries were built at the western end of the island at Cliff End, The Needles, Hatherwood and Warden Point, with barrack accommodation at Golden Hill. On the south-east side of the island, there was a concentration of batteries near Bembridge: Redcliff, Yaverland, Sandown and Barrack Batteries protected that quarter, with Bembridge Fort providing barracks. Finally, Puckpool Mortar Battery near Ryde provided additional fire-power. Portsmouth and its harbour was now entirely ringed with forts – and was for a time one of the most strongly defended places in the world. These fortresses were nicknamed 'Palmerston's Folly' by successive generations of Portsmouth folk on a series of grounds, not least that Lord Palmerston himself had grossly over-reacted to the threat posed by France. The Spithead forts were not completed either until 1880 – long after the threat posed by France had passed away. In fact neither the Spithead forts nor the forts on Portsdown Hill ever fired a shot in anger except perhaps during air raids in the Second World War. Most absurd, in the eyes of Palmerston's critics, was the fact that the forts on the hill faced the wrong way – inland! It was not fair criticism. In 1860 the threat from France seemed real enough

17. Horse Sand Fort, completed 1880, photographed 1980.

to most professional, informed opinion and if a landing took place on any part of the neighbouring coast, a defensive line looking north was essential to protect Portsmouth's rear.

The works executed following the 1860 Royal Commission were the last great defensive schemes carried out in the Portsmouth area. Minor works were done up to and including the two world wars but nothing new was built. In fact, the lines round the towns of Portsmouth and Portsea, being redundant, were systematically demolished during the 1870s and 1880s, with the exception of the seaward defences of what is now Old Portsmouth. There, the line from King's Bastion to Square Tower and Point Battery continued to provide important sites for guns until the end of the Second World War.

The loss of the town's fortifications was mourned by many who appreciated their picturesque qualities. Sir Walter Besant captured something of their magnificence in *By Celia's Arbour*:

> We were standing . . . in the north-west corner of the Queen's Bastion, the spot where the grass was longest and greenest, the wild convolvulus most abundant, and where the noblest of the great elms which stood upon the ramparts . . . threw out a gracious arm laden with leafy foliage to give a shade . . . If you looked out over the parapet, you saw before you the whole of the most magnificent harbour in the world; and if you looked through the embrasure of the wall, you had a splendid

framed picture – water for foreground, old ruined castle in middle distance, blue hill beyond, and above blue sky . . .

The evening sun 'proclaimed the death of another day' from the Duke of York's Bastion

with a loud report, which made the branches of the trees above us to shake and tremble. And from the barracks in the town; from the Harbour Admiral's flagship; from the Port-Admiral's flag-ship; from the flag-ship of the Admiral in command of the Mediterranean Fleet, then in harbour; from the tower of the old church, there came such a firing of muskets, such a beating of drums, playing of fifes, ringing of bells, and sounding of trumpets, that you would have thought the sun was setting once for all . . .[32]

The glacis, to the right of the Landport Gate, 'whereupon scavengers and others lay the town dung', as the author of the 'State of Government' noted cheerfully in 1745,[33] was described in 1840 as 'about half a mile in length. . . . with cattle grazing upon it, together with a row of fine elms on the inner lines . . . well adapted to deceive the mind into the belief of its being a fine open park attached to the mansion of a nobleman . . .'[34] It was its use and potential use as open space for recreation purposes which attracted similar comments from other writers.[35] When the walls came down, however, levelled by convict labour, the land was retained by the War Office and turned over to a variety of military, civic, and commercial purposes, chief amongst them the building of new barrack accommodation and recreation grounds for both officers and men.

Of the dung, distributed so liberally over the glacis by past generations, it is reassuring to learn that not long after the author of the 'State of Government' made his comments, the Governor, Sir Philip Honeywood, ordered that: 'the Dung-Heaps that lie before the Glacis from Landport Gate to Southsea Castle, be removed within six weeks, as being of dangerous Consequence for covering the Approaches of an Enemy'.[36]

Interestingly, it was not the potential hazard to health which prompted Sir Philip Honeywood to issue his order. It was the security of the town which dictated building styles for many years and certainly dictated the quality of life in both Portsmouth and Portsea. At one time houses had to be built in such a way that they did not obscure the governor's view of the fortifications. According to W. G. Gates, these houses were two-storied with grouted walls and small, leaded windows with diamond panes. Apparently, some still existed in the mid-19th century.[37] Inevitably, the premium on space in the old town of Portsmouth meant that people were forced to live cheek by jowl with their neighbours, and as the density of the population increased in the 19th century the pressure became intolerable on the wealthier classes, who forsook Portsmouth for the new middle-class suburb of Southsea, and the old town of Portsmouth itself became an increasingly unpleasant place in which to live. The moats themselves were open sewers and before the introduction of mains drainage were extremely offensive in mid-summer. The poorer classes were, inevitably, concentrated in over-crowded premises, and the narrow streets and alleys, inadequately lit, poorly paved and drained and without a satisfactory water supply, were breeding grounds for disease. Robert Rawlinson in his *Report to the General Board of Health on the Borough of Portsmouth 1850* actually said that because Portsmouth was a garrison town and great naval station, its sanitary conditions ought the more rigidly to be attended to, that the health and efficiency of the troops and sailors might be better preserved. Unfortunately, he noted, 'the soldiers' wives and families inhabit some of the most wretched, crowded and unhealthy quarters of the town . . .'.[38]

The necessity of keeping garrison hours was also extremely irksome to those townsfolk wishing to be out of town late. Dr. Henry Slight highlighted this problem in a manuscript note attached to his volume on 'Interments', in which he records that, when he and his brother, Julian, were delivering a course of literary lectures at Southampton and did not leave that town until well after 10 o'clock at night, they could not reach Portsmouth, travelling in their own chaise, before one in the morning and 'It not being able to pass the gates at Portsmouth after Midnight we put up the Horse and Carriage at the Bush Hotel Southsea . . .'.[39] Henry Everard, the hero of *The Silence of Dean Maitland*, was equally inconvenienced by the locked gates. The victim of a miscarriage of justice, he was working with a gang of fellow-convicts on the demolition of the defences of the old town when he was able to make his escape. With the connivance of a sympathetic sentry, he reached the ramparts where he slipped between the elms until he reached the steps, but descending them, he discovered to his horror that the gates were locked. He had overlooked this crucial fact. His only course now was to climb the gate

> which he could not do without noise, and which was in no case an easy feat, the plain boards of which the gate was made being high, and the top thickly studded with those dreaded crooked nails, which look like alphabets gone wrong, and do dreadful damage to hands and clothing.
>
> Fortunately the moon had set, the sun was not yet risen, and the darkness favoured him . . . He struggled up with as little sound as possible. . . . Then, having gained the top – not without some rents in his scanty clothing – he grasped the nail-studded ridge and sprang down.[40]

From what survives of the fortifications, it is not easy to say a great deal about their architectural qualities. They were utilitarian structures first and foremost. The first town walls were simple structures of earth and timber, and later of stone, limestone, probably from Portland which was within easy reach of Portsmouth by sea. The town gates, however, were comparatively elegant structures. The Landport Gate for example, which still stands in St George's Road, was built in 1760, of Portland stone, in the style of Hawksmoor. The original gate, a little to the east of the present gate, was described by Leland as 'a Gate of Tymbre'. It was replaced in 1585 when the town's defences were remodelled. The small crown over the arch on the inside of the gate facing St George's Road is believed to have been the keystone of this Elizabethan structure.

The forts on Portsdown Hill were as functional as the town's defences. They were built basically of chalk; the chalk from the moats being used to construct the ramparts. Masonry was used only where necessary for inner walls, the caponiers and barrack accommodation. What little decoration exists is on the entrances, for example at Fort Nelson where the stone shafts and capitals of the supporting arch of the main entrance are Romanesque in style. There is restrained decoration elsewhere in the ironwork of grilles and lamp brackets but, again, it is strictly functional. The architectural effects of the hill forts – and this must surely have been the case with the town defences, too – resulted from their scale and strength.

Work on the defences of Portsmouth was supervised from medieval times by specialised engineers, men familiar with and practised in the science of fortification. Robert Rodyngton and Robert Barbot are two of the earliest names associated with the supervision of works at Portsmouth. By Elizabeth's reign the post of 'Surveyor of the Works of Portsmouth' was associated with such men as William Ridgeway and Richard Popinjay. They were engineers supervised by and responsible to the Privy Council. A warrant to the Treasurer and Chamberlains of the Exchequer for the payment of £15 to Popinjay, 'Master of the Workes at Portsmouth', allowed him for his costs in coming to court on business to do with the works at Portsmouth 'and for drawinge of plottes [plans] for the said works' provides an illuminating insight into the Tudor administrative machine.[41]

Anciently, every soldier was expected to be able to turn his hand to engineering, but by this time the duties of an engineer had been split into field and permanent fortifications. The former were executed by officers appointed specifically for that purpose for the duration of a campaign, while permanent fortifications were more likely to be erected in peacetime by engineers who were not necessarily army officers. Richard Popinjay was such a man.

The office of Chief of the King's Engineers appeared in the early 17th century. The office was usually held by three men at the same time. When this complement was not adequate,

18. Pencil sketch of King William Gate, built 1833-4, and its Guardhouse, which still stands in Pembroke Road. In the background are St Paul's church and King's Terrace, n.d. mid-19th century.

19. King William Gate before demolition of the defences began in the 1870s. Stone, brick, and earthen ramparts are clearly visible as well as one of the famous elm trees on Portsmouth's walls. The large building on the skyline was the Green Row Wesleyan Methodist chapel.

additional engineers were taken on temporarily and subsequently discharged when their services were no longer required. It was an erratic system. No one body bore overall responsibility for building military works. In 1683, however, a warrant was issued which laid down that the Ordnance Office was to have responsibility for such works. The establishment was to be made up of a Principal Engineer, a Second Engineer, a Third Engineer and two ordinary engineers. The Principal Engineer was Sir Bernard de Gomme. By 1698 the establishment had grown to nineteen. In 1716, a Corps of Engineers was formed of 28 men, increased a year later to twenty-nine. They were based at the Tower of London. A properly- organised Drawing Room establishment began to emerge now, and the splendid maps of Portsmouth and its defences which were produced from this time by the Drawing Office testify not only to the fine draughtsmanship of the men in that office but are of course further evidence of the town's importance in the nation's scheme of defences.

A 'School for Practitioner Engineers' was established in 1741, the precursor of the Royal Military Academy, which gave a further fillip to the science of military engineering. In 1757, the members of the Corps were given army rank, the Chief Engineer being designated a colonel. The Corps was reorganised in 1782. The old engineer ranks were abolished with the exception of that of Chief Engineer, and the new establishment was made up of a Chief Engineer and Colonel, six Colonels-Commandant, six Lieutenant-Colonels, 18 Captains of whom nine were Captain-Lieutenants, 22 First Lieutenants and 22 Second Lieutenants. Finally, in 1787 the Corps was designated the Corps of Royal Engineers.[42]

The Portsmouth Garrison was itself abolished in 1960. Portsmouth City Council has (since the late 1950s) set about acquiring what survives of the town's defences. A precedent of sorts had been set as long ago as 1932 when Lumps Fort was purchased by the corporation, with the object of preventing the site being used as a fun fair. A competition was organised among architects for the best seaside amenity scheme. The competition was won by Messrs. Wesley Dougill and E. A. Ferriby of Liverpool whose plans for the competition have come into the ownership of Portsmouth City Records Office. The scheme was never implemented however. The war intervened and today Lumps Fort is a pleasant and restful rose garden. As for the other remaining defences, the city council purchased Point Battery, the Round Tower, Long Curtain Battery and the King's Bastion in 1958, and in 1960 acquired Southsea Castle on a long lease and purchased the Square Tower. There were many schemes for these sites at this time and feelings ran high between the commercial lobbies and local organisations anxious to preserve the sites for their own sake as historic buildings. The latter won the day and these sites have been faithfully restored by the council to provide public amenities. More recently, Fort Widley was acquired by the council and has been partly restored and opened to the public. Fort Purbrook has also been purchased by the city council. It is used partly as a store for reclaimed materials and partly for youth activities. Fort Nelson has been acquired by Hampshire County Council. It is in the process of being restored and there are long-term plans for an artillery museum there. Only Fort Southwick plays any role in the nation's defences today, being the headquarters of the Commander-in-Chief, Naval Home Command. The process of acquisition continues. In April 1986 Portsmouth City Council purchased the last part of Hilsea Lines which they did not own and thus were able to begin a comprehensive scheme to restore that link in Portsmouth's system of defences.

The city council's aim is quite simply to exploit these historic sites as tourist attractions and hence revenue-earners. Their full potential was not appreciated until comparatively recently. Two separate events served to concentrate official minds. The Dartington Amenity Trust was commissioned in the late 1970s to look at the tourist potential of Old Portsmouth. Their report, 'The Defence of the Realm', went well beyond that original brief and demonstrated that those 'surviving fragments' of Portsmouth's military past were of more than local significance. At the same time the accelerated run down of the dockyard made it clear that the town would have to realise that potential for all it was worth. It is remarkable that the very fact that Portsmouth was once one of the most heavily-defended areas not only in Britain but in northern Europe is still important today.

The Square Tower, with Semaphore.

Chapter Five

Port and Garrison Town

Portsmouth, it was said in Charles I's charter of 1627, was 'a port and frontier town . . . situate and lying near the high sea, the strength and security of which it is therefore the more necessary we should earnestly study and provide for'.[1] It was a succinct description of the place's significance, applicable not only in the early 17th century but also during much of its history.

From the first, the port rather than the fort predominated. During the Middle Ages, the harbour and its adjacent roadstead was one of the most important assembly points for English fleets preparing to transport armies to France. Edward III's successful Crécy campaign of 1346 was only one of many which began with ships, mariners, retinues of fighting men and lumbering supply wagons converging on Portsea Island from many parts of England and Wales. During the 15th century the harbour seems to have been used less frequently, and it was not until the end of the 17th century that it was restored to favour.[2] In 1698, a government survey of the Channel coast concluded that the harbours and waterways of south-east Hampshire 'seem to offer all that is to be desired for the susteining and preserving the greatest navall strength in the world'. With official acknowledgement of its advantages, Portsmouth after 1700 became the rendezvous for almost every major expedition sailing from Britain.[3]

The concentration by historians on the naval function of the port has resulted in serious neglect of its less-glamorous commercial development. Although only a subsidiary theme, it deserves greater recognition than it has hitherto received. Portsmouth's other role, that of 'frontier town', which became increasingly important after Henry VII's accession, has been touched upon in the previous chapter. But the stone walls had to be defended, and the existence of a governor and garrison for several centuries inevitably had a profound impact on the civilian population whose lives were circumscribed. This chapter will consider the development of Portsmouth's seaborne trade, and some aspects of the municipal and social consequences of the naval and military presence.

There is a serious lack of information about medieval Portsmouth's overseas trade, but it seems clear that such commercial traffic as was carried on was insignificant compared with that at Southampton, of which port it was a member. Moreover, in 1199, the town of Southampton acquired the right to collect not only its own local (as distinct from royal) customs, but also those of Portsmouth, the burgesses of which, after some resistance, agreed in 1239 to a compromise solution. The arrangement seems to have lasted several centuries, but the whole subject of the economic relationship between the two towns remains obscure and awaits detailed investigation.[4] In 1565 it was stated that the landing places at Portsmouth (i.e. the Camber) were within the liberties of the town, 'and the mayor for the tyme beinge hathe the governemente of the same porte and landinge places, notwithstandinge there dothe no vesselles lade or unlade there any maner of merchandise but onlye by the lysence and auctoritie of the Quene's Majestis costomers of Suthampton'.[5]

A rare glimpse of Portsmouth's medieval trade is found in a local port book of 1435-6. A very small number of ships is shown passing through the harbour carrying negligible quantities of merchandise which included rye, wheat, fish, canvas, iron and wool cards. Payments of local custom and tolls amounted to 47s. 5d.[6] Other evidence from the Middle

Ages suggests an unadventurous overseas trade confined mainly to France and Spain, with merchants exporting wool and wheat and importing wine, woad, wax and iron.[7]

Commerce throughout the Middle Ages was hazardous, and piracy and French incursions into the Solent must have severely hampered the development of legitimate trade during the 13th and 14th centuries. Portsmouth, not yet fortified, was sacked by the barons of the Cinque Ports in 1265 and by the French on several occasions during the 14th century, the most serious raid being that of Nicholas Béhuchet in 1338, when Southampton was also devastated.[8] Such was the dislocation caused at Portsmouth on this occasion that no local dues were collected the following year, and in 1341-2 the total was still only 28s. Extra customs which the king granted the men of Portsmouth in 1342 'towards enclosing, paving and improving their town' proved to be of little consequence since 'men and merchants . . . do not care to come to the town'. In 1360, Portsmouth, Southampton and Winchester were excused tax because of 'the poverty which they are undergoing in these days'. During the second half of the 15th century, when the total yearly yield at Southampton ranged from about £200 to £300, the local port books failed to record customs levied at Portsmouth and all the other member ports except Lymington. This, according to one authority, was probably because 'they were not considered to be worth collecting'.[9]

After the great burst of naval activity under the early Tudors Portsmouth suffered a long period of stagnation, during which the few merchants who lived there lacked the resources to undertake much more than a modest seaborne trade. A fragment of a portolan chart dating from the mid-16th century, if not earlier, and now in the City Records Office, shows principally the coastline of western Europe from Normandy to the Straits of Gibraltar (Plate 20), and this seems to have been the geographical extent of most local trading voyages at that time.[10] Yet despite the limited enterprise of Portmuthians, the harbour was frequently busy, since London merchants found the town a useful departure point for many of their commercial ventures, including pioneering voyages to Brazil and north and west Africa.[11] London money also financed many of the privateers which used Portsmouth as their base during the last years of Elizabeth I's reign.[12] It was from there, too, in 1587, that the settlers bound for Raleigh's second Virginia colony departed, and to which, the previous year, the remnants of the first colony had returned.[13]

A clearer picture emerges of Portsmouth's overseas trade during the 17th century because of the survival of a number of port books. Exports included such items as Hampton and Taunton serges, bays and perpetuanas (i.e. new draperies), and woollen and worsted hose. The total volume annually, however, was negligible compared with that of the import trade, but even that was relatively modest and subject to wild fluctuations in value from year to year. Foreign ships were frequent visitors, especially when substantial quantities of naval supplies were required.[14] During Channel storms, or when England was under threat or at war and enemy ships were prowling off the coast, Portsmouth was frequently used as a place of refuge by merchant vessels, some of which belonged to the major trading companies based in London. Details of three Levant Company ships which arrived during the summer of 1648 help to put into proper perspective the comparatively limited cross-Channel and north European traffic of the local merchants. The *Northumberland* and the *Edward* had come from Scanderoon (i.e. Iskenderun in modern Turkey), and the *Harry* from Leghorn in Italy. Whereas the port-based merchantmen were rarely above 30 tons, the Londoners' were around 400 tons. Out of them were brought huge quantities of cotton, raw silk, fine fabrics, gall and kidskins, most of which were almost certainly transported overland to the capital. The impact of such a fleet is clearly seen in the customs receipts for the four quarters of 1648: £8 0s. 9¾d.; £6 17s. 1½d.; £2,452 10s. 5d.; £7 0s. 1d.[15]

Portsmouth's coastal trade was slight at the beginning of the century, but the port book for 1662-3 shows a greatly expanded traffic carried on principally with the capital and the

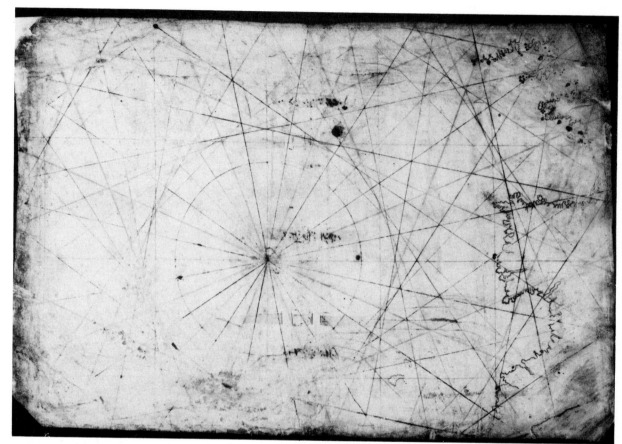

20. A Portsmouth mariner's chart of c.1550, showing the coast of Western Europe and part of North Africa.

ports of the south coast and the north-east. The commodities handled were very varied, but foodstuffs and coal predominated, the latter being brought from Newcastle and Sunderland by a host of colliers, a large proportion of which belonged to Brighton.[16] In 1682-3 the total import of coal into Portsmouth from Newcastle totalled 1,670 chaldrons, but in 1730-1 this had almost doubled.[17] The port was not included in a list of the 17 major collier-owning places in 1702-4,[18] and throughout the period the total tonnage of Portsmouth-based ships of all kinds remained comparatively small.

The contribution of Portsmouth merchants to the port's trade during the early Stuart period was minimal. After the Restoration the names of local men such as Thomas Hide, Richard Lardner and Samuel Williams appear more regularly in the records. Among those found importing timber from Norway in 1661 was Josiah Child, who had come to the town in 1655 as victualler and deputy treasurer of the fleet, and been elected mayor in 1658-9, when he had also acted locally on behalf of the East India Company. A few years later he moved to London, where in time he became one of the most famous merchants of his age.[19]

King Charles II's Portsmouth provided little scope for a man of Child's abilities. Although during the Third Dutch War of 1672-4 such was the increase in trade that four tidesmen were added to the customs establishment, in 1676 it was said that few or no merchants lived in the town and that traffic in peace-time was negligible. Two of the tidesmen were consequently withdrawn.[20] When England was at war once again in the 1690s, however, Portsmouth enjoyed another boom period commercially. John Weaver, customs officer, petitioning in 1696 for an increase in salary for himself and his clerk, pointed out that the annual receipts, once £800 or less, had risen to £6,000.[21]

Accidents to warships in and around Spithead have become part of local naval lore, but merchant ships, too, were often victims. In 1697, for example, the *White Phoenix* of Flushing, which had survived the perils of the Atlantic, was wrecked off Southsea Castle.[22] Eight years later, the *Elizabeth and Mary* of London took on board at the new salterns a cargo of 3,753 bushels of white salt and five bushels of bay salt. While 'rideing at ancker att Spithead expecting to saile with convoy . . . a sudden violent storme arose' during which the ship was in collision with another and driven on to Southsea beach. Sea-water 'ranne into her hold and there washt away and consumed all the said salt'.[23]

Prospect of Portsmouth, the Isle of Wight Gosport, Portchester &c Sep. 13. 1723.

A. *The Isle of Wight.* B. *Southsea Castle.* D. *Portsmouth.* E. *Landgard fort.* F. *Gosport.* G. *Portchester.* H. *Portsdown hill.*

21. Portsea Island, Portsmouth Harbour and Spithead viewed from Portsdown Hill, 1723.

During the 18th century much of the port's seaborne trade retained its traditional pattern, but the geographical range widened in response to Britain's colonial expansion. Portsmouth became the country's second largest exporter of wheat, but was a poor runner-up to London, since the amount handled *c.*1736 was less than a third of the capital's total. Smaller quantities of malt and barley were also shipped, so that Portsmouth was the fourth most important port for these three commodities.[24] From Ireland, especially after about 1760, came butter which was distributed inland by Hampshire and Wiltshire middlemen; and, mainly for victualling the fleet, although some was re-shipped to the West Indies, salt beef and pork, which increasingly replaced home-produced meat.[25] Quantities of bullion came into Portsmouth from Portugal in settlement of that country's trading accounts with England and the North American colonies.[26] Portsmouth also continued to be one of the places to which, in time of war, London and some other ports sent their merchant ships to await escorts. From Spithead, despite problems caused at times by westerly winds, sailed the slave traders, the mighty East Indiamen, and ships bound for the Caribbean.[27]

At the end of the 18th century, the port of Portsmouth, which extended from Bosham

Creek to Hill Head, was still considered to be subordinate to Southampton, although the total customs receipts of the two places, 1710-70, were not greatly dissimilar (Table 1). Portsmouth finally overtook its neighbour at the time of the American Revolution, and although it slipped back again after the peace, resumed its growth during the French Wars of the 1790s.[28] Smuggling, which tended to distort official statistics, was always difficult to detect in the many creeks and harbours of the Portsmouth area. East India Company goods, apparently uncustomed, were discovered in a haystack outside the town in 1662,[29] and in 1728 it was reported that men from several places, including Portsmouth, 'through ignorance or inadvertency', had 'either run, imported, or bought, goods, which had not paid the duties'. As a result they had been imprisoned. Some, given bail, had fled, while others, still languishing in gaol, had not the means, in most cases, of ever regaining their freedom.[30] In the late 18th century smuggling was probably on the increase, and despite the war English contrabandists were often in collusion with the French authorities. Goods were sometimes landed illicitly on Southsea Common or at Eastney. On one occasion in the 1780s, sixty or more armed men with blackened faces were intercepted by soldiers from nearby Fort Cumberland, but only four were caught.[31] The old custom house in Oyster Street was replaced by a building in Broad Street in 1785. That in turn about 1832 gave way to premises on Camber Quay.[32]

Table 1 – Customs Revenue every tenth year, 1710-80

PORTSMOUTH

	Gross £	s.	d.	Net £	s.	d.
1710	5,984	16	$0\frac{1}{4}$	3,884	6	$1\frac{1}{4}$
1720	3,598	5	$2\frac{1}{2}$	1,346	12	$6\frac{1}{4}$
1730	12,111	18	$0\frac{1}{4}$	9,014	11	$1\frac{1}{2}$
1740	14,872	5	$7\frac{3}{4}$	11,983	7	10
1750	18,724	3	4	8,749	14	$8\frac{1}{4}$
1760	22,636	2	$4\frac{3}{4}$	11,656	12	$4\frac{1}{4}$
1770	17,461	16	4	13,109	6	$9\frac{1}{4}$
1780	78,854	17	$1\frac{3}{4}$	39,933	8	$1\frac{1}{4}$

SOUTHAMPTON

	£	s.	d.	£	s.	d.
1710	6,469	10	$3\frac{1}{4}$	4,878	8	$5\frac{1}{4}$
1720	11,078	18	$6\frac{1}{4}$	8,306	6	$1\frac{1}{4}$
1730	14,818	0	$8\frac{1}{2}$	12,165	18	$7\frac{3}{4}$
1740	16,674	11	$3\frac{1}{2}$	13,818	7	$10\frac{1}{2}$
1750	14,475	11	7	9,576	14	3
1760	16,577	2	11	12,799	10	7
1770	22,877	2	10	17,811	11	$6\frac{3}{4}$
1780	34,865	19	$4\frac{1}{4}$	30,324	12	4

Deductions from gross receipts consisted of (1) drawbacks and bounties; (2) allowances for damage and over-entry; (3) management charges.

Source: BL, Add. MS. 8,133A, ff. 128, 137.

An examination of harbour dues collected during February and March 1830 shows 92 vessels entering the port bringing cargo from 33 places. These included Sierra Leone (timber), Cherbourg (eggs), Guernsey (potatoes), Waterford (butter, bacon, oats), Colchester (oysters) and London (timber, beer, groceries). Twenty-seven colliers came from Sunderland.[33] Imports of livestock from the West Country and the Isle of Wight, and wine from the continent were also commonplace at this period. Much of the coal brought in was used locally; the rest was distributed inland or re-shipped to other coastal places, very little being sent overseas. During one decade about this time, the amount of coal discharged at the port increased by 30 per cent.[34]

The re-emergence of Southampton as a major port dealing with passengers as well as with cargo was a considerable threat to Portsmouth after the accession of Queen Victoria. Various improvements were made to the Camber, but far-reaching schemes to construct large commercial docks were frustrated because the civil port had to take second place to the needs of the armed forces. Already in 1849, Southampton with its greatly improved facilities had expanded its trade to the point where the total tonnage of ships clearing its wharfs was more than three times that of its neighbour.[35] Between 1841 and 1881, its merchants were more numerous, although its total population was much smaller than that of Portsmouth.[36] Both ports, however, showed a spectacular threefold increase in coal imports between 1828 and 1868.[37]

The departure in May 1787 of the fleet carrying the first convicts to Botany Bay initiated a new phase in the port's history. By the time that the practice of transportation had ended in 1853, many thousands of convicts had sailed from Portsmouth to the penal colony.[38] East India ships awaiting convoy at Spithead still picked up supplies there, as well as officials and passengers who had travelled overland from London. Their successors, the 'Blackwall Frigates', continued the practice even in peace-time.[39] In 1840 nearly one hundred incoming ships dropped off their letter bags at Portsmouth, and 106 outward-bound vessels stopped to take in passengers.[40] The success and continuance of this arrangement depended upon good inland communications, and the failure of the railway builders to provide a direct line from the town to London until 1859 was a major handicap. To the chagrin of Portmuthians, the long-familiar Indian troopships were transferred to Southampton in 1894. Each of these graceful vessels bore the motto of the Star of India, 'Heaven's Light Our Guide', which now adorns the city arms.[41]

During the quarter-century before the First World War, Portsmouth seems to have shown no significant increase in commercial activity, if the number of ships using the port is adopted as the criterion. Between 1893 and 1914, the annual total ranged between 6,085 in 1893 and 11,598 in 1902. A very high proportion of these consisted of small craft plying within the Solent area. In 1913, for example, they accounted for 6,366 of the 7,569 vessels which arrived. Another 1,030 were coasters and only 173 engaged in overseas trade. The commonest foreign ships were Norwegian and French. With the outbreak of war in 1914, there began a rapid decline in numbers. Recovery in the 1920s was slow and reached only the lowest pre-war levels. Major developments in docking facilities since the Second World War have boosted commercial traffic. By the early 1960s about a million tons of merchant shipping were being handled each year. Coal, timber, oil, bricks, fruit and vegetables were among the most important items entering the port, while scrap-iron, cars, chemicals and general cargo were prominent exports. The continental ferry port at Mile End, which was opened in 1976, rapidly became the most important English cross-Channel passenger port after Dover.[42] Its development has made even stronger the traditional maritime link with France, and especially Normandy. Eight hundred or more years ago, kings, barons, and bishops left Portsmouth to make the hazardous Channel crossing to visit their continental possessions. Today, great numbers of less exalted travellers embark on the same journey, often simply to do a day's shopping.

The military affairs of Portsmouth during the Middle Ages were normally the responsibility of the constable of Portchester Castle, but with the growth in importance of the town and its fortifications under the early Tudors, a separate officer was appointed. Known as the governor (or lieutenant-governor), he was a significant figure until the post was abolished in the 19th century.[43] This important official commanded a permanent garrison said to be 'daily attendant', which at the end of Elizabeth I's reign consisted of 100 soldiers, 30 gunners (one of whom was designated master gunner), and five 'officers', a term used to describe an ensign, an armourer, a surgeon, a drummer and a fifer. For most of the time up to the Civil War the regular garrison strength seems to have remained at approximately the Elizabethan level. Southsea Castle, under its own captain, had a separate garrison which in 1623 consisted of a porter, a pensioner and 10 men who were described as 'neither gonners nor soldiers'.[44]

The commanding officers of the Portsmouth and Southsea Castle garrisons, who were men of rank and proven loyalty, each received a fee and living accommodation. In the early 17th century the former was entitled to 10s. a day and an official residence in buildings attached to the medieval Domus Dei; the latter, who received 2s. a day, almost certainly had apartments within the castle. The actual presence of the military commanders could not always be relied upon, especially in peace-time when their role was essentially ceremonial, and in practice they often operated through deputies.[45] During the 18th century the Portsmouth governor's official residence fell increasingly into disrepair, and in 1826 it was demolished. From 1833 until about 1884 he was provided with an elegant house in the High Street.[46]

Some members of the garrison were like William Chapman, a long-serving gunner who was described in 1605 as 'lyveing and abyding here in the town of Portesmowth'.[47] Others, however, were often billeted on the local inhabitants, as were military personnel awaiting departure on overseas expeditions, and craftsmen brought in to work on the fortifications or in the dockyard. Billeting was deeply resented by householders when it was compulsory and occurred repeatedly over a prolonged period. Thus, during the late 1620s, semi-mutinous troops, many sick and unpaid, were on several occasions forced onto unwilling hosts who were themselves not reimbursed for their pains.[48] Despite the Petition of Right (1628) and the Disbanding Act of 1679 in which this widespread abuse was recognised and theoretically rectified, the practical problems of accommodating a large contingent consisting of several hundred men, in an area with a comparatively small population, were virtually insoluble without some recourse to compulsion.[49]

The worst abuses resurfaced during James II's reign when, according to the borough authorities, the inhabitants were oppressed by a lawless 'Irish and Popish' garrison, members of which had made themselves 'absolute masters of our homes and goods and by free quartering upon us have utterly impoverisht our towne and places adjacent . . .'. With the accession of William III, it was acknowledged that only after the barracks and local public houses had been filled should soldiers be quartered in private houses, and then only with the occupants' consent and under strict supervision.[50]

The precise location of the earliest barracks is now uncertain, but it seems very likely that a military hospital set up on part of the vicar's glebe c.1680 had been converted into living accommodation before the Glorious Revolution. Situated in the northern quarter of the town near the Landport Gate, they were known as the Colewort or New Barracks, and contained 144 beds in 1745, by which time further accommodation was available. The Fourhouse Barracks on the site of the old brewhouses in St Nicholas Street had 160 beds, the smaller Landport Barracks, the location of which is unknown, 76, and Southsea Castle, manned at this time by detachments sent from Portsmouth at the discretion of the governor, another twenty-seven. There were also eight beds at Portsbridge Barracks.[51] Whether these were single or double beds is not clear. In the late 16th century, when craftsmen who came into the town to work in the dockyard were billeted on householders, or lodged at the Queen's storehouse at the Camber, they slept two to a bed between sheets provided by the crown.[52]

The Armory

All the Old Armory is under the Reparations of Ball, shott, etto, ffuses, & combustible Boxes, Barrack Bedding, and sundry other Stores for the use of this Garrison.

Barracks

To entertain the Garrison are Barracks for 300. men particularly mentioned as follows.

Easst Street House Barracks
consisting of 2 Buildings (one an Infirmary) and containing 4 Rooms on each Room on the Ground ffloor, and 3 Beds above in each . . . . . . 108 Beds

Landport Barracks
consisting of one Building and an Infirmary with 4 Beds in each Room on the Ground floor, and 3 above, in all 70

Colt Garden Barracks or
Colewort Garden the New Barracks
Consisting of one Building of 3 stories, and Divided into four Separate apartments, viz.t one for Commission Officers containing 12 Rooms with 3 small Kitchens and Closets Communicating)
the other three apartments contains 36 Rooms with 4 Beds in each Room in all . . . . . . 144.

Total of Beds in the Barracks to entertain the Garrison 380.

1.

State of the Government of Portsmouth 1745

Portsmouth Garrison

The Garrison consists of a Governour, Lieut. Governour, Town Major, Chaplain, Physician, Town Adjutant, Surgeon, Marshall, Gunr. Porter, Mr. Gunner and 15 Gunners.

The Town is fortified with 5 Bastions, and two Demi Bastions, with other works, and 133 Guns mounted thereon the particulars whereof are as follows viz.t

Kings Bastion
3 fforty five pounders are mounted on the point of this Bastion, and 7 of the same natured on the faces, and 2 Eighteen pounders, and 4 nine pounders . . . on the flanck . . . 16 Guns in this Bastion.

Pembroks Bastion
3 Eighteen pounders on the point of this Bastion, and 4 nine pounders . . . the flanks.

East Bastion
3 Eighteen pounders on the point of ye Bastion and 6 Eighteen pounders with 5 nine pounders in the flanks.

22. Pages from a survey of the fortifications and garrison of Portsmouth, 1745.

With the French Wars in the latter half of the 18th century the fortifications were extended, and large numbers of troops were frequently present in and around Portsea Island. The 1851 census shows that by then Portsmouth town, with a total population of 10,329, had no fewer than 1,679 resident servicemen, while the more extensive Portsea parish had a further 1,049.[53] Living accommodation in the various forts which had been constructed in the area during the 18th and 19th centuries, and in the existing barracks, proved to be inadequate, and over a period of a hundred and fifty years or so an extensive construction programme was undertaken, convict labour often being used. The Colewort Barracks were considerably extended in stages, while in the neighbourhood of the old Fourhouse Barracks there developed a huge block of military establishments which swallowed up much of the land within one sizeable quarter of the town, and included the Clarence (previously called Marine) Barracks at the end of Peacock Lane, rebuilt c.1824, and the adjacent Cambridge Barracks. The latter had originated as commissariat offices which had been erected on a disused timber yard at the top of Penny Street during the Napoleonic Wars. Converted into barracks c.1825, they were greatly extended in the 1850s, when the Portsmouth Theatre and several substantial houses in the High Street were demolished to make way for the new buildings. In addition, other accommodation was provided during the first half of the 19th century for different branches of the military at Point and in Portsea. The construction of permanent Royal Artillery Barracks at Hilsea in 1854 ended a period beginning in George II's reign when only temporary or semi-permanent camps were put on the site. In the 1880s the great complex of barrack buildings to the east of the High Street was further extended across the area of the recently demolished fortifications. The new Victoria and enlarged Clarence Barracks were the last in a series of major architectural projects designed to cope with the great numbers of troops passing through Portsmouth during Britain's imperial heyday.[54]

Meanwhile, the Royal Marine Artillery Division, which had been based in several different premises over the years, was finally, during the 1860s, installed in austere buildings overlooking the sea at Eastney. In 1923 they were joined by the Royal Marine Light Infantry from Gosport. The Royal Navy, which for centuries had maintained its men on shipboard in the harbour, decided in the late 19th century to accommodate them on land. On the north side of Queen Street the Admiralty constructed (1899-1903) an extensive group of buildings which absorbed the existing Anglesea military barracks (built 1847-8) and part of the land previously occupied by the Portsea defences. Now known as H.M.S. *Nelson* and much rebuilt in recent years, the establishment remains as a functioning entity, although one by one the military barracks on Portsea Island have been closed and for the most part demolished.[55]

From the early Tudor period one of the principal themes in Portsmouth's history was the precise nature and extent of the power exercised by each of the civil and military authorities. Although it was generally accepted that in wartime, or during periods of national emergency, the word of the governor was paramount, there were countless opportunities for disagreement when the country was at peace. Much depended upon the personality of the governor. Sir Adrian Poynings (1559-71) and the enigmatic Colonel George Goring (1639-42) were irascible men openly contemptuous of the townspeople. Often the dispute concerned buildings erected by the military on waste land without reference to the mayor, or the arbitrary demolition or removal of structures to the detriment of the inhabitants, on the basis that easier access to the defences was needed, or because the gunners' field of vision was hampered. In the 1630s the mayor's attempts to assess members of the garrison for ship money without consulting the military authorities caused the sergeant-major to complain bitterly that the burgesses had acted 'like most spleenetive men as they allwaies had shewen it to the garrison . . .'. Anger was also caused by the attempts of members of the garrison to breach the burgesses' privileges by opening alehouses and carrying on trade within the liberties without licence. In 1630, when the dispute was at its fiercest, the soldiers argued that without being allowed to trade they could not survive on their pay of 8d. a day which, in any case, was seriously in arrears, a common grievance among servicemen at this time.[56]

Under what conditions a member of the garrison could possess burgess rights is difficult to establish from the confused evidence available. In 1618, Thomas Mondaie, who had been a freeman for nine years, was disfranchised because he had 'bought a souldier's place and is under the governement of the governor of the garrison which is contrarye to the auncient orders and constitucions of this towne for anie burgis to be'.[57] Despite this there is ample evidence that an individual might be subject to both authorities. The best-known example is Joshua Savour, the master gunner, who became a freeman in 1594 and was admitted to the ruling body in 1603. His was clearly an active role and just before his death at the age of 43 in 1605 he was a candidate for the mayoralty. In his will his gifts to the Corporation included 'my best peece of plate' (a standing cup which still graces civic functions), and 'haulf a dozen of my best silver spoones', several of which have been lost. Savour is known to have had influential friends, and his social standing may well be the reason why he was allowed to infringe the ancient order.[58]

Some of the senior officials of the dockyard are also known to have possessed burgess rights from late in Elizabeth I's reign, and the double allegiance appears to have posed few practical problems, even though these men were active participants in local government. Between 1650 and 1686, seven senior dockyard men were elected to the mayoralty and collectively served on no less than 11 occasions.[59] But if a tradition of harmony seems to have developed, it did not avert occasional friction. In 1697, when the mayor and councillors found the dockyard gates closed against them during their annual perambulation of the liberties, they had no hesitation in ordering them to be broken down.[60]

One of the consequences of a naval and military presence on Portsea Island was the occasional outbreak of serious disorder. Large numbers of ill-assorted combatants, often drawn from the worst elements in society, might, because of their restlessness while awaiting embarkation, create panic and terror among the local inhabitants. Indeed, the borough of Portsmouth was born amidst such confusion in 1194 when Richard I granted the first charter of liberties. While the ships in his punitive expedition against France were being prepared, the king left Portsmouth to go hunting in Stansted Forest. Almost immediately he was recalled to discipline his mercenaries, among whom fighting had broken out.[61] The murder of Bishop Moleyns by disaffected sailors outside the Domus Dei in 1450 was an outrage which had serious consequences for the townspeople, who were held responsible.[62] Again, in 1628, at the time of the proposed second La Rochelle expedition, many of the seamen rioted in the High Street and were quelled with difficulty by the Duke of Buckingham and his officers.[63] For every one of these more famous incidents there must have been scores of less momentous riots.

Many of the disturbances which occurred were a form of protest occasioned by the government's failure to hand over the servicemen's pay or alleviate their appalling living conditions. Others, which were due to inter-service rivalry, high spirits, or alleged sharp practice by tradesmen, were no less serious. In 1758, for example, about two hundred sailors, armed with clubs, 'went to the back of the Point . . . to a public house, which they pulled almost down; they threw the beds and furniture about the street, and stove all the beer in the cellar', after which they rampaged through the town doing considerable damage.[64] Drunkenness was to be found almost everywhere and petty crime was commonplace. But these offences were not associated particularly with servicemen. While soldiers and sailors mugged civilians, civilians also mugged soldiers and sailors. Really serious offences against the person by members of the forces seem generally not to have been excessive. In the 19th century some young officers engaged in pranks which the townspeople found tiresome. They smashed street lamps, threw detonating crackers against shop windows, disrupted performances at the theatre and abused the peace officers. Duels were frequently fought, Southsea Common being a popular venue.[65]

During the French Wars, according to one contemporary, there were some twenty thousand prostitutes operating in the Portsmouth area.[66] Although this estimate is probably an exaggeration, there is little doubt that during wartime hordes of women and girls roamed the streets or operated from well-established brothels. The attorney Daniel Howard reported that in the late 18th century four of the best-known establishments were the *Green Rails* in Oyster Street (which was later converted into a Methodist church), the *Spring Clock* and the *Hole in the Wall* close by the Square Tower, and the *Brass Knocker* in Keppel Row.[67] 'Devil's Acre', outside the main gate of the naval base, was a popular resort for those seeking to relieve sailors of their purses. In 1802, the *Hampshire Telegraph* suggested that sailors should be paid at their home towns rather than at Portsmouth immediately after disembarking. 'These poor fellows are generally robbed of their money in a few hours after they receive it by a gang of prostitutes and their male abettors.'[68] From time to time the magistrates attempted to clean up the streets by punishing the most blatant culprits with hard labour, but 'gross scenes' were still said to occur.[69] The abolition of Free Mart Fair in 1847 eliminated one of the most serious causes of public concern, but it is clear from the minutes of the Watch Committee that in the early 1850s the problem was still as acute. The attention of the police was drawn to 'the great numbers of common prostitutes who infest the public streets', 'the nightly assemblage of prostitutes on Southsea Common', and 'the disgraceful scene which occurs every Sunday on the passage of the military along the ramparts to and from divine service'. Women of ill-repute, it was said, loitered at Beeston's Bastion. The police took note, but one member of the constabulary was dismissed after having been seen entering the *Green Dragon* with a prostitute, 'where he remained some time'.[70] In 1865 there were still 1,355 known 'common women' in Portsmouth, although the Contagious Diseases Act of 1864 saw a steady reduction in numbers, especially of child prostitutes.[71]

The moral welfare of rank and file servicemen was the subject of much debate in the mid-19th century, but little of practical value was done until the Royal Sailors' Home was set up in Queen Street, Portsea, in 1851. Seafarers were provided for the first time with a clean and comfortable hostel and social centre where they could relax in their off-duty hours without having to frequent the more sleazy districts of the town.[72] In the 1870s two formidable women appeared on the Portsmouth scene and independently, with great courage and determination, set about further improving the servicemen's lot. Sarah Robinson opened the Soldiers' Institute in the disused *Fountain* inn in the High Street in 1874, choosing Portsmouth because it was 'the worst place I know of'. It was not the first attempt to improve soldiers' amenities, since a modest and short-lived establishment bearing the same name and resembling a Mechanics' Institute had been set up in Old Portsmouth in 1856 by The Revd. W. Carus Wilson. Sarah Robinson encountered much local opposition which culminated in her being burnt in effigy on Southsea Common on Guy Fawkes' night, but she persevered and eventually gained widespread respect as 'The Soldiers' Friend'. In 1915 the Y.M.C.A. (established in Commercial Road in 1857), took over the running of the Institute, which, during the First World War, was said to have been used daily by an average of twelve hundred men.[73] Miss Robinson's fellow spirit, Agnes Weston, who had already set up a sailors' rest at Devonport, complemented the work of the Institute by founding a similar centre in a disused Landport music hall, later moving to better premises nearby and greatly expanding the facilities. Opened in 1881, Agnes Weston's Royal Sailors' Rest, with its hundreds of cabins, restaurant, baths, writing room, concerts, film shows, banking facilities and evening classes, became world famous. Moreover, Miss Weston's

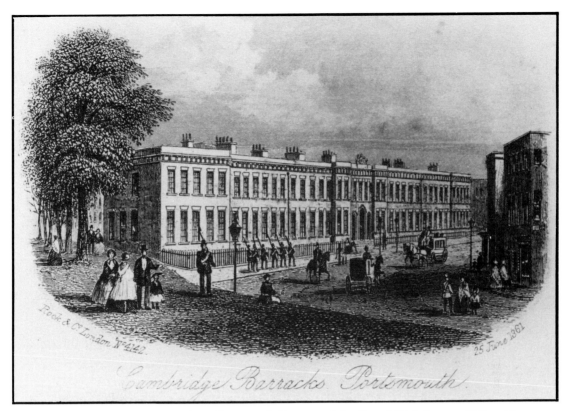

Cambridge Barracks Portsmouth.

23. The Cambridge Barracks (now Portsmouth Grammar School) and High Street, *c.*1861, with fortifications in the foreground before the construction of the Cambridge Road which breached them in 1864.

24. A military parade outside the Royal Garrison church, formerly the Domus Dei, *c.*1846. In the background is King William Gate, built 1833-4.

The Garrison Chapel & Parade Ground, Portsmouth.

concern for the bluejackets included their families, whose welfare she greatly improved through relentless pressure on the authorities. Both Agnes Weston and her lifelong friend and fellow worker, Sophia Wintz, were created dames and at their deaths were buried with full naval honours.[74] During the late 19th century, the moral regeneration of the new urban areas was attempted by many others, including the Salvation Army (who described their own religious and social work in Portsea as 'a plunge into one of the darkest and most heathenish neighbourhoods in the land'), and by Father Robert Dolling and The Revd. Reginald Shute.[75] Inevitably, their efforts affected members of the forces as well as civilians.

Until modern times, the Royal Navy, like the merchant marine and fisheries, depended to a large extent on recruits from coastal towns and villages, and it was a common practice in many Portsea Island homes to send one or more sons to sea. The large proportion of seafarers among local families meant that in the event of a naval disaster whole districts were not only plunged into mourning, but also suffered severe economic distress, since a sailor's pay stopped immediately he was reported dead. When the *Royal George* sank at Spithead with few survivors in 1782, the tragedy was made worse by the fact that on board were not only the normal crew of 800, but also some two hundred wives and children, hangers-on and local purveyors who had gone out from the town in the familiar bum-boats.[76] With the growth of the Royal Navy, losses – still suffered to a considerable extent by certain traditionally seafaring communities – could be devastating, and news of a shipwreck would spread like wildfire through the town. Among the most poignant tragedies was the unnecessary sinking by collision of H.M.S. *Victoria* off Tripoli in 1893 with the loss of three hundred and sixty or more men, many of whom came from Portsmouth.[77] The greatest wave of emotion undoubtedly occurred in 1916, after the Battle of Jutland, when a large number of local sailors were among the six thousand who died. 'Scarcely a family was to be found in which there was not one dead', wrote W. G. Gates, 'one who had been called husband, son, brother, or friend'. In one street alone 40 women became widows overnight. At a memorial service, the Bishop of Winchester reminded the congregation 'that Portsmouth was bearing three times the burden in death and sorrow that all England bore through her fleet at Trafalgar'.[78]

Portsmouth's contribution to the army in this war was also substantial. During 1914-15 the town raised three voluntary battalions, each 1,100 strong. The soldiers departed for active service amidst scenes of great euphoria, marching confidently through the streets to the main railway station. Not one battalion returned. The men who survived the awful carnage were transferred to the depleted ranks of other regiments. At the final count, the roll of honour of Portsmouth men who had died during the conflict contained more than five thousand names.[79]

Those left at home were often in the front-line, too. Whenever England was at war, Portsea Islanders were acutely aware that at almost any time an attempt might be made by the enemy to seize and destroy the naval base and the town which sustained it, thereby more easily securing control of the Channel. Fortunately, such expeditions were not lightly undertaken, even by the most impulsive of powers. During the first phase of the Hundred Years War, when the French sacked Portsmouth on several occasions, lack of adequate defences made the town an easy prey. By the early 16th century, however, a frontal attack had become much more hazardous because of the developing system of fortifications and England's growing naval strength. When the French king despatched a large army to assail the town in 1545, it could do no more than despoil the Isle of Wight. Accident or incompetence, not French gunnery or tactical skill, caused the loss of King Henry's much-prized *Mary Rose* in the Battle of Spithead.[80] The more famous Spanish Armada of 1588 did not have as an objective a landing in south-east Hampshire. However, a hastily revised plan which entailed the Spanish fleet taking temporary possession of the Spithead anchorage and occupying the Isle of Wight was foiled by superior English seamanship.[81]

The French Wars of the 18th century produced a whole series of schemes designed, in the words of Dumouriez (the future victor of Jemappes), 'to deprive England for ever of her finest port and greatest naval establishment'. Wild rumours of imminent attack frequently circulated in the town, but it was not until 1779 that a complex plan to capture and hold Portsmouth as a kind of northern Gibraltar was attempted. A critical situation was saved when the Franco-Spanish fleet returned home prematurely, ravaged by sickness.[82] In the early 1800s Napoleon Bonaparte fruitlessly sought to invade England, but the seizure of Portsmouth and the Isle of Wight did not receive priority in his grand strategy.[83] Suspicion of Gallic military ambitions continued to worry the government during the Second Empire, and resulted in the construction of the great defensive ring of forts popularly known as 'Palmerston's Folly'.[84]

25.   Fort Widley, completed 1868, on the site of the former Portsdown Fair.

Somewhat ironically, the only time the fortifications of Portsmouth came under fire was in 1642 at the beginning of the Civil War, when the governor, Colonel George Goring, declared for the king. The ensuing short siege by Parliamentary supporters was something of a comic opera affair. Southsea Castle and the town were swiftly taken, largely because of the governor's indolence and the lack of will of the townspeople and many of the garrison. For the rest of the war and during the Commonwealth Portsmouth remained a Parliamentary stronghold.[85]

With the development of aerial warfare in the 20th century, civilians living in military and naval towns became even more vulnerable. When a zeppelin dropped four bombs harmlessly into the harbour in 1916,[86] few could have foreseen the immense destruction and loss of life that would occur in the city during the Second World War.[87] In 1944 Portsmouth was at the heart of the D-Day operations. The huge allied force which sailed from the waters round the Isle of Wight to liberate Europe was the last and greatest of the many war fleets which, since Norman times, had mustered there to sail to France. The wheel had finally come full circle.

King James' monogram from the fortifications.

Chapter Six

The Way People Lived

Before the early 18th century, the area circumscribed by the modern city boundaries was inhabited almost entirely by men and women whose livelihood was derived from farming. The traveller who came over Portsdown Hill looked down on fields and commons which stretched far into the distance. Only when he had crossed Portsea Island and reached Portsmouth town was there a transition from a rural to an urban environment; but even within the town, despite the influence of commerce and craft, a strong vestigial interest in agriculture was retained well into the 18th century.

The way of life of the medieval inhabitants is mainly a matter of conjecture. There is no doubt that in the 11th century much of Portsea Island was sparsely populated and comparatively poor. The largest settlements were in the north of the modern city on the somewhat ill-defined manor of Cosham and its more populous neighbour, Wymering, which stretched from the slopes of Ports Down across Port Creek to modern Hilsea.[1] The simple timber-framed houses of the peasants have left no traces, but Wymering church and manor house still retain evidence of their medieval origins, and they and the vicarage, still in close proximity, transmit faint echoes of the early manorial community despite the all-encompassing roar of modern suburbia.

From about the mid-13th century surviving records begin to provide fuller details of the local economy. Thus a glimpse of Wymering with its windmill and two salterns is to be found in a manorial extent of 1259-60.[2] Even more revealing are the almost contemporary accounts of Stubbington grange, an outlying possession of Southwick priory and one of the most important agricultural units in the area. Mrs. Margaret Hoad, who has examined the roll for 1267-8,[3] has shown how the estate consisted of some 152 cultivated acres managed from the principal farmhouse, which stood approximately on the site of the modern Church of the Ascension in Stubbington Avenue, North End. Probably a hall-type timber building with extensive barns and outhouses, it was re-roofed that year with 4,000 stone tiles. Simon, the monks' steward, who was almost certainly the permanent occupant, was attended by four domestic servants. Somewhat surprisingly at this early date, coal was used for heating and cooking, although ample logs must have been available in the extensive local woodlands. Tallow was bought for candles, and salt for culinary purposes. Nearby grew vines under the supervision of a vine-dresser.

The farm seems to have had nine regular workers, namely an overseer-cum-carter, two ploughmen, two cheese-makers, a shepherd, a swineherd, a cowman and a dairyman, whose wages, in addition to various payments in kind, ranged from 8s. to 12s. a year. Casual labourers were employed to assist with harvesting and harrowing, and this year a blacksmith was 'hired from the market' to make ironwork for two ploughs. Crops grown included wheat, rye, barley, oats, peas, beans and vetches. The livestock, which was listed in detail, and seriously depleted by disease, included horses, cattle, sheep, pigs and geese, and there were 520 birds in the dovecot. Much of the farm produce went to feed the monks at Southwick. Of the cheeses made after haymaking, 35 were sent to the priory and six eaten by servants and visitors at Stubbington grange. The workers at harvest-time consumed a further one hundred and eight. Southwick also received 62 fleeces, and on one occasion the prior was sent 12 lb. of almonds. Surplus produce was sold, and this year receipts totalled £38 10s. 1¼d., slightly less than the farm's expenses (£39 13s. 1¼d.).

The new settlement which was established at the harbour entrance in the late 12th century rapidly became a cohesive social unit, although even half a century later it was still probably little more than a line of narrow burgages fronting the High Street and stretching back to the rough lanes behind. By then a substantial proportion of the tenements and plots had been acquired, probably through benefactions, by the monks of Quarr Abbey on the Isle of Wight. Some twelve rents payable in money or wax are listed in a charter of 1257, and other sources have yielded four more.[4] The houses of some of the inhabitants must have been comparatively small. When that of Hugh de Stoke collapsed in 1245 from the excessive weight of the bacon flitches which had been stored there awaiting dispatch to Gascony, he received 20s. compensation for its reconstruction.[5]

Much more impressive than any of the burgesses' houses was the king's hall, with its own chapel. Intended to accommodate occasional royal visitors – although better facilities must have been available at Portchester Castle – it was almost certainly the finest domestic building on Portsea Island despite its thatched roof, which was less modish than the tiled rafters of Stubbington farmhouse. Dating from Richard I's reign, it is said to have stood on a site later known as Kingshall Green, behind the present Portsmouth Grammar School.[6] It has apparently left no archaeological evidence, but a substantial aisled hall of about 1250-1400, with an attached L-shaped stone structure and traces of a garden or courtyard, has been revealed by excavation near the Camber.[7] Only two heavily-restored buildings, the east end of Portsmouth cathedral, c.1188 (part of the original cruciform parish church), and the former Domus Dei, c.1212, have survived from before the disastrous French raids of the 14th century. Constructed of stone, they were able to withstand the fiery onslaught which probably reduced to ashes most of the wood and plaster houses of the inhabitants.

Although Portsmouth townspeople still had their roots in agriculture, their special privileges, including a weekly market and an annual fair, enabled them to develop the potentiality of the site as a business centre. By the mid-13th century they had their own merchant gild,[8] and the variety of occupations is revealed in contemporary documents, where inhabitants' names include Stephen the butcher, John the baker, Alan the tanner, Henry the fisherman, Richard the roofer and the merchants Hugh, Warin, Philip and John. Some, like Robert le Franceis and William Gomes, were presumably of alien origin.[9]

By the accession of the Tudors, Portsmouth town had changed comparatively little. The simple fortifications which had developed during the Hundred Years War enhanced the community's separate identity, but much of the intramural land was still empty of buildings, and most of the houses remained concentrated along the High Street and in the vicinity of the parish church.[10] Today, a walk round the streets of Old Portsmouth reveals no obvious evidence of the 16th-century buildings, but traces of timber framing and wattle and daub have been found in recent years behind the later façades of several of the existing houses, including 63 High Street.

Many of the inhabitants continued to hold land in the common fields that lay outside the town walls. The victualler John Palmer, for example, had at his death in 1573 five hogs, and three acres of wheat, four of barley, and four of peas and vetches. Owen Tottye, shipowner and glover, and five times mayor, held 30 acres of the town's lands in 1567.[11] Tudor Portsmouth, with pigs wandering the streets, a hayward, a cowherd and a poundkeeper among its officials, retained a semi-rural atmosphere. At first light the residents' animals were driven out through the gates and at night returned to the byres and stables in the back lanes. Sheep worrying by stray dogs, infringements of the ploughing regulations, and over-grazing of the commons were matters as important to the town governors as the control of craftsmen and shopkeepers.[12]

The streets were largely unpaved, and it was the responsibility of each resident to keep clean the section in front of his or her house. Theoretically the open gutters were scoured once a week, starting at the top of the street and working down house by house. Unfortunately, too many of the inhabitants neglected their duty or swept their rubbish on to their neighbour's property. The need to maintain a good supply of drinking water was also recognised, but the fouling of public wells was commonplace.[13] To the imperfectly understood dangers arising from insanitary practices was added the recurrent peril of plague. Especially virulent were the outbreaks of 1563,[14] when a high percentage of the townspeople must have succumbed, and 1666, which, according to one estimate, claimed about one in eight Portmuthians, although the rural settlements of Portsea Island seem to have remained largely unaffected.[15]

During Henry VIII's reign the medieval Domus Dei was closed and converted to secular purposes,[16] but the impact on medical care and poor relief is not likely to have been very great, since by then such institutions were generally in decline. In the years that followed, however, mariners and soldiers discharged from overseas expeditions, and itinerant craftsmen at work on the fortifications for long periods without pay,[17] added to the already difficult problem of relieving the town's indigenous poor. Portsmouth's wealthiest men were not particularly philanthropic[18] and provided no substantial benefactions to underpin the local system of public charity, about which we now know little. The general impression is of neglect until after the Restoration.[19] In 1599 Honor Waite of Wymering endowed a small almshouse at Cosham,[20] but it was not until the next century that a similar institution was founded on Portsea Island.[21]

With a population in 1603 of about three hundred, Wymering was an extensive manor which stretched across Port Creek to Hilsea. A further one hundred and fifty or so people lived at Widley and about one hundred and twenty at Farlington.[22] Gatcombe manor, home of the Ernley family, sat astride the parish boundaries, so that the lord's house had its hall in Wymering and its parlour in Portsea.[23] One of the more substantial yeomen farmers on Portsea Island during the early Tudor period was Thomas Carpenter, who occupied some ninety-one acres of the former monastic grange at Stubbington, and apparently paid for the building of Portsmouth's first town hall.[24] Most of the farmers, however, were men of more modest means, frequently copyholders for a term of three lives.

Such was John Fawkner, who was born in the 1520s and who, at the end of the century, had a messuage and about ten acres in Fratton manor. He was still alive in 1612, but by 1617, Anys, presumably his widow, had taken possession, having been required at his death to provide a heriot (i.e. his best beast or the monetary equivalent) for Prince (later King) Charles, the lord of the manor. A widow was allowed to farm the land until her death unless she remarried. At harvest time Anys was expected to provide free labour on the lord's desmesne. The commons and waste of the manor had ponds and marshes where carp, tench and perch, and countless wildfowl abounded, and the heaths were rich in rabbits, but in Anys's day the exclusive right of fishing and trapping was vested for life in the captain of Southsea Castle, Sir Robert Lane.[25] As late as 1659, a widow Fawkner, copyholder, was still farming in this manor on what appears to have been the same holding.[26]

The development of Portsea new town and other urban communities during the Georgian period[27] stimulated the growth of market gardening, but away from the immediate influence of the towns, extensive areas continued to be farmed on traditional lines. Mr. Moody still had two teams of oxen at work in 1801, although at Stubbington Farm the progressive Mr. Fitzherbert was one of the first local farmers to obtain a threshing machine.[28] In the 1850s about four-fifths of Portsea Island was still devoted to agriculture, but by the early 20th century this had declined to little more than one-fifth. Many of the once-fine farmhouses were then in a state of near dereliction since, according to a contemporary, 'there is the ever present fear of being gobbled up by the speculative builder'. Even Middle Farm, Milton (now Milton Park), 'the gem of Portsmouth homesteads', where peacocks had once strutted about the beautiful lawns, was empty and neglected, and its former estate of several hundred acres reduced to a few small fields.[29]

Apart from the tower and original nave of Portsmouth Cathedral,[30] there is now little visible evidence of any extensive rebuilding in the town during the half-century after the Civil War. Even the fashionable Dutch-gabled houses on the corner of Lombard Street and St Thomas's Street belie their late Stuart appearance, since they, like many others in Old Portsmouth, are almost certainly examples of the more conservative trend of up-dating houses of an earlier age by constructing modern façades.[31] During the Georgian period, however, the heart of the town was transformed. The principal thoroughfares began to be lined with fine new mansions, such as that built in the High Street by Philip Varlo (1721-78), which in the 1790s became Admiralty House and later the official residence of the lieutenant-governor.[32]

26.   Regency terraces, Southsea, *c.*1847. In the foreground is the site of the modern Pembroke Park.

Scattered across Portsea Island were also many rural retreats where ex-officers and retired businessmen, and those of independent means, lived comfortably amidst fields and commons. Such was Kingston House, 'the most complete villa of its size in the island',[33] and Milton House, the walled garden of which alone survives.[34] During the middle decades of the 19th century the needs of the urban well-to-do were changing, a fact which was

27. Part of the 1867 25″ O.S. map showing Thomas Ellis Owen's Southsea.

recognised by the talented architect and property developer, Thomas Ellis Owen (1804-62), who transformed the nascent suburb of Southsea. With vision and imagination he created a miniature garden city consisting of terraces and villas of distinct character which were more in keeping with the times than the urban mansions crowded within the walled towns.[35] General Jones left his fine Highbury Street house with its Italianate sculptured marble chimney pieces, and ceilings with enriched cornices,[36] and moved to the more fashionable 'Woodside' in Queen's Crescent; and Emanuel Emanuel, the wealthy High Street goldsmith, retired to Grove House (now part of St John's College) in 1865, where, in the garden, his authoress daughter Katie married the Victorian educationist, Philip Magnus.[37] When Sir Frederic Madden returned to his home town in 1866 after several years' absence, the new developments both amazed and puzzled him. 'It is really marvellous how people can come and live here', he wrote. 'The town of Portsmouth is deserted for Southsea.'[38]

Skilled craftsmen, minor tradesmen and members of the lower middle class often occupied narrow, several-storeyed town houses with shallow bow windows. Residences of this kind which are still to be found in Portsmouth would be familiar to Jane Austen's heroine, Fanny Price, since they are similar in design to the family home to which she returned from Mansfield Park;[39] and Dickens's Nicholas Nickleby would recognise the kind of house where Miss Snevellicci held court in Lombard Street, and into which Mr. Crummles and his talented family were crammed in St Thomas's Street.[40] Indeed, the same basic design was adopted c.1800 by the builder of Mile End Terrace where Dickens himself was born in 1812.

Smaller, meaner versions were to be found in the poorer districts, but many of the least-favoured inhabitants lived in low, weather-boarded cottages packed together without the most elementary facilities.[41] The Highbury Street home of John Pounds is a classic example of the inferior housing that existed little more than a stone's-throw away from the mansions of the rich.[42] But it was not only in the older areas that dwellings were sub-standard. One of the most notorious congeries of courts and alleys lay in the post-1815 suburb of Landport, in an area which lay athwart Commercial Road to the north of the railway line. Many of the ill-built, insanitary dwellings were said to be 'scarcely better than hovels'. Upper Church Path, a narrow but busy pedestrian thoroughfare which gave sole access to innumerable crowded courts, was built up on each side for almost half-a-mile. In places it was straddled by buildings, so that the lane was popularly known as 'The Arches'. Matrimony Row contained about twenty houses, 'the overflow from the privies' of which ran through into the kitchens 'and is a very great nuisance to the inhabitants'.[43] An important advance was the construction of main drainage in 1865-70.[44] When auctioneers King and King advertised for sale numbers 16 and 17 Matrimony Row in 1877, it was stated that both had been joined to the new system. Let individually at a weekly rent of 2s. 8d., these two-roomed cottages were bought for £35 by William Mortimore of Buckland.[45]

On the whole, however, the character of this area changed little during the next 40 years. An article published in 1914[46] strongly condemned the appalling conditions that still prevailed. Although some houses were well maintained, the great majority were dilapidated and verminous, and swarms of 'unkempt, ill-fed' children were forced to grow up in what the coroner at an inquest described as 'a pestilential spot'. The reforming zeal of Father Robert Dolling and other campaigning inhabitants drew attention to the appalling catalogue of social and moral problems in these deprived areas, but they were of such magnitude that inevitably improvements were slow to come about.[47]

By the 1870s a piped water supply was available for those who could afford it in virtually the whole area covered by the modern city. But until comparatively late in the 19th century many of the poor continued to depend on communal standpipes, public wells subject to all manner of contamination, or the proverbially insolent water-carriers who, since at least the

17th century, had toured the streets in carts selling by the bucketful. In the 1840s some of the residents were too under-privileged to afford even this basic necessity. 'We get water where we can', said one woman. 'We have frequently to steal it.'[48] Even the almshouse in Highbury Street, erected in 1831, had only a single outdoor privy and no internal water supply throughout Queen Victoria's reign. Elderly inmates who were lodged on the upper floor had to struggle to their rooms as best they could with their splashing buckets. It was not until 1907 that a tap was fitted on the upper landing. At the same time, only 13 years after the construction of a generating station near the Camber, the ten almswomen were provided with electric light.[49] Gas had come to Portsmouth in 1821,[50] but on the eve of the First World War many of the inhabitants still depended upon candles and oil lamps for their lighting.

The essentially rural character of Portsea Island until the 19th century and the availability of fish in coastal waters meant that much of the food consumed by the inhabitants was produced locally. Two mills were a feature of the original town as early as 1200, and another dominated Wymering in the mid-13th century.[51] Several windmills produced flour both for the residents and the armed forces during the 19th century, the last being demolished as late as 1925.[52] From 1194, when Richard I granted his charter, if not earlier, surplus agricultural produce was sold in the weekly market situated close to the parish church. Goods brought from a wider area by travelling merchants were available each summer at the Free Mart Fair, which lasted for 15 days.[53]

Resident craftsmen had wares to sell, too, and gradually Portsmouth's first shopping centre developed close by. The earliest shop windows still to be seen are in Peacock Lane and probably date from the 17th century.[54] Business premises in the High Street tended to be modernised in response to boom conditions, such as those which prevailed during the French Wars, and by 1815 Portsmouth's principal thoroughfare had become one of the most fashionable shopping centres in the south of England. Its long, slightly-curving rows of Georgian fronts are well shown in contemporary prints and drawings, and especially in a panoramic view published in 1842.[55] Several of these handsome buildings still remain, but little survives of Portsea's Georgian Queen Street, which by Nelson's day had become a serious rival, and where, in 1851, one large store had 32 male assistants and four apprentices.[56]

Some local businesses were so successful that they became household names far beyond Portsea Island. The best known are those of Jeremiah and Charles Chubb the locksmiths,[57] Timothy White, who sold medicines and builders' supplies in Commercial Road,[58] and James Gieve, the naval and military tailor who in 1887 became the sole proprietor of the firm which had been started by the grandfather of George Meredith, the novelist,[59] who was himself born above his father's High Street shop in 1828.[60] Another distinguished author, H. G. Wells, was from 1881-3 a draper's assistant at Hyde's emporium in King Street, Southsea, another new shopping centre. It was not a particularly happy period of his life, but later it provided background material for *Kipps* and more especially *The History of Mr Polly*, in which Portsmouth appears as Port Burdock.[61]

A significant development in the early 1790s was the founding by a group of dockyard workers of a consumers' co-operative movement. Over the next few years their ambitious schemes to provide members with cheap food and drink involved the acquisition of a windmill, a bakery, and a brewery. Unfortunately, little is known about the progress of this remarkable pioneering venture, which seems to have lost its impetus about the time the Toad Lane experiment was launched in Rochdale (1844). Even so, in 1859 the Dock Mill Society and Bread Company (established 1814) was said to have 'several retail shops'.[62] In 1873 the modern Portsea Island Mutual Co-operative Society was set up, its first shop being opened in rented property in Charles Street, Landport.[63]

The perennial, inescapable problem of poverty was greatly intensified in Portsmouth from the late 17th century by the expansion of the dockyard, the growth of new urban communities, the influx of displaced agricultural workers and, especially during wartime, the floating population of undesirable hangers-on. At the peace, or during a severe recession, social dislocation was often acute, with the authorities having to deal with large numbers of unemployed dockyard workers, demobilised ex-servicemen, widows and orphans of the war dead, impoverished minor tradesmen, and countless beggars and vagrants.

28.   The first Portsmouth workhouse, Warblington Street. built 1725 and demolished 1847.

Poor relief was the responsibility of the churchwardens and overseers, and in St Thomas's parish in 1725 they established a workhouse in Warblington Street, the cost (about £1,000) being met from voluntary subscriptions. A few years later the Portsea officials built a similar institution on a site near the modern Flying Bull Lane, Landport.[64] Early in the next century, both Wymering and Farlington parishes also had poorhouses, the former being situated in Cosham.[65] On his visit to Portsea Island in 1795, Sir Frederic Morton Eden reported that the Portsmouth workhouse was 'neither well contrived nor well managed', but that the Portsea building was 'kept very clean'. The poor there, whose chief occupation was picking oakum, 'appear to live very comfortably'. In addition, a substantial number of paupers received parish out-relief.[66]

When, as a result of the New Poor Law (1834), the two medieval parishes of St Thomas and St Mary were united into the Portsea Island Union, there was strong opposition from Portmuthians, who were allotted only seven of the 21 places on the Board of Guardians.[67] The mainland parishes of Wymering and Widley to the west, and Farlington to the east, were included in the Fareham and Havant Unions respectively. With the severe economic depression and increase in distress early in Queen Victoria's reign, the two existing Portsmouth and Portsea workhouses were considered to be inadequate, and to replace them a more spacious building was erected in St Mary's Road, Milton, in 1845. Costing £20,000, it was 'in an elevated and pleasant situation' and had 13 acres of cultivable ground on which the able-bodied inmates were expected to work.[68]

The Portsea Island Union was the most populous in Hampshire and dealt with the largest number of paupers. Capable of housing 1,200 inmates, the workhouse already contained 1,041 in 1851. During the late 1890s the enlarged building had to cope with over 1,700 needy inhabitants. Poor rates were high. In the three years before the setting up of the Union, the total average annual expenditure on relief by the two independent parishes had amounted to £15,104. In 1851 the Union needed almost double that amount and in 1856 the total rose to £37,448. This heavy burden was resented by the inhabitants, especially because until 1860 the government made no contribution despite its immense range of interests on Portsea Island.[69]

After the Civil War an increasing number of private charities also contributed towards poor relief, and innumerable self-help organisations sprang up, the best known being the pioneering Beneficial Society, founded in 1754, and St Thomas's Amicable Benefit Society which had 920 members in 1859. There were boot and burial clubs, Foresters and Odd-fellows, even a Society for the Relief of the Ruptured Poor. At times of extreme poverty the well-meaning local gentry and business fraternity set up soup kitchens, opened public subscripions, and patronised benefit performances at the local theatre and other charity functions.[70] The Board of Guardians was not finally abolished until 1930, when the local authorities were made responsible for the welfare of the poor.[71]

Closely associated with the problem of poverty was that of public health. After 1666 plague was no longer the major threat it had been in the past, but smallpox remained to imperil both the resident population and the transient servicemen. In February 1746 it was reported that whereas during the previous two months 65 members of the Hampshire Regiment stationed in the town had been infected, only five had died, a fact which was considered worthy of report.[72] By the late 18th century, Portsmouth, Portsea and Gosport were served by a substantial number of medical men who founded their own professional society, which met quarterly. But local physicians adopted vaccination with caution, since some highly respected practitioners, notably William Goldson of Portsea, had doubts about its efficacy.[73] Others, however, were convinced of its value and in 1816 the Council gave its support by allowing the town hall to be used as a temporary clinic where the poor might be vaccinated free of charge.[74] For much of Queen Victoria's reign there was a constant struggle to keep the contagion at bay and as late as 1871-3 an epidemic caused 598 deaths. Thereafter the number of cases fell dramatically and between 1874 and 1914 only 14 fatalities occurred.[75]

Until comparatively late in the 19th century the treatment available for the sick was makeshift and unscientific. In 1687 James II had 'touched for King's Evil' (scrofula) while on a visit to Portsmouth,[76] and in 1794, when many were dying from what seems to have been a virulent strain of influenza, tobacco, red wine and camphor were recommended as 'successful antidotes'.[77] When cholera appeared for the first time in the early 1830s, and more particularly in 1848-9, the medical profession could offer no effective treatment. In the latter outbreak, upwards of one thousand people died on Portsea Island before the disease had run its natural course.[78]

The first known civilian medical institution to be established in Greater Portsmouth in modern times was the dispensary set up in St George's Square c.1822 to provide the poor with free treatment for disorders of the eyes and ears. A year or so later a general dispensary was also functioning there, either as part of, or in association with, the earlier institution. In 1836 Dr. Engledue suggested that the dispensary might become the nucleus of a general hospital, but it was not until 1849 that the building later to become known as the Royal Portsmouth Hospital was opened. There followed St James's for the mentally sick (1879), the Infectious Diseases Hospital at Milton (1883), and the Eye and Ear Infirmary in Pembroke Road (1884). St Mary's evolved from the Poor Law Infirmary which was originally part of the greatly enlarged Portsea Union workhouse, and Queen Alexandra's from the Edwardian military hospital on Portsdown Hill.[79]

In 1863 the Local Government Act of 1858 was adopted, thereby giving the Council greater responsibility for public health. Slowly, improvements in the water supply and drainage began to have an effect. Portsmouth's first Medical Officer was the remarkable Dr. (later Sir) George Turner, who had been born in Portsea and who died in 1915 after spending several years fighting leprosy in Africa and contracting the disease himself. During his time as Portsmouth's Medical Officer of Health (1873-80), he was an outspoken critic of the deficiencies in the town's medical facilities and gave the authorities a difficult time.[80]

An analysis of the number of deaths from the principal zymotic diseases[81] between 1861 and 1914 shows an appalling annual toll of victims, a high proportion of whom were children. In 1876, 457 died from scarlet fever, and in 1881, 205 from diphtheria. In 1886 there were 102 deaths from whooping cough, 124 from typhoid and 191 from diarrhoea.[82] The total number of inhabitants was increasing rapidly, however, and over the years there was a steady improvement in the standard of public health. Whereas the average annual death rate per thousand in 1841-7 had been 25.37, in Dr. Turner's last year in office it had fallen to 16.51, and in 1914 to only 12.41, which was the lowest recorded in Great Britain in any town of over 200,000 inhabitants.[83]

Although it is known that as early as 1277, William, a Portsmouth boy, was a student at Merton College Grammar School, Oxford,[84] it is not until the 17th century that references to schoolmasters and the education of local children become at all frequent in the borough records. Several teachers, some unlicensed, were then domiciled within the town,[85] probably providing in most cases little more than elementary instruction in the basic skills. A classical education was to be had at the 'old Latin school', which stood in the north-western corner of St Thomas's churchyard. Little is known about this building, which in the 1770s was apparently converted into the parish fire station,[86] but it seems possible that it was already functioning as a school in the mid-17th century, when a certain Mr. Warder was warned about allowing his pupils to play in the churchyard.[87] It must have become defunct during the next half-century or so, because in 1717 the leet jury lamented the want of a grammar school, 'which we look upon as the onely ornament and advantage of a place'.[88]

This deficiency was remedied in 1732, when a former mayor, the physician William Smith, left land on the Isle of Wight to endow such an institution. Situated in Penny Street and not opened until the early 1750s, his school was a modest establishment which, despite a pressing local demand, seems to have fallen into desuetude by the end of the Napoleonic Wars.[89] One of the reasons for this failure was undoubtedly the fierce opposition that it faced from several well-run private enterprise academies in the vicinity. These included the school attached to St George's church, Portsea, where Sir Frederic Madden completed his education alongside Sir Walter Besant's father.[90] Uncertainty about Dr. Smith's wishes led to a protracted lawsuit in the early 19th century which resulted in the Master being required to accept a number of free scholars in addition to those who paid fees. Few suitable boys were forthcoming, and the school continued its erratic and undistinguished progress until the late 1860s, when it virtually closed down.[91]

Free elementary education began in the new town of Portsea when the Beneficial Society decided to pay for the tuition of a small number of poor boys. In 1784 a schoolroom was constructed on the lower floor of the Society's new headquarters in Kent Street. Numbers rose dramatically in the 1820s, when fee-paying pupils were admitted. During the next 140 years, thousands of Portsea boys received their education in this building, including Henry

Ayres, who became premier of South Australia seven times, received a knighthood, and gave his name to Ayres Rock.[92]

An era of expansion in elementary education began in 1812 with the opening of the first Lancasterian (non-denominational) school in what is now Guildhall Walk, and the first Bell (C. of E.) school in Pembroke Road.[93] By 1859 nearly all the local Anglican churches had National Schools attached to them. Pupils paid a small weekly fee unless voluntary charitable provision enabled them to enjoy a free education.[94] The 1851 census recorded 9,514 Portsmouth children attending a wide range of day schools,[95] but Henry Slight's description of 26 of them paints an appalling picture of overcrowded, ill-ventilated classrooms lacking the most elementary amenities.[96]

The children of the very poor without the means or the incentive to attend these schools had, in the immediate post-war years, received encouragement and rudimentary instruction from John Pounds (1766-1839), a poor, semi-literate cobbler who had been crippled at the age of 15 while an apprentice in the dockyard. Half-starved street arabs, whom he described as 'they as nobody cares for', were attracted into his tiny Highbury Street shop by the hot roasted potatoes and food scraps he always had ready, and there he encouraged them to learn to read and write. Sometimes he took them on nature rambles on Ports Down. His work foreshadowed, and probably helped to inspire, the Ragged School movement, and after his death several such schools were established in Portsmouth and Portsea.[97]

Private schools, ranging from the ubiquitous Dame Schools run for the most part by women of dubious competence to superior academies, continued to thrive throughout the 19th century. White's 1859 *Directory* lists 87 of the more reputable, 22 of which took boarders.[98] In the great days of empire, many officers and colonial administrators left their children to be fostered locally while they and their wives were abroad. Thus in 1871 the six-year-old Rudyard Kipling and his sister Alice (or 'Trix') were left with an old naval captain and his ill-tempered wife at Lorne Lodge, Campbell Road, and attended Vickery's (or Hope House) School. The sensitive boy hated his six years in Southsea, and his temporary home, which he called his 'House of Desolation',[99] was depicted in the early chapters of *The Light That Failed*, as well as in a short story, *Baa Baa, Black Sheep*. For would-be naval officers there were 'crammers', such as North Grove House, Southsea, where Charles Dickens's son Sydney was a pupil.[100] The tradition of private boarding establishments continued well into the 20th century. In the 1920s the future film actor David Niven was sent briefly to a school for 'difficult' boys in Southsea.[101]

A landmark in social history was the Elementary Education Act of 1870, which set up elected School Boards whose task was to supplement the existing system where necessary by building the first local authority schools. In May 1871 a report showed that 12,180 Portsmouth children were officially in attendance.[102] Every Noncomformist school either closed or became the responsibility of the local Board, but the majority of the National (Anglican) Schools remained staunchly independent. By 1902, when the Board was disbanded, a total of some twenty-seven thousand children had been provided for in the newly-opened elementary schools. The 10 surviving voluntary schools contained almost five thousand more.[103]

The great expansion in educational facilities was a response not only to the growing awareness of the need for universal literacy, but also to the spectacular increase in the local population during the period 1860-1914. Dr. Smith's school was refounded and reopened as Portsmouth Grammar School in 1879 in modern buildings (now the Lower School) on land formerly part of the fortifications near the Landport Gate. Associated with it at this period was the Pares family, one of whom, for a short time a languages master, was Professor Sir Bernard Pares, the authority on Russian politics and history. In the 1880s a boarder was Cyril Garbett, later to be archbishop of York. In 1926 the Governors acquired the disused

29. John Pounds (1766-1839) teaching some of his 'little wagabonds' in his workshop.

section of the Cambridge Barracks in the High Street, to which, a year later, the school removed.[104]

The provision of education for girls before the 19th century has left little trace, but respect for a degree of literacy is evident in 1593 in the will of Henry Turgis, a Cosham yeoman farmer who left £4 a year 'for the good education of my said daughter (Marie) untill shee shall accomplishe the age of eleven yeres'.[105] After infant school, boys and girls in 19th-century Portsmouth were invariably taught separately, girls' places being surprisingly numerous. In 1837 the Beneficial School, hitherto concerned solely with the education of boys, provided facilities for girls, too. Within a few months there were 136 on the register.[106] The daughters of gentlefolk were catered for by several private academies from which tradesmen's daughters were often excluded. Partly for this reason, a number of local people invited the Girls' Public Day School Company to extend its activities to Portsmouth. Opened in Osborne Road in February 1882, the new High School was in 1885 able to move into purpose-built premises in Kent Road, where, greatly expanded, it remains.[107]

The growing demand for technically-minded boys as naval and dockyard engineering apprentices helped to prompt the creation in 1888 of a Higher Grade School. In 1904 this became a secondary school, and a parallel girls' school was also established.[108] Four years later, a group of five de la Salle brothers opened a Catholic school for boys at 27 South Parade. In 1912, St John's College, as it was called, with 75 pupils, took over more spacious premises in Grove Road.[109] Between the wars educational facilities continued to expand and included the creation in 1921 of the Northern Secondary School for Boys,[110] where a future prime minister, Lord (James) Callaghan, was one of its earliest pupils.

The first steps towards higher education were taken in 1894 with the founding of a technical institute in Arundel Street; but it was its much-expanded successor, Portsmouth Municipal College (opened 1908) which was the antecedent of the modern Polytechnic (1969), into which, in 1976, was absorbed the Portsmouth College of Education, originally founded in 1907 as a women's day training college. The Highbury Technical College was opened in 1963.[111]

Cultural institutions were non-existent in Portsmouth before the 19th century, and began formally in 1818 with the launching of the Portsmouth and Portsea Literary and Philosophical Society by George Stebbing, Dr. John Porter and some of their friends. Meetings were held at various venues before the opening in 1831 of a splendid, purpose-built headquarters on the corner of Highbury Street and King Street in Old Portsmouth. A middle-class institution, it failed to cater for the large number of intelligent artisans who sought enlightenment, but it was to the credit of some of the leading members, notably Henry and Julian Slight, that a Mechanics' Institute was founded in 1825, with, after 1836, its own meeting place, the Athenaeum, in Bishop Street, Portsea. Like the Lit. and Phil., and the dockyard workers' Watt Institute, founded in 1848, the Mechanics' Institute had a library and reading room, and provided a regular lecture programme until its demise about 1870. A few years earlier, the flagging Lit. and Phil. had also been wound up and its headquarters converted into a Masonic Hall.[112] In 1869, however, a new Literary and Scientific Society was formed which, in the 1880s, included among its members two local G.P.s, Dr. Arthur Conan Doyle and a certain Dr. Watson.[113.]

Portsmouth's overland link with the capital had always been very important, but until the coming of the railway to Portsea Island in 1847, the journey was wearisome and dangerous. The road from the town to Sheet, just north of Petersfield, which near Butser Hill was often impassable in the winter, became the responsibility of one of the earliest turnpike trusts in 1711. Even so, the normal journey to London still took two days, with passengers sleeping overnight at Guildford. When a direct rail route was opened in 1859, the distance could be

30. The headquarters of the Portsmouth and Portsea Literary and Philosophical Society, opened 1831. The building was sold to the Freemasons c.1860 and demolished a century later.

covered in about three hours, much less than half the time taken by the fastest Royal Mail coaches in their heyday (1785-1841).[114]

For many centuries, a small fleet of wherries transported travellers across the harbour. In 1840 this monopoly was shattered when a company opened a safe and regular passenger and vehicle service from Portsmouth Point to Gosport by means of a steam-driven floating bridge. Some of the watermen, not to be outdone, acquired small steam launches, and organised themselves into two companies which were the forerunners of the Portsmouth Harbour Ferry Company established in 1962. The floating bridge ceased to function in 1959 and vehicles once more had to take the long land route to the Gosport area.[115] After 1864 a tow-boat for vehicles linked Portsmouth and Ryde (later changed to Fishbourne). This was replaced by a purpose-built car ferry in 1927. A regular passenger service by hovercraft from Southsea to the Isle of Wight began on 24 July 1965, and is now the oldest of its kind in the world.[116]

Within Portsea Island there were horse-drawn omnibuses from about 1840. Later, horse-trams were introduced and, when the service became a municipal matter in 1901, it was immediately electrified. It continued until 1936. Trolley-buses were in favour from 1934 until 1963, but increasing reliance was placed on the motor bus. A service of sorts had been in operation between the piers as early as 1899, but it was only after the First World War that a proper municipal system was developed and this functioned directly under the Council until 1986.[117]

Between 1932 and 1973 Portsmouth Municipal Airport provided limited facilities for private and commercial aircraft, including, from 1948, a service to the Channel Islands. For some years after 1933, Airspeed Limited, of which Neville Shute the novelist was managing director, manufactured aircraft on the same site in a factory built for it by Portsmouth Corporation.[118]

Communications with the outside world were revolutionised in 1885 when the National Telephone Company set up an exchange in Commercial Road. At first calls were confined to a limited area, but lines to Southampton and London were opened in 1889 and 1896 respectively. From 1901 until 1913, when it was taken over by the Post Office, Portsmouth had its own municipal telephone system with, latterly, 2,528 subscribers.[119]

The regular circulation of news locally seems to have begun with the *Portsmouth and Gosport Gazette,* which was published from 1745 until about 1790. The *Portsmouth Gazette and Weekly*

31. The Portsmouth and Gosport Floating Bridge, *c.*1840.

Advertiser followed in 1793, but ceased to operate on 8 February 1802 when it was acquired by its youthful, and at the time inferior, rival, the *Portsmouth Telegraph, or Mottley's Naval and Military Journal*, founded in 1799. During the next few years, its ambitious owner, James Charles Mottley, beat off or bought up all competitors, and his weekly newspaper, renamed the *Hampshire Telegraph and Sussex Chronicle, or Portsmouth and Chichester Advertiser*, went on to become the principal vehicle of local news not only in Portsmouth but also in south-east Hampshire and south-west Sussex, until, towards the end of Queen Victoria's reign, its fortunes were dramatically changed with the revolution in popular journalism.[120]

In its heyday the *Hampshire Telegraph* was one of the most famous provincial newspapers, liberal in outlook and particularly noted for its naval information. It had the distinction of printing, on 2 December 1805, the earliest known plan of the Battle of Trafalgar[121] and the French Admiralty, which kept a file on every British warship, was said to have obtained much of its intelligence from its columns.[122] Read by Jane Austen[123] and to be found in most middle-class homes in the area, its weekly circulation in 1823 was 3,200 copies. In 1826 this had risen to 3,700, an exceptionally high figure for a provincial weekly at this period, putting it in the same class as the *Manchester Guardian* with its circulation of about 3,200 in 1827. But while the newspapers in the northern industrial towns continued to expand, the *Hampshire Telegraph* by about 1840 had reached its peak and in the next few years settled down to about three thousand copies a week.[124] The coming of the railway to Portsea Island in 1847 meant that London newspapers were available in Portsmouth early on the day of publication, and fiercer local competition, especially from the Portsea based *Portsmouth Times and Naval Gazette*, founded in 1850 by J. S. Tibbitts, also threatened the *Telegraph*'s supremacy.

A landmark in the history of the Portsmouth press was the founding in 1877 of the first local evening newspaper, the brainchild of a young Scot, James Graham Niven. The *Evening News* was produced in a disused butcher's shop in Arundel Street, which was only just big enough to accommodate the six compositors, the clerk, and the proprietor, who, as well as being manager, editor and reporter, helped to distribute the paper by dog-cart. The flat-bed printing press

32. The first *Evening News* office, Arundel Street, 1877.

was operated in a former slaughter-house at the rear of the building. Three months after the first issue, when Niven's venture hovered on the brink of bankruptcy, the editorial staff doubled with the appointment as junior reporter of the 21-year-old ex-sailor, W. G. Gates. Gradually the *Evening News* gained recognition, so that by the end of the year 24,000 copies a week were being sold.

During the next few years the paper went from strength to strength. In 1883, however, a serious crisis arose when the *Hampshire Telegraph* was sold by the Harrison family to a group of wealthy businessmen, Andrew Carnegie, J. Passmore Edwards, and Samuel Storey, M.P., who immediately launched a rival evening paper; but this was short-lived and Carnegie and Edwards speedily withdrew from the scene, leaving the *Hampshire Telegraph* and the *Evening News* to combine into one organisation with Storey as the dominant figure. Both publications continued to be produced in the cramped Arundel Street premises until 1895, when a new building was acquired in Stanhope Road.

From 1884 the Liberal *Evening News* faced strong opposition from the Conservative *Evening Mail*, founded by the proprietors of the *Portsmouth Times* and purchased by Alfred Harmsworth, later Lord Northcliffe, at the time of the 1895 election, when he was a local Conservative candidate. Despite the superior resources he could bring to bear, the *Southern Daily Mail*, as it became known, finally amalgamated with the *Evening News* in 1905. The acquisition of the *Portsmouth Times* in 1928 ended the long run of the *Hampshire Telegraph*'s principal rival.

With its two newspapers triumphant over all competitors, the company moved in 1968 to the spacious, modern News Centre at Hilsea. Unhappily, the long-established *Hampshire Telegraph* succumbed to economic forces in 1976, but *The News*, changed in name from *Evening News* in 1969, remains, as it has for more than a century, one of the most influential forces in Portsmouth life.[125]

The house where the Duke of Buckingham
was assasinated.

Chapter Seven

The Way People Worshipped

Little obvious evidence exists today of the activities of the early church on Portsea Island. St Mary's, Portsea, was endowed *c.*1164 but the present building of 1887-9 by Sir Arthur Blomfield is the third St Mary's to be built on that site. The transepts and chancel of St Thomas's, Portsmouth, are all that survive of John de Gisors' original endowment of *c.*1180, and the shattered remains of the old hospital of Domus Dei or the Royal Garrison Church, as it is better known, endowed *c.*1235-38 but extensively restored by G. E. Street in 1866 and almost completely destroyed by enemy bombing in 1941, are the sole remnants of that building. Other religious sites on Portsea Island have all but disappeared, surviving, unknown to the general public, in a street or place name or as a note on an old plan or an oblique reference in a book.

Stubbington Avenue, in North End, perpetuates the memory of Stubbington Grange, a farm belonging to the Austin Canons of Southwick, a religious house founded by Henry I

33. St Mary's church, Kingston. A watercolour by R. H. C. Ubsdell of the medieval church painted *c.*1840. It was demolished in 1843.

in 1133, originally at Portchester. Surviving 13th-century account rolls of the bailiff indicate that there was a surprisingly sophisticated system of agriculture here and that the canons enjoyed a not uncomfortable lifestyle.[1] St Andrew's Road in Southsea is an echo of the chapel of that name which once stood in Fratton. Its origins are obscure; however, there is a reference to the chapel in a grant of Guarin de Plaiz made in the 1190s to the Bishop of Winchester, Godfrey de Lucy, in which de Plaiz gives to the canons of Southwick 'the Chapel of St Andrew which is in my fee in the parish of Portsea'.[2] The exact location of the chapel is not known. Subsequent references are few. There is a note of the chapel in Pope Nicholas's Taxation of 1291 where it is clearly subservient to and, it would seem, part of St Mary's parish. The last known reference to the chapel in a document occurs in 1573 when the lands of 'the late Chapel of St Andrew were sold'. The name survived in the common field in Fratton called St Andrew's Field but with the breakdown of the common-field system and enclosure in the 17th and 18th centuries even that faint memory of the past faded.[3]

More of a mystery, because of the dearth of sources, is 'the Chapel of Our Lady of Closze': a note on the important Portsmouth map of 1584 in the British Library.[4] It has been confused on some occasions, being in the same vicinity, with the 19th-century St Mary's, Portsmouth, built by the well-known 19th-century local architect and entrepreneur, Thomas Ellis Owen, in St Mary's Street and subsumed earlier this century into the power station site. According to Henry T. Lilley and Alfred T. Everitt in *Portsmouth Parish Church*, the chapel was still standing, if only a ruin, by the reign of Elizabeth I. It was probably built *c*.1320 when Walter de Corf was vicar of Portsmouth and the town suffered successively from the visitations of the French in 1336 and 1337 and the Black Death in the late 1340s. Certainly, there is no reference to the chapel in Pope Nicholas's Taxation nor in 1316 when Archbishop Reyolds inspected the charters of Southwick. In his subsequent inspection of 1324, however, he does mention a chapel in the parish of Portsmouth and in a rent roll of 1333 at Winchester College, a certain house is described as 'being in the street towards the new Chapel of the Blessed Mary'. There are also two references in a rent roll of 1469 in the City Records Office: to a tenement 'in the way where the Chapel of St Mary of Clos is' and a reference to the fraternity of the 'Be' Marie de Portes' which would seem to indicate that the chapel was used, if not founded, by a gild of some sort. More, we do not know.[5]

We know even less about the Magdalen Chapel, so called, mentioned in the first surviving Election and Sessions Book in the City Records Office, on 8 October 1543 when John Rydely, 'gentleman Captain of the Tower', leased of the mayor and burgesses 'Magdalen Chapel and all those Crofts of Pasture Land called Maudlin ground' as well as other land in the common fields for 40s. per annum for 12 years.[6] According to Robert East, author of *Extracts from the Portsmouth Records*, Magdalen Chapel was a small roadside chapel used by travellers and pilgrims which stood on or near the site of the old Board of Guardians offices, now the home of the Registrar of Births, Marriages and Deaths, in St Michael's Road. There is an earlier reference to 'Magdaling' furlong lying in the common fields of Portsmouth in a survey of the common fields made by Richard Palshid *c*.1531.[7] No other information about this chapel survives – to the best of our knowledge.

Better documented, though long since disappeared, is the chapel built *c*.1508 by the townsfolk of Portsmouth to the memory of Adam de Moleyns, Bishop of Chichester,[8] who was murdered in the town in 1450, supposedly by seamen. The Bishop had been a prominent state servant being not only the King's Confessor but Keeper of the Privy Seal and, less well known, the author of *The Libelle of English Policy*, one of the first economic text books ·ever written. He had been at the centre of the political intrigues of the period but was now purported to be sickened by affairs of state and, having resigned his See, determined to quit the country and live abroad, quietly. He was waiting for a boat for France at Portsmouth.

It is more likely he was aware that if he was to preserve his own skin in the clamour raised against those who counselled giving up our French territories, as he had, then he would be wise to go abroad. The known facts, however, are that de Moleyns was set upon in the town and murdered, and the people of Portsmouth were held accountable for what was probably a political crime and were, accordingly, excommunicated. The *English Chronicle* claimed that de Moleyns was in Portsmouth to pay the seamen's wages and that 'he fil in variaunce with theym and thay fil on him, and crueli there kilde him'. Popular tradition claims that the crime took place in the Domus Dei, by night, while de Moleyns was ministering at the altar. Archdeacon Wright in *The Domus Dei* has demonstrated satisfactorily that this was somewhat unlikely.[9] He fixes the exact spot of the incident at a point to the south of the church where a small chapel was built by the townsfolk on the reputed site of the assault, as part of the penance they were required to do in 1509 to expiate their crime. The chapel is marked as such on the 1584 map of Portsmouth[10] and can be distinguished clearly on the Cowdray print of the sinking of the *Mary Rose*. The process by which the excommunication was lifted and the people of Portsmouth were readmitted to their church is a rare survival, there being, according to Archdeacon Wright, no similar known record surviving of such an event. The account is contained in Bishop Fox's Register, now in the Hampshire Record Office.[11]

There is little else known of these now obscure religious sites. The two major churches on Portsea Island, however, St Mary's, Portsea, and St Thomas's, Portsmouth, and the hospice of Domus Dei are better documented. Curiously, there is no mention of any church building on Portsea Island in the Domesday Survey of 1086. There are just three churches mentioned in the Survey in south-east Hampshire: Fareham, Boarhunt and Bedhampton, despite the fact that the largest and most populous Domesday manors in the area were ecclesiastical land-holdings: Hayling, Havant, Brockhampton and Bedhampton in the east, and Alverstoke and Fareham in the west. St Mary's, Portsea, was built and endowed by the de Portsea family on a site roughly equidistant from the then existing communities of Fratton, Copnor and Kingston, as the Domesday settlement of Buckland was called. There is no foundation deed as such. The details of the endowment have to be disentangled from the deeds concerning the subsequent transfer of the church to Southwick Priory and its endowment recorded in the Southwick Registers.[12] The first of the deeds is a notification by Baldwin de Portsea to Henry of Blois, Bishop of Winchester, that he is giving the church and tithes of Portsea with half a hide of land at Stubbington to the prior and canons of Southwick in memory of, amongst others, his father, Alexander. When the actual grant was made an even larger endowment was given consisting not only of the church and tithes and the half hide at Stubbington but also half a virgate of land in Buckland and pasture for 100 sheep and 15 other animals. From diplomatic evidence the date of the endowment would seem to be approximately 1164.

The early history of St Thomas's, Portsmouth – and indeed the foundation of the town of Portsmouth itself – is to be found, similarly, in the pages of the Southwick Registers. The moving spirit was John de Gisors, a wealthy Norman merchant, who seems to have held land on both sides of the Channel, according to the Red Book of the Exchequer and the Testa de Neville, including the manor of Titchfield and the manor of Buckland which he acquired *c*.1160. The manor of Buckland included the area we know today as Old Portsmouth. It was known then as Sudewede, i.e. south-wade or water. John de Gisors must have seen the potential of the area round the Camber as a good natural harbour, protected as it was from the prevailing winds by the shingle spit of what was later known as Point and with deep water channels nearby. Accordingly, he set about founding his new town in the vicinity of the Camber by granting 'places' to tenants and providing land for the canons of Southwick Priory to erect a chapel upon, 'to the glorious honour of the martyr Thomas of

Canterbury, one time archbishop, on my land which is called Sudewede in the island of Portsea . . .'. It is not possible to date this deed but in a later deed from Richard Toclive, Bishop of Winchester, 1174-88, to Guy, Prior of Southwick, the Bishop refers to 'the Chapel of the blessed martyr Thomas . . .' and in 1185 Pope Urban III refers to 'the Church of Portsea with its Chapel'. These references would all point to a foundation date of c.1180. Subsequent grants of land to the canons including, 'the whole tithe of my water mill next the arm of the sea on the north part of my town of Portsmouth', formed the original endowment. We know more about the physical characteristics of John de Gisors' chapel than we do of any other medieval church on Portsea Island for the transepts and chancel of the original building survive in the present cathedral church of St Thomas. There may also have been a spire on this first building because alongside the copy grant of a messuage containing four perches for the repair of the chapel made c.1185-9 by de Gisors to the canons of Southwick in the Southwick Registers is a recognition mark or sketch of a spire, which would seem to indicate that St Thomas' once had a broach spire, probably of timber sheathed with lead.

This early chapel was not a parish church, for Portsmouth was not yet a parish. It was a dependency of St Mary's, Portsea, the mother church until the 14th century and, like St Mary's, the property of the canons of Southwick. The work of St Thomas's was carried on by two canons, a chaplain and two clerks in minor orders. They seem to have lived in a clergy house at the corner of St Thomas's Street and Lombard Street. The chaplain was replaced by a perpetual vicar early in the 13th century. The first perpetual vicar of whom anything is known is Thomas de Sengleton. He entered into a contract with the canons in 1260 whereby they relieved themselves of all responsibility for St Thomas's chapel reserving to themselves the right of presentation and an annual pension of 100s. to be paid them quarterly by the vicar. He received in return both the small and great or rectorial tithes and the clergy house, and agreed to bear the charge of keeping the chapel and books in good order. This agreement was to last for almost two centuries.

St Thomas's was not a particularly wealthy living. At the time of Pope Nicholas's Taxation of 1291, the annual value of the living was put at 10 marks (£6 13s. 4d.). Farlington was worth twice and Havant four times as much. St Mary's, Portsea, was worth almost £40. The town was fired by the French in 1336 and again in 1337 when the whole place was destroyed except St Thomas's and Domus Dei. The vicar had to be excused that year from paying any taxes as his houses, his goods and chattels, and those of his parishioners had been destroyed. The vicar of Portsea was similarly excused from paying taxes.

It was not unknown for the vicar of Portsmouth to be preferred to the vicarage of Portsea, as was Walter de Corf in 1348. He did not enjoy his new found wealth and prestige for long, however: he seems to have been a victim of the Black Death, as was his successor at Portsmouth, for a new vicar was inducted at Portsea on 1 April 1349 and at Portsmouth on 19 April. In fact few vicars of Portsmouth spent much time in their posts in the last years of the 14th century. Livings were exchanged frequently by clergy denounced by their bishop, Wykeham, as 'choppe-churches'. It was a sign of the times and the clergy on Portsea Island were no different from those elsewhere. Possibly as a result of the Black Death men were restless, the economy was unstable and labour at a premium. The clergy had to struggle to make ends meet and improve their positions. An energetic man could take a neglected parish, work it up and move on, at a profit.[13]

Domus Dei, 'a fair Hospitale' according to Leland c.1540,[14] was one of a number of similar institutions established in coastal towns or near the sea to receive pilgrims and strangers on their way to a famous shrine. Portsmouth was of course conveniently placed for the great shrines at both Winchester and Chichester. The town's significance as a gateway to English territories in France, and in particular Normandy, should not be overlooked either and may have been a consideration of the founder, Peter de Rupibus, Bishop of Winchester, when he endowed Domus Dei *c.*1212. Certainly, royal expeditions departed or returned regularly almost annually throughout the reign of Henry II. Established usually within the town walls, or township, the inhabitants of the town itself would also have recourse to such establishments as Domus Dei in times of sickness.

There is some debate about the dedication of the hospital, which generally varies between St John the Baptist and St Nicholas although in 1214 King John granted a charter of confirmation to the hospital 'just recently built at Portsmouth' in honour of 'the Holy Trinity, the Blessed Virgin, the Holy Cross, the Blessed Michael and All Saints'. By the end of the 14th century, however, the dedication had settled in favour of St Nicholas. The common plan of such buildings consisted of a long hall which was divided into bays by pillars. At one end was a porch and at the other a chapel. The central part of the hall was left free and the occupants were housed or nursed in the aisles. Remarkably, this plan is still preserved today in St Mary's Hospital in Chichester. The government of such institutions was vested in a master. Brethren, assisted by sisters, nursed and cooked, and the spiritual care of the hospital was entrusted to a series of priest chaplains. Conflict arose early between St Thomas's and Domus Dei because the hospital was attracting fees and legacies away from the former. The dispute was settled finally only in 1229.

Other religious houses with property and rents on Portsea Island before the Reformation besides Southwick included Titchfield Abbey, a Praemonstratensian house, and the Cistercian Quarr Abbey on the Isle of Wight. Between 1342 and 1360, John Edindon gave his manors of Portsea and Copnor to Titchfield Abbey. Praemonstratensians were expected to devote a considerable amount of their time to the study of the scriptures and other literature: theology, philosophy and the humanities. Titchfield, a daughter house of Halesowen in Shropshire, was not a wealthy religious house but by 1400 had a large and valuable library. There is an account of the library, as catalogued in 1400, in the second Titchfield Register. There were 224 volumes and probably more books because many of these manuscript volumes contained a number of theses which would be bound today as separate items.[15]

Quarr Abbey owned property and rents in Portsmouth from an early period due most likely to the considerable amount of coming and going which went on between Portsmouth and the Isle of Wight. The former always relied heavily on the latter for regular supplies of foodstuffs as well as stone for building. The abbey, founded by Baldwin de Redvers in 1132, was a suitable religious foundation to endow. Portsmouth's medieval records do not survive but there are 16 documents surviving in the Public Record Office which give some notion of the sort of sums involved in annual rents of money and wax payable on various properties in Portsmouth.[16]

On the eve of the Reformation, the religious houses paid more rent to Portsmouth Corporation than any other group. The Prior of Southwick paid a total of 54s. 10d. and three pounds of pepper, the Abbot of Hide 3s., the Abbot of Quarr 2s., and the Custodian of Domus Dei 51s. 2½d. and two pounds of pepper.[17]

Titchfield was the first of the local religious houses to be dissolved. Promised to Thomas Wriothesley, a loyal servant of Henry VIII, its surrender was secured with the compliance of its abbot on 28 December 1537. Its gross value p.a. was £280 19s. 10½d. according to the *Valor Ecclesiasticus.*[18] Some notion of the state of the house by the time it was surrendered may be gauged from the letter written to Wriothesley by the king's commissioners, Crawford and Lathum. The library had clearly gone, the church had been stripped of its valuables, there were no oxen and but a dozen rusty platters and hangings worth 20s., while the land had fallen into ruin. There were debts of £200. Amongst the lands Wriothesley acquired were the manors of Portsea and Copnor.

Southwick and its possessions were surrendered by its prior, William Norton, on 7 April

1538. Southwick was worth, gross, £257 4s. 4d. according to the *Valor*. Amongst the possessions were the rectories of Portsea and Portsmouth. They were acquired eventually in 1543 by Winchester College.[19]

Domus Dei had been held since 1522 by Dr. John Incent, described by Dom Frederick Hockey as 'a spectacular pluralist'.[20] The *Valor* described Domus Dei as having a gross annual value of £79 13s. 7½d. and a clear value after distribution of alms of £33 19s. 5½d. The work was done by the chaplain of the hospital chapel, John Wood, on a salary of £5 13s. 4d. It was another good example of the rife non-residence and pluralism which was a typical feature of the times and brought such institutions into disrepute. Incent was a close friend of Wolsey, his vicar-general when the latter held the See of Winchester and the occupant of a number of other benefices in Hampshire including the mastership of St Cross, Winchester. The house was surrendered in 1540. While the majority of the buildings soon fell into disrepair, the chapel was spared, used first as a chapel royal attached to the Governor's House when the complex was taken in hand and restored during Elizabeth's reign as a home for the governor of the garrison, and later serving as a chapel for the garrison itself.

Henry VIII died on 28 January 1547, still a Roman Catholic who in the last years of his life had positively reasserted Catholic doctrine. Edward's accession brought changes – and the first instances of image-breaking. Amongst the earliest acts of iconoclasm was an incident in St Thomas's, Portsmouth, in May 1547 when a group of soldiers pulled down images of Christ and the saints.[21] The Bishop of Winchester[22] was forced to go to Portsmouth to calm down matters. His exhortations worked. There were no further incidents.

Sources for the study of Portsmouth's ecclesiastical history during Elizabeth's reign are in short supply. Although the first set of instructions for the keeping of parish registers was issued in 1538, neither Portsmouth's nor Portsea's registers survive before 1653-4 and no original administrative material, such as churchwardens' accounts or the records of the collectors for the poor. Only transcriptions of some miscellaneous churchwardens' accounts for the years 1560, 1567 and 1570 survive, printed in Robert East's *Extracts from the Portsmouth Records*, printed in 1891 and quoted extensively by Lilley and Everitt in *Portsmouth Parish Church* in 1921. East does not indicate where he discovered the original documents, which do not survive today, to the best of our knowledge. The accounts for the year 1560 record, however, that the churchwardens, Owen Totty and Stephen Winder, incurred considerable expenditure on 'serteyne Reparacyons don to the churche and churche yard': the bells and clock were repaired, the churchyard was tidied up and enclosed and the gates repaired. Work was also done on the main fabric of the church including the steeple. This is the first firm evidence we have that there was a steeple. The pulpit was mended and a table of the Ten Commandments provided. There are also the usual notes of expenditure incurred for bread and wine for communion. The accounts for 1567 record expenditure on paper and ink for entering up the registers and keeping the accounts and for making transcripts of the registers 'to send to Winchester'. Funds were raised by a variety of means which included stripping the lead from the roof and substituting stone slates, and, in 1567, holding a church-ale.[23] Few incumbents held office for long. Between 1560 and 1564 four men came and went in close succession, one dying in office. In 1564, Christopher Threder was admitted to the livings of both Portsmouth and Portsea and actually remained in possession of them both until his own death in 1579. He never became a rich man. He left in his will only 12d. for the poor box of each church, and to his daughter, a 'sounding board', two pewter plates, two pewter dishes, a bacon hog, a goose and a gander. He was buried in the chancel of St Thomas's. Another five men came to St Thomas's in quick succession before John Ravenscroft was admitted to the vicarage of Portsmouth in 1589. He remained in there until the end of

Elizabeth's reign and it was during his period of office that the Queen herself visited Portsmouth, 28 August to 2 September 1591, and attended divine service at St Thomas's.

Original records survive in greater numbers from the mid-17th century. Churchwardens' accounts survive for the parish of St Mary's, Portsea, from 1632.[24] They are housed today in the City Records Office. The parish registers of both St Mary's, Portsea,[25] and St Thomas's, Portsmouth,[26] also survive – from 1653-4. The first records of Dissenters appear, too. Historians continue to be indebted, however, to Lilley and Everitt. They note that the register book of St Thomas's once held a note inside the cover that 'My Lord Ducke's boweles wear buried the 24th of August 1628' and thus allude to an event in Portsmouth's history of national importance: the assassination of the Duke of Buckingham on 23 August 1628. Buckingham's sister, the Countess of Denbigh, placed a memorial to her brother against the north wall of the chancel, behind the altar. The memorial can still be seen in the chancel, placed now against the east wall.

What little evidence we have of the churchmanship of these times survives chiefly in the pages of Lilley and Everitt. They record that at Easter 1567, a copy of Archbishop Parker's *Advertisements* was purchased which prescribed the surplice as 'the minimum of clerical ornament'. In 1570 the church-wardens placed a copy of the Bish-ops' Bible in the church and a cover for the communion cup to be used also as a paten. Later we learn that in 1613 some fine hangings were presented. In 1633, yet another new bible – the Authorised Version of 1611 – was purchased at a cost of 13s. and a new tablecloth of white linen damask to cover, at com-munion, the gold cloth: signs per-haps of Laudian inclinations. The churchwardens' accounts of St Mary's, Portsea, which survive in their original form from 1632, indi-cate that Holy Communion was ad-ministered at least nine times a year during the 1630s: on Whit Sunday, 6 August, 10 October, Christmas, 19 February, Palm Sunday, Good Friday, Easter Day and the Sunday after Easter. It is also clear that the incumbent wore a surplice and a cloth was provided for a com-munion table. But whatever the in-clinations of the incumbents of St Mary's and St Thomas's in the dec-ade or so before the Civil War, their style of doing things does not seem to have pleased all the townsfolk, for in April 1643 the Grand Jury in their presentment pleaded 'that the devine service of common prayer

34.   Interior of St Thomas' church, Portsmouth by R. H. C. Ubsdell, painted *c*.1840. Both the medieval chancel and the 17th-century chancel arch and nave are clearly visible.

with the history of the Church heretofore used by the Statute of Primo Elizabeth may be againe read and used in this the parish Church of Portsmouth according to the purport, intent and meaning of the saied statute'.

During the Civil War, St Thomas's was virtually destroyed by parliamentary forces in September 1642 when the tower was shot through and shot which fell short of the tower went through the roof of the building and into the nave. The parishioners were forced to adjourn to the Garrison Chapel for the duration. The incumbent at the time of the siege was Walter Flay. He was ejected in 1643, as were the incumbents of Alverstoke, Bedhampton, Fareham, Warblington, Havant and Rowner. A succession of Presbyterian ministers included Nathaniel Tucker, 'a seditious Levite' according to the Royalist newspaper, *Mercurius Auticus*, in August 1643, quoted by Lilley and Everitt, and Benjamin Burgess, who was admitted in 1658. Burgess clearly accompanied Haselrig, Walton and Morley to London in December 1659, for the Rump ordered that 'Mr Burgesse of Portsmouth be desired to assist in carrying on the work of Fasting, Humiliation and Prayer' on 4 January 1660, which day they had set aside for thanking God for his blessings. Such fame or rather, notoriety, did not do poor Mr. Burgess much good, however, for he in his turn was driven from office – by the Act of Uniformity of 1662. Of St Mary's during these troubled times, we know little. There are no accounts surviving of churchwardens' expenditure during the period 1642-47, and from 1651, though there are accounts, they are very badly kept until the turn of the century when a fine italic hand and legible, properly recorded, meetings of the vestry appear.

The first properly-documented sources for the activities of Nonconformists survive from the mid-17th century. The Quaker Sufferings Book 1655-1792, preserved today in the Hampshire Record Office, contains sobering accounts of attempts by the Society of Friends to meet undisturbed not only in the town of Portsmouth but elsewhere in the county.[27] Friends suffered the most appalling ill-treatment during these years. Fines were exacted from them 'for not contributing towards repairing steeple houses', i.e. parish churches, during the Commonwealth, but this was comparatively mild treatment compared wih that meted out to them after the Restoration. On Christmas Day 1660, Friends were much abused by their fellow townsfolk for opening up their shops, and their goods were despoiled with dirt. When a sympathetic bystander remonstrated with the crowd on behalf of the Friends, he in turn was abused for his pains, and one William Lunn was taken out of a Friends' house, imprisoned all night and the next morning turned out of the town with 'a kick on the breach' from a soldier. He was probably connected to the Widow Lunn who during the Commonwealth had taken from her by Captain Robert Peacock, a pair of shoes worth 4s. towards the 9s. demanded from her for repairing the steeplehouse. Other incidents recorded in the Sufferings Book include the story of William Rutter who was taken out of a meeting and committed to prison for refusing to take the oath of allegiance, and died there on 14 March 1661. Other cases are recorded of first-day meetings broken up and the man of the house and his men friends being taken to the Main Guard,[28] where they refused to take the oath and were confined in a place known as Felton's 'hole', in the Main Guard, for a number of days. When they were finally released, they were usually kicked and pushed through the streets and put out of the town at the Landport Gate. During the governorship of Colonel Legg[29] the Quakers were treated particularly brutally and many of them were confined in Felton's hole, described in the Sufferings Book as 'so badd that some of the soldiers confest they would not put a dogg there' (it was susceptible to inundations from the sea).

The story of the Presbyterian Church in Portsmouth goes back to the time of Mr. Benjamin Burgess's incumbency of St Thomas's Portsmouth. Dismissed from office in 1662, he did not leave the neighbourhood. He seems to have taken up residence initially in the parish of

Portsea and served as a Collector for the Poor.[30] About 1667, he was holding Presbyterian meetings in a malthouse at Gosport, and after 1672 and the Declaration of Indulgence[31] he was licensed to preach in both Portsmouth and Gosport. Premises in Penny Street were replaced eventually in 1718 with premises in the High Street associated more usually today with the Unitarians, but only because the Portsmouth Presbyterian congregation eventually adopted Unitarian principles. The Carter family were great benefactors of the High Street Chapel. John Carter (1672-1723), a merchant who laid the foundations of the family's wealth and prosperity and, incidentally, brought the news of Queen Anne's death to Portsmouth and was promptly put in chains for his trouble by the governor, Colonel Gibson, contributed greatly towards the cost of erecting the chapel. His grandson, Sir John Carter, who was mayor nine times between 1769 and 1804, proved an equally staunch supporter. It was Sir John who worked closely with the minister of the day, The Revd. Thomas Wren, between 1777 and 1782 to relieve American prisoners of war at Forton Prison. Between them, they provided clothing, money for food, books and may have played a part in helping some prisoners to escape. In due course Mr. Wren was in fact awarded the degree of Doctor of Divinity by Princeton 'for services to American Prisoners at Portsmouth, England'. He was the first Englishman to receive such an honorary degree after the American Revolution.[32]

Baptist preachers were active in Portsmouth from at least the 1640s. Like the Quakers, they were imprisoned frequently and, later, fined heavily for preaching and teaching in seditious conventicles and refusing to take the oath of allegiance. However, with the Act of Toleration,[33] they opened for public worship a chapel in St Thomas's Street, Portsmouth, in 1693, and later another chapel was built in Kent Street, Portsea, for the congregation of Gosport Baptists who had adjourned there. Some notion of the size of the local Dissenting population towards the end of the 17th century may be gauged from the Compton Census of 1676.[34] There were few Dissenters then, perhaps two to two and a half per cent of the population. By 1725 that figure had increased four-fold, according to the visitation returns of that year preserved amongst the records of the bishops of Winchester, to just over nine per cent of local 'souls'.[35] In Portsea, there was a meeting house 'of the Anabaptist persuasion', and of 1,500 parishioners the parish officers calculated that there were perhaps nearly two hundred Protestant Dissenters. In Portsmouth, it was calculated that there were 8,000 parishioners, one meeting of Presbyterian Dissenters consisting of about seven hundred persons, of whom five hundred belonged to the parish and the rest to neighbouring parishes, chiefly the Common in the parish of Portsea, i.e. the growing suburb soon to be known as Portsea. There was also a meeting of Arminian Baptists of about one hundred and fifty persons, of whom approximately one hundred belonged to Portsmouth parish, a Quaker meeting of about twenty persons and twenty families of Calvinistical Baptists who met at the Common.[36] The Nonconformists were also well-represented by this time on both the aldermanic bench and amongst the burgesses. Between 1716 and 1735, nine aldermen were registered as Dissenters and about thirty burgesses.[37]

There appear to have been no Catholic Dissenters to speak of in the town before the late 18th century. A list of communicants compiled during the year 1603 preserved in the British Library records that there were no recusants at all in the parish of Portsmouth and only two, and they were women, in the parish of Portsea.[38] The 1725 visitation indicates that in the parish of Portsea, there was 'no Papist of any consequence . . . and not above two or three labouring persons that are such' and in the parish of Portsmouth, only two families professed to be Papists and they were 'mean and obscure'.

The history of the Church in Portsmouth from the beginning of the 18th century is tied up increasingly with the growth of the town. In 1704 the first St Ann's was built in the dockyard 'for the use of Officers and Artificers belonging to the said Dock, as also for officers and men belonging to the Ordinary of the Navy in this Harbour'.[39] In 1785, the church moved to its present site when the dockyard was enlarged. In 1752, a memorial presented to the corporation by 21 inhabitants of Portsea requesting the mayor, aldermen and burgesses to grant them a piece of land for the purposes of erecting a chapel, indicates that the parish church of St Mary's was no longer adequate for the needs of the growing population:

> the Parish of Portsea is a large and populous parish, and that part of the said parish which is now commonly called or known by the name of the Common is of late years very greatly increased in the number of houses and inhabitants, and is situate more than a mile distant from the Parish Church, whereby many of the old, decrepit, infirm and sickly persons are disabled from attending Divine Service and doing their duty to Almighty God.[40]

The corporation looked favourably upon the petitioners and granted them a piece of waste land in what is now St George's Square. The foundation stone of St George's Church as it was called was laid on 11 May 1753. The total cost of the building including boundary wall was £2,208 9s. The bulk of this sum was raised by a general subscription for seats, which became the property of the subscriber. The parish church remained the mother church and the appointment of a minister was vested in the vicar of Portsea.

St John's, Portsea, was built in 1787-8. A proprietary chapel where the pews could be bought and sold, St John's stood in Prince George Street, Portsea. The presentation was vested in trustees who had to be not only proprietors themselves but residents of the borough and communicating members of the Church of England. These building efforts did not solve the problem of the ever-growing suburb, however. The local population was 32,166 in 1801 according to the census. This includes of course both Portsmouth and Portsea. From 1816, complaints occurred regularly in the archdeacons' visitation returns that the parish church of St Mary's, Portsea, was very old and too small for the population. In 1817, we learn that the church at Portsea will hold only six hundred persons and that the local population now amounts to thirty-six thousand.[41] It is worth recalling that about one hundred years before, in 1725, the population numbered some fifteen hundred 'souls'.[42] In 1819 the complaints recur but reference is made to 'two new chapels . . . about to be erected'.[43] St Paul's, Southsea, was consecrated in 1822 and All Saints, Landport, in 1828. They were both built by parliamentary grant. Other steps were taken. The parish church of St Mary's, Portsea, was rebuilt in 1844 with a combination of voluntary subscriptions, public grants and the help of its patron, Winchester College. St James Milton was opened in 1841 in the south-western corner of the parish, and within the walls of the town of Portsea the church of Holy Trinity opened in the same year. It was still not enough. Archdeacon Wigram calculated in 1851 that in the seven Anglican churches in the parish of Portsea, with its population of some fifty thousand, there were sittings for only 8,700, of which between three thousand and three thousand five hundred alone were free and, therefore, available to the poor. By contrast, the Archdeacon calculated that the 360 beer shops and 296 public houses in the parish could accommodate some twenty-four thousand people![44]

One of the major obstacles to progress at this time was the obstructive attitude of the vicar of Portsea, J. V. Stewart, who feared that any radical solution of the parish's problems might severely affect his income from fees and whose consent was still required to any changes which might affect his position. The result was that only four new parishes were established between 1851 and Stewart's death, aged 85, in 1878. By the end of the 19th century and the beginning of the 20th century, however, a network of church buildings did exist covering the built-up and newly-developed parts of Portsea Island. The combined efforts of Evangelicals, Ritualists and Anglican middle-of-the-road churchmanship all played their part.[45]

Evangelical churches were probably amongst the best-attended. At St John's, Portsea, The Revd. John Knapp not only increased the sizes of his own essentially middle-class congregations during the years of his ministry, 1858-81, but set out to capture the minds of

35.   The Sunday Evening Service at the Circus church, Portsmouth, from John Knapp's *The Church in the Circus*, (London 1858).

the working classes. He had some experience already of gospel services in London and determined to promote something similar in Portsmouth. He obtained the use of a vacant circus building in Landport and gospel services began in June 1857. They were immensely popular from the start. On the first evening there was a congregation of two thousand. Services were experimental: on Sunday mornings, there was either Morning Prayer or Holy Communion, both with sermons, and in the evening, the Litany, popular hymns and a 'rousing' sermon. On Wednesday evenings the service included a reading of the most interesting portions of a newspaper for about three-quarters of an hour. There were also prayer meetings, bible classes and Sunday schools. Knapp's achievements were lauded in the Evangelical press. He was a most understanding man. He thought that Sunday morning services should be held as late as possible so that the working man who rose very early

Monday to Saturday might find 'the Sabbath day . . . a day of rest, physically for the body, as well as morally and spiritually for the mind and soul'. He believed very firmly in hymn singing and a simple, straightforward address. The Circus Church was immensely successful. In 1863 Knapp handed over complete responsibility to his curate, John Martin. A permanent building was erected in Surrey Street in 1864; it was destroyed by enemy action in 1941.

A rare insight into life at St John's Parsonage survives in the letters which passed between Mrs. Anne Knapp, John Knapp's wife, and their eldest daughter, another Anne, in Barbados with her husband, William Mayo, between 1872 and 1875.[46] Amongst the minutiae of domestic existence: smoking chimneys, bad drains, a leaking roof, recalcitrant children and lazy servants, her own, the children's and their neighbours' many ailments, there are details of organ recitals, bible classes, sales of work and parish outings and, at the centre of events, 'poor Pater'. She wrote of him tenderly: 'every year seems to make him dearer to us all; he is so kind, and tenderly considerate for all of us'.[47] Mrs. Knapp also relayed delightful snippets of news to her daughter including the tale of the sudden demise of Mr. Charles Stewart, the brother of the obstructive vicar of Portsea:

> Mr. Chas Stewart (formerly of St Paul's Square) – is dead, he married his second wife, a Miss Strong, some few weeks ago, and went to Paris for his wedding trip. On returning, a drunken soldier got into the railway carriage and excited Mr. S. so much that he had an apoplectic fit on his return and died.[48]

He was 74 years old.

Two new Evangelical parishes were established in the 1860s: St Luke's and St Simon's. St Luke's was a predominantly working-class district. The first incumbent, Basil Aldwell, served his parish for nearly forty years. He was succeeded by his son in 1895 who in turn worked in the parish for a lengthy period, resigning in 1920. Basil Aldwell was particularly interested in educational matters. When he died, the parish schools had some one thousand children on their registers and were reckoned to be among the best in the diocese. During his incumbency, he also established a soup kitchen, a Visiting Society for the relief of the poor, youth groups, branches of the Band of Hope and Scripture Union, an industrial society and a mothers' meeting. At St Simon's, the first vicar, Frederick Baldey, established a similar pattern of activities: a mission church was established in Albert Road, an industrial society was formed, a blanket and coal society, and a soup kitchen. During the summer months, Baldey, who was keen on revivalist meetings, conducted regular services on the beach for both residents and summer visitors.

Ritualist activity began in Portsmouth in some of the poorest and most deprived areas. The first Ritualist was Thomas Platt, appointed to Holy Trinity, Portsea, in 1854 although he did not in fact introduce eucharistic vestments until Christmas 1865. He soon established a pattern of parish teaching, visiting and care for the poor and deprived similar in most respects to his evangelical neighbours. His curate, Reginald Shutte, established the Mission of the Good Shepherd in Whites Row, one of the most socially deprived parts of Portsea, behind The Hard. There, Shutte held daily services and weekly celebrations of Holy Communion, established a Sunday school, ragged schools, coal and clothing clubs. The Mission developed eventually into the church and parish of St Michael's. St Michael's was a long time building. Although the foundation stone was laid in 1872, the nave was only completed in 1882 and the chancel, begun in 1886, was not completed until 1891. The bulk of the money was raised by his working-class congregation and therefore, not surprisingly, was gathered only slowly but Shutte was also hampered by the attacks made on his Ritualism.

Shutte was a somewhat self-effacing man. Nigel Yates in his work on the Ritualists[49] in Portsmouth regards him as 'one of the most undervalued of Portsmouth's Victorian religious

36.   Interior of St Agatha's, Landport, early 20th century.

leaders', and it is true that most students of Portsmouth's 19th century religious life have chosen to concentrate their attention on Robert Dolling, priest-in-charge, between 1885-96, of the first Winchester College Mission in Portsmouth, St Agatha's, Landport. Dolling was certainly not self-effacing. His activities during his fairly brief time in Portsmouth have so stamped themseves upon the city's consciousness that even today he is still a vivid memory. His own *Ten Years in A Portsmouth Slum*, published in 1896, and C. E. Osborne's *Life of Father Dolling* (1903), are dramatic accounts of his struggles not only to improve the quality of life of his parishioners but to advance the Ritualist cause. He kept open house with his sister at their home in Clarence Street. He established a gymnasium for the young men of his parish, and a panoply of organisations, which was common to both Evangelical and Ritualistic parishes. He campaigned vigorously to improve the lot of the shop worker and to combat alcoholism and prostitution in his parish and, indeed, the town. He was a keen advocate of sacramental confession, used incense, was fond of extempore prayer, introduced almost immediately on his arrival daily celebrations of Holy Communion and, later, extra-liturgical devotions. Despite infuriating many local clergy and prominent citizens of the town, Dolling was tolerated by the first two of the three bishops of Winchester who held office while he was at St Agatha's: Harold Browne and A. W. Thurold. He came to grief during the episcopacy of Randall Davidson, who took issue with him over the three altars, one of which was to be used exclusively for requiem masses, which he erected in the new permanent church of St Agatha which had replaced the first mission church. Dolling resigned in 1896. Perhaps one major reason why his memory is still so fresh lies in the fact that 'his' church still survives in defiance of bishops, the Blitz, and, until recently, municipal indifference.

Equally colourful is the story of another Ritualist, Bruce Cornford, vicar of St Matthew's, Southsea, 1896-1940. His particular brand of high churchmanship, at the same time both anti-Protestant and anti-Roman Catholic, attracted huge congregations to St Matthew's throughout the Twenties and Thirties.

Anglican middle-of-the-road churchmanship was exemplified in the missionary activity of St Mary's, Portsea, in the last quarter of the 19th century. There Edgar Jacob, who had succeeded J. V. Stewart on the latter's death in 1878, set to with a reformer's zeal to 'turn round' his huge parish. He found a church, albeit rebuilt for Stewart in the 1840s by local architect Thomas Ellis Owen, not capable of seating even a thousand people – in a parish with a population of about twenty thousand. There was no parish school to speak of and no parish organisation at all. In an initial 'holding' operation, he repaired the parish church and managed to squeeze in sufficient additional seats to take his average Sunday evening congregation to some twelve hundred. And with the opening of St Barnabas's Mission in July 1879 and St Faith's Mission in December, he secured a further 900 seats. Parish life flourished: mothers' meetings, savings clubs, temperance organisations, soup kitchens, music groups. More mission churches were planned. Baptisms increased threefold between 1876 and 1880, numbers of communicants increased dramatically and so did Sunday school attendance. Jacob also set about rebuilding his parish church. The foundation stone was laid by the Dowager Empress of Germany, the former Princess Royal, in 1887 and the building was completed finally in 1889.

Jacob also set in train the quite remarkable system of parish administration which, perfected by his successors, Cosmo Lang, Bernard Wilson and Cyril Garbett, became the hallmark of St Mary's and a valuable training ground for several generations of Anglican priests up to at least the end of the Great War. The parish was split into districts, one assigned to the parish church and one to each mission. Two or three curates were responsible for each district and were expected to carry out regular and systematic house-to-house visiting. Church councils were introduced in each district, which sent representatives to a general council for the whole parish. St Mary's became a model for other Anglican parishes. *The Work of A Great Parish*, edited by Cyril Garbett and published in 1915 with an introduction by Cosmo Lang, by then Archbishop of York, celebrated the 25th anniversary of the consecration of the present St Mary's. It is also a record of the quite remarkable achievement of Jacob and his successors who 'out of chaos . . . brought order and out of sheer apathy and indifference . . . created a strong and vigorous Church life'.[50] The ritual used was restrained, 'simple', to quote Garbett. He claimed that there was 'a strong Puritan tradition in the town and parish hostile to religious ceremonial'.

Accordingly, the vicars of Portsea had, he said:

recognised the vehemence in and strength of this sentiment; they had not hesitated to introduce changes which were clearly necessary in the interests of reverence and order, but they were careful not to move in the minor matters of ceremonial in advance of the goodwill of the people, and they have avoided unnecessary innovations which were sure to cause pain and anxiety to many of their workers.

It was a wise policy which ensured that St Mary's avoided controversy and built upon the foundations laid by Jacob when he took up office in 1878. Garbett was succeeded by Canon J. F. L. Southam, a man whose reputation, undeservedly, is still far too low. His career has yet to be studied in detail by historians of St Mary's. He was the man, however, who lit the candles which Garbett did not choose – or dare – to light upon the High Altar of St Mary's. He was also vicar when the decision was made not to make St Mary's the cathedral church of the new diocese of Portsmouth. Was his influence decisive? He was certainly well aware of the sacrifices the parish would have to make should it become the cathedral church.[51]

With the launch of the Six Churches Fund by Bishop Talbot in 1913 and the construction of new churches in the northern and eastern parts of Portsmouth: St Saviour's, Stamshaw, St John's, Rudmore and the Church of the Ascension in the north and St Alban's and St Cuthbert's in Copnor, to the east, the pattern of Anglican church building on Portsea Island was virtually complete. In 1927 the parish church of St Thomas's, Portsmouth, became the cathedral church of the new Anglican diocese of Portsmouth, created out of the ancient diocese of Winchester. Partially extended in 1938-9 by Sir Charles Nicholson, who also designed St Alban's, Copnor, St Thomas's still awaits completion. It is in fact one of only two uncompleted cathedral buildings in England.[52] There was an abortive attempt to

37. The vicar of Portsea, Cyril Garbett, with the Archbishop of York, Cosmo Gordon Lang (vicar 1896-1901), from Charles Smyth, *Cyril Forster Garbett, Archbishop of York* (1959).

complete the extension in the mid-1960s with plans by Seely and Paget and Pier Luigi
Nervi as consultant engineer, but the scheme came to nothing. In 1985, the Provost of
Portsmouth, David Stancliffe, published a new scheme for completing the building following
a long period of consultation and development of the brief between 1983 and 1985. Described
by him in *Church Building*[53] as a geometrical form reminiscent of the work of Sir Edwin
Lutyens, the new scheme provoked a predictable series of reactions. Subsequently refined
in the light of comments and other practical considerations, the scheme was presented to
the public again in 1988 and fund-raising began.[54]

More traditional in style is the Catholic Cathedral of St John the Evangelist in Edinburgh
Road. Interestingly, the Roman Catholic diocese was created in 1882 and is the senior of
the two dioceses by forty or more years. In fact, the city is probably unique amongst towns
and cities in this country in having two bishops bearing its name simultaneously. The
Roman Catholic Diocese of Portsmouth was carved out of the western portion of the Roman
Catholic Diocese of Southwark, itself constituted only in 1850 following the re-establishment

38. St John's Roman Catholic Cathedral with Victoria Park in the foreground and the Royal Naval barracks, the
dockyard and Whale Island behind, early 20th century.

of the Roman Catholic hierarchy in this country. The new diocese of Portsmouth was given the counties of Hampshire, Berkshire, the Isle of Wight and the Channel Islands. As the author of the recent history of the diocese, Gerald Dwyer, has put it, this is an area almost co-terminus with the pre-Reformation diocese of Winchester.[55] The Cathedral, which in 1882 was already under way to serve as a large parish church, is described by Dwyer, as 'a great act of faith'. The congregation was not big. It had never been very considerable. The two or three families noted in the Visitation Returns of 1725 had grown into a congregation sufficiently large by the end of the 18th century to support a small chapel of their own but it was a very modest affair, tucked away behind two houses in Prince George Street, Portsea, and only enlarged again in the early 1850s when, apparently, there were only some nine hundred at mass. The priest-in-charge in 1877, Father Horan, wanted something splendid and he set about achieving it. His new church, built near the newly-developing centre of the town, was known as the 'penny brick' church, being built with no great endowments aside from a gift of £4,000 from the Duke of Norfolk but with the many small contributions of the congregation. Of deep-red brick, the building stands out prominently across Victoria Park. The interior is well-proportioned with attractive Gothic nave arcades, slender piers, foliated capitals and delicately moulded arches. The original architect, 1877-82, was J. Crawley. Later additions were by J. S. Hansom.

The local Jewish community was also established for many years in this part of town.[56] The first references to Jews in surviving local records occur in Sessions Papers from 1736 and tradition has it that a synagogue existed, probably in a room in a rented house, in Oyster Street from 1732. There are certainly several Jewish householders listed in Oyster Street in rate books of this date.[57] Also, the Jewish burial ground was purchased in 1749, which would seem to indicate that an established Jewish community was in existence by this time. Hard evidence of the existence of the synagogue survives only from 1780. A lease dated then confirms that there was quite definitely a synagogue in Portsea, in White's Row, and that it had been in existence for some years in a converted house.[53] This house was to be pulled down now and a proper synagogue built in its place. This synagogue was the home of the local Jewish community until 1936, when it moved to the present synagogue at The Thicket, Southsea, to the north of St John's College.

Between approximately 1780 and 1936, however, the local Jewish community was concentrated near the Dockyard Main Gate and along the length of Queen Street. Trading opportunities – with the Navy – brought the Jews and their families to Portsmouth. Aubrey Weinberg has calculated that this local Jewish population was always very small. He has identified only forty-odd adult males in 1776 when the local population already constituted approximately ten thousand. By the beginning of the 19th century, he had identified some thirty trades practised: those of lodging-house keeper, silversmith, watch-maker, slop-seller and pawnbroker. The community declined in numbers in the depression which followed the end of the Napoleonic Wars but rose again in the last half of the 19th century as a result of the flight of many Jews from persecution in Europe.

Jews emerged to play a prominent part in the political life of the town in the mid-1930s. Despite the passage of the Municipal Reform Act, which conferred voting rights on all ratepayers and entitled Dissenters to be elected to local corporations, Jews were still debarred from standing for election. Interestingly the corporation petitioned parliament regularly from 1836 to remove Jewish civic disabiliies and to allow Jews to stand for parliament and enter the universities. The first Jew to be elected to the town council, Emanuel Emanuel, in 1841, did in fact risk being challenged as religious disabilities were not removed officially until 1846.

No survey of the religious life of the town and, in particular, the Evangelical Revival of the 18th and early 19th centuries is complete without an examination of the activities of the

Methodists.[59] They were an important influence. All three branches of Methodism were represented prior to the Union of 1932: Wesleyans, Bible Christians from 1824 and Primitive Methodists from 1849. John Wesley himself was a frequent visitor to the town. He made some 22 visits in 38 years, normally in October. In July and October 1753 he was particularly distressed by 'that accursed itch of disputing' which had practically broken up the local congregations. But of the ordinary townsfolk he wrote in July 1753 that 'so civil a people I never saw before in any sea-port town in England'. He preached frequently in the open air. His audiences were most receptive to his message. 'Never did I see any receive the word with greater earnestness', he wrote in 1768, and again, in 1770, he wrote, 'the people in general here, are more noble than most in the south of England: they receive the word of God with all readiness of mind, and show civility, at least, to all that preach it'. The earliest Methodist chapel in existence in Portsmouth was in Warblington Street, from 1767. This chapel was replaced by another in Oyster Street in 1788, which was replaced in its turn by the Green Row Chapel. In Portsea, there was probably a chapel in existence from at least 1768. It was closed and a new chapel opened in Daniel Street, in St Peter's Chapel, premises which had belonged hitherto to a now dissolved breakaway Anglican congregation. The chapel does in fact still exist on Whitbread's Queen Street site and its pediment can be seen over the brewery wall.

The Bible Christians opened their first chapel in Little Southsea Street in 1822 and, soon afterwards, another in York Street, Landport. Throughout the 1820s, they sent missions out to the surrounding neighbourhood: Copnor in 1825 and 1826 and Hayling Island, Chichester and Selsey in 1829. The Primitives held their first meetings in Dock Row in Portsea. The Wesleyans were always the wealthiest of the three groups, but were of course more numerous. It is interesting to note that in 1851, while the Methodists were the strongest denomination nationally after the Church of England, this was not true of Portsmouth where the Baptists and Congregationalists, their roots reaching back beyond the 18th century, were strongest.

The last quarter of the 19th century saw considerable expansion of Methodist church-building activities, in parallel with the activities of the Church of England in the town. Older centres sponsored new, daughter churches. Arundel Street sponsored Buckland in 1875, Wingfield Street in 1878, Havant in 1889, Twyford Avenue in 1903, Copnor in 1911, Drayton in 1914 and, later in the 20th century, Wymering in 1934. Daniel Street sponsored Victoria Road in 1878 and Trinity in 1901, and Pembroke Road sponsored Victoria Road and South Street in 1878, Eastney between 1877 and 1886, and Rivers Street in 1887. This proliferation of daughter churches proved, however, to be at the expense of the membership and finances of the older churches. The building of Central Hall in Fratton was a later response to the problems of urban growth and to the recruitment difficulties of depopulated churches in town centres. The last years of the 19th century saw also increasing emphasis put upon 'the pleasant and social' aspects of Church life. Many records survive of musical soirées and entertainments, and, most particularly, the *café chantant*.

Note should be made, too, of the Wesleyan Sunday school movement and indeed the Sunday school movement in general. In their time, the Wesleyan Sunday schools must have provided literally thousands of local children with the only education they ever received. The earliest schools were in Warblington Street in 1803 and Oxford Street, Landport, in 1805. Additional schools were also established subsequently in Portsmouth, Portsea, Landport, Fratton and Stamshaw. Daniel Street claimed to have educated nearly six thousand children by 1841. The great local inspiration was of course the crippled cobbler, John Pounds, the man said to have inspired the Ragged School movement who in the early years of the 19th century gathered round him in his little shop in St Mary's Street many of the youngsters who haunted Portsmouth's streets. He taught them all he knew as well as providing them with fresh clothes and a modicum of social graces. Books were supplied by ministers of the Unitarian Chapel in the High Street and, when a Sunday school was set up there in 1835, John Pounds sent his best pupils.

Another prominent local figure in the Sunday school movement was George Bayne.[60] For thirty years, between about 1846 and 1876 when he died, he ministered to the young of Landport. At his own expense, he opened and equipped a Sunday school in Clarendon Place in Landport 'which in a short time became one of the most popular in the town'. In 1868 he opened a Sunday Night Ragged School. On his death, the *Portsmouth Times* wrote:

> Hundreds of sailor lads who are today ploughing the main owe their start in life to Mr. Bayne. Many a promising soldier, industrious mechanic and studious clerk will cherish his memory as one who saved them from the perils of the streets and afforded them the means to gain vantage ground on the battlefield of life.

He also established a day school in Clarendon Place. The Education Act of 1870 usurped to a great extent the role of the Sunday school as the provider of basic education in reading, writing and arithmetic for the children of the poor. Sunday schools of all denominations continued to have a respected role to play, however, providing religious education, usually on Sunday afternoon.

The Salvation Army played a role as important as the Sunday school movement in the social life of the town from the late 1870s, not only evangelising but through their work running hostels for soldiers and sailors, the needy and destitute. The definitive history of the 'Army' in Portsmouth has yet to be written but, according to Gates,[61] the Salvation Army was established in Portsmouth *c*.1878 in Lake Road. Apparently the early history of the movement was a troubled one, 'the open-air meetings being considerably interfered with . . .'. Adjacent to the Lake Road Citadel was a home with accommodation for 100 naval and military men where they could stay away from their ship or barracks. The Southsea Citadel was opened in Albert Road, Southsea, on 5 September 1897. It was capable of seating 750 people and the school-room adjoining could accommodate 366 children. The new citadel was clearly needed. A report in the *Hampshire Telegraph*, 1 May 1897, refers to hundreds being turned away from the doors of the temporary accommodation at the Rosebery Hall in Duncan Road.[62] Gates, writing *c*.1900, the year his *History* was published, mentions other 'Army' activity: their Rescue Home in Nobb's Lane where women and girls taken off the streets worked in a laundry established there. Gates also noted that 'within the last few years' other Salvation Army halls had opened for worship in North Street, Portsea, and Hyde Park Road, Southsea. On 27 March 1913 a new naval and military home, known as the Princess Henry of Battenburg's, opened in Queen Street, Portsea. The Lake Road Citadel was destroyed on the night the Guildhall was reduced to a gaunt shell, 10-11 January 1941. The new citadel on the same site was opened by the Lord Mayor on 14 June 1958. According to *Records of the Corporation*, the new building was made to resemble the original building as far as possible. It is an imposing building seating some four hundred and fifty people and cost £31,000, much of which was contributed by the War Damage Commission.[63]

Successive borough boundary changes beginning in 1895 brought within Portsmouth's limits by 1932 parts of the ancient parishes of Portchester, Wymering and Farlington. Portchester was given by Henry I in 1133 to his new house of Austin Canons as their priory church and the church building was probably begun and completed soon after this time. The advowson and rectorial tithes remained with the canons who removed shortly afterwards to Southwick and remained there until the dissolution of the religious houses. The advowson remained in the hands of the crown until 1865 when it was bought by Thomas Thistlethwayte of Southwick House with whose descendants it still remains. There are some especially interesting mixed registers surviving for Portchester, in particular the volume covering the years 1694-1803 which contains a wealth of information on the local economy, social conditions and individuals.

References to the parish of Wymering survive from the 13th century. Again, the advowson belonged to the canons of Southwick until the dissolution of the religious houses. Thereafter, it followed the descent of the manor of Southwick until 1817 when it passed to Thomas Thistlethwayte and Winchester College. Wymering vicarage was consolidated with the rectory of Widley in the early 19th century and the right of presentation was purchased by F. T. Nugee in 1847. It is still in the hands of his descendants. F. T. Nugee's younger son, George Nugee, was the incumbent between 1859 and 1872. He was a very advanced Ritualist not only in liturgical matters but in his interest in monasticism. He established communities of men and women in his parish. Most of the principal landowners of the parish, led by John Deverell of Purbrook Park who held land in the parish, were antipathetic to these activities and complained forcefully to the Bishop of Winchester. Charges of impropriety and immorality led to Nugee resigning in 1872.

There was ritual conflict in the parish of Farlington in the mid-19th century, too. The earliest reference to a church at Farlington seems to be in 1200. The advowson followed the descent of the manor to the end of the 18th century. For most of the 19th century it was in the hands of the Richards family as patrons, incumbents or both. Liturgical disputes between The Revd. E. T. Richards, rector of Farlington between 1826 and 1887, and, again, John Deverell, in his capacity this time of lord of the manor of Farlington, divided the parish for much of the century. The legacy of these disputes survives today in a series of churches built in the ancient and then under-populated parish between 1831 and 1874: St George's, Waterlooville, Purbrook and Christ Church, Portsdown. At Farlington itself Richards rebuilt the church almost entirely between 1872 and 1875 using the services of G. E. Street, who had already carried out extensive works at the old Domus Dei or Royal Garrison Chapel in Portsmouth. St Andrew's, Farlington, is today a splendid Tractarian period piece. Street was also employed by Nugee in the restoration of Wymering church, 1858-61.[64]

A number of churches were destroyed or badly damaged during the Second World War. Fortunately, only one set of church records was lost completely: those of St Paul's, Southsea. St Paul's stark and distinctive silhouette dominates the surrounding, mixed townscape in surviving photographs of the devastation. After the war there was a modest rearrangement of Anglican parishes on Portsea Island. The parish of St Matthew's, Southsea, was combined with that of St Bartholomew's and the church rebuilt and reopened in 1958 as Holy Spirit, Southsea. St Bartholomew's church was sold off for redevelopment. St Paul's was not rebuilt, the parish being dissolved and absorbed by neighbouring parishes. The Circus Church was destroyed, too. Its assets were sold and used to establish the parish of St John's, Fareham. St John's Roman Catholic Cathedral survived the air-raids relatively unscathed, but the bishop's house was destroyed and with it much of the early history of the Roman Catholic Diocese as the muniments were stored there.

The Church in Portsmouth in the last decades of the 20th century is still very much an active force in the local community. The latest figures available for the Anglican Diocese of Portsmouth, for 1985, indicate that some 2.3 per cent of the population are in church on Sunday, i.e. some sixteen thousand people.[65] Some forty per cent of Roman Catholics in the Catholic Diocese of Portsmouth attend Mass on Sunday, i.e. approximately twenty-one thousand, five hundred individuals.[66] A businesslike approach to finances and church building characterises all denominations. A discernible post-war trend has been the recognition not of differences between the various churches but of how much they have in common. In outer Portsmouth the first shared Anglican and Methodist church was built at Hart Plain in 1967 and, since 1982, the various denominations in Emsworth have shared in the work of the Pastoral Centre at the Methodist church there. On Portsea Island itself, groupings of local churches as well as gatherings of people of different denominations meeting in their own homes are endeavouring to come together in a shared experience as they move towards the 21st century.

The High Street Unitarian Chapel, 1840.

Chapter Eight

The Voice of the People

On 23 April 1904, Alderman Power[1] purchased from Messrs. Sotheby, Wilkinson and Hodge's, London Lot No. 1,073, for £45. This lot comprised the earliest extant Portsmouth charter, which was granted by Edward II in 1313 and confirmed the privileges granted in the earlier charter of Richard I which survives no longer. The story of the Edward II charter is curious.[2] It went missing at some time in the mid-19th century. It was offered for sale to Sir Frederick Madden[3] in June 1863 by a Mr. Solomon of Broad Street. Sir Frederic refused to buy the charter because he regarded the asking price of £100 as quite absurd. By 1891 it was in the possession of Mr. W. B. Thorpe, a barrister of the Middle Temple with strong antiquarian inclinations who offered it to the Town Council during the mayoralty of Alderman Scott Foster.[4] The asking price was still too high, however, and there matters rested until 1904 when, following Mr. Thorpe's death, his collection of manuscripts was dispersed and Alderman Power was able to bid successfully for this important 'stray' from the corporation's archives.

Charters have been used since Anglo-Saxon times as a means of granting privileges. Their use increased as the advantages of written evidence over oral declaration became obvious. In the Middle Ages, charters were granted not only by the king but by great landowners and religious houses. Royal charters were distinguished by the double-sided Great Seal depicting the monarch on horseback on the obverse and enthroned on the reverse. Before leaving the Chancery, transcripts were made of the original documents for possible future reference and rolls made of the transcripts sewn end to end into a continuous strip. These are the Charter Rolls preserved today in the Public Record Office.

Portsmouth has been granted 26 charters during the last 900 years. Only 14 have survived, however. The most important are on display today in the Guildhall on the Lord Mayor's corridor. The charter of 1313 granted by Edward II confirms the privileges granted in the earlier but no longer extant charter of Richard I. The charter of Richard I is generally acknowledged to be the town's first royal charter. The *Report on the Borough of Portsmouth* published by the Commissioners on Municipal

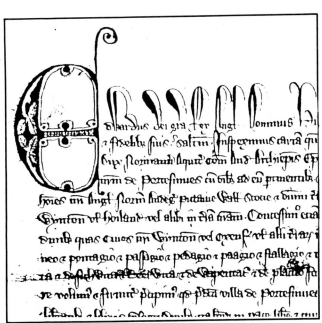

39. Opening greeting of the charter of Edward II, 1313, the earliest surviving charter in the city's possession.

121

Corporations in England and Wales in 1834 alludes to a supposed charter of Henry I granted in 1106. The first reference to this document occurs in the Herald's Visitation of Hampshire in 1686 preserved today at the College of Arms. The entry states that the town was incorporated by charter of Henry I in the sixth year of his reign by the name of 'Approved men of Portsmouth'. No other record of this charter exists nor is it ever recited in the innumerable charters granted subsequently to the town. This is suspicious in itself. Recent research on the early history of Portsmouth has also demonstrated not only how the heralds could have made their mistaken statement but also that Portsmouth as such did not exist in 1106 and certainly was not known by that name.[6] The town was in fact established in the 1180s by a Norman merchant, John de Gisors, who forfeited all his lands to the king in 1194 for his part in Prince John's rebellion.

Richard knew Portsmouth. Although he visited England only twice during his reign, in 1189 and in 1194, he came to Portsmouth on both these occasions and would have been quick to see the potential of de Gisors' settlement not only as a port, but as a port of embarkation for his French territories. This must account for the fact that he did not alienate the town but 'retained' it in his own hands as his charter recounts – and in that same charter granted the townsfolk their first taste of independence as a borough from the county of Southampton. They were granted the right to hold a fair annually for 15 days and a weekly market, on Thursdays. Widespread exemption from tolls was also granted and a number of privileges relating to landholding in the borough.

King John confirmed his brother's charter in 1200 and these two charters were confirmed successively by one monarch after another between the 13th and 16th centuries. These charters are called 'Inspeximus' charters ('we have inspected'). The town was thus in practice governed by the charters of Richard and John until the end of the 16th century, when the next significant charter was granted by Elizabeth I. While the town clearly had a corporate existence soon after its foundation, this was the first definite charter of incorporation. Portsmouth henceforth was a free borough, and its inhabitants a body corporate under the name of 'mayor and burgesses'. The mayor was to be elected annually by the burgesses from amongst their number. They were granted a common seal. They could also acquire lands and privileges and plead and be impleaded in the courts in their corporate name. The mayor and three burgesses were also henceforward to be Justices of the Peace and execute those duties now falling to the lot of those who held this office in the county. These duties appertained chiefly to the administration of criminal justice and, as the 16th century advanced, the implementation of certain aspects of the Poor Law, e.g., hearing disputed cases relating to settlement.

The town fell into decay in the 16th century. In 1625, the mayor and the inhabitants petitioned for the renewal of their privileges and certain trading advantages. Charles I's charter of 1627 accordingly enlarged considerably the privileges of Elizabeth's charter and gave the inhabitants a licence to weave, make and sell all kinds of kersies[7] and broadcloths.[8] There were some changes, however. The mayor was to be chosen now from amongst the aldermen, of whom there were to be 12, selected from amongst the burgesses. Together, the mayor and aldermen were to form the borough council and were empowered to make bye-laws. This charter also empowered the borough to hold a court of record[9] and provide a borough gaol.

The charter of Charles I was surrendered in 1682 – as were the charters of other similar authorities – while Charles II and his ministers attempted to deal with the independently-minded municipalities. The new charter granted in its place was unique in that Gosport was now united with Portsmouth in an uneasy alliance. The crown also had absolute control now over the borough: mayor, aldermen and burgesses could be removed henceforward by the king's sign manual. However, in 1688, James II withdrew all borough charters granted in 1682. The surrender of the charter of Charles I had never been enrolled through official oversight and therefore it became once again the governing charter of the borough and remained so until 1835, when the old boroughs were swept away with the passage of the Municipal Reform Act.

Subsequent grants of privileges have included letters patent granted by George V in 1926 which raised the borough to the dignity of a city and again, in 1928, a further grant which directed that the chief magistrate of the town should be styled Lord Mayor. More recently, letters patent of the present queen, Elizabeth II, completed the city's arms with the grant of a crest, supporters and badge in 1970. Finally, in 1973, with the approaching reorganisation of local government in England and Wales, the new district of Portsmouth was granted borough status and, in 1974, the privilege of continuing to style its leading citizen, 'Lord Mayor'.

Who actually governed the town? Aside from the charters, the earliest references to local government in Portsmouth occur in the Southwick Cartularies, or Registers as they are known sometimes: collections of deeds relating to property owned by the canons of Southwick. According to Margaret Hoad in her work on the origins of Portsmouth in *Hampshire Studies*,[10] the Registers reveal that early key figures in the town were the bailiffs, first mentioned in the early 13th century. The Registers also indicate that there was a curia or burgemote, i.e., a borough court, from a very early date. They also refer frequently to a *prepositus*. Mrs. Hoad believes that the *prepositus* which, translated literally, means 'the one set before' but has often been translated by historians of the town as 'reeve' or 'mayor', was in fact the senior of the two bailiffs. If there was indeed a tradition whereby two individuals had control of the town's affairs, it might explain why, from the time records survive in the early 16th century until 1835, two men were always put in nomination for the position of mayor. The bailiffs' duties included collecting the rents and customs as well as the farm of the borough.[11] They also heard pleas, received writs, acted as the king's escheators[12] in the town, heard recognizances of debt and sealed conveyances of lands within the borough. By the late 13th/early 14th century the office of 'mayor' appears to be gaining in importance and references to bailiffs gradually disappear. Certainly in Elizabeth's charter it is stated that whereas in former times the town was governed by a mayor, two bailiffs, two constables and other public officers, henceforward the corporation was to be described, we must assume more accurately, as 'the mayor and burgesses of the borough of Portsmouth'.

The burgesses were certainly a decisive influence in the borough's affairs until the growth of the office of alderman in the 17th century. Their number varied greatly from time to time. The earliest surviving list, of 1575, notes 54 names.[13] There were 25 burgesses and 12 aldermen in the reign of Charles I. There was no limit on the number of burgesses who could be elected each year. No qualifications were necessary and non-residence was no disqualification. Soldiers of the garrison and dockyard officers were elected in the 16th century but this custom had declined by the early 18th century. Burgesses were chosen by the common consent of the mayor and existing burgesses in the borough court before 1627. From 1627 until 1835 they were chosen by the mayor and aldermen, as they thought fit. Fines were paid for what was in fact the freedom of the borough from at least the 16th century. Francis Bodkin gave 10s. in 1546 and Richard Jenens 26s. 8d. in 1593. Many famous men were made honorary freemen or burgesses: Sir Christopher Hatton,[14] Sir Julius Caesar,[15] General George Monck,[16] Samuel Pepys[17] and Admiral Byng[18] to cite but a few. For a brief one hundred years between approximately 1540 and 1640, the corporation acquired several handsome pieces of plate from men newly elected freemen. Possibly the finest piece in the collection is the Lee Cup, which bears a London hallmark for 1590. Of silver-gilt, the cover is surmounted by a small female figure bearing a shield. The thistle-shaped bowl is engraved with flowers, foliage and roundels. The donor, Robert Lee, was a

40. (*above*) The Savour tazza or standing dish, 1582,
presented by Joshua Savour, Master Gunner of the Garrison.

41. (*right*) The Lee Cup, 1590, presented to the town by
London merchant Robert Lee when he was made a burgess.

London merchant, sheriff in 1594 and lord mayor of London in 1602. He gave the cup when he was made a burgess of Portsmouth in 1590.[19]

Burgesses had a number of privileges. From the time of Richard I's charter, they were free from toll and passage[20] and other dues paid by travellers, they were free from suit in the shire[21] and hundred[22] courts and from pleas of the forest.[23] They also possessed considerable trading advantages. They could buy and sell without a mayor's licence. They could also vote for the two members of Parliament until 1832. In brief, the burgesses had a decisive role to play in the life of the town – and with the mayor, were responsible for running the town before 1627.

The *Victoria County History* suggests that this was in fact a rather cumbersome system and that, inevitably, a small group of burgesses, *de facto*, gradually formed an executive council with the mayor. This executive group would seem to have been in existence by the late 13th century, as the 'jurats' mentioned in the first Customs and Usages.[24] There are assorted references to mayors' 'assistants' from the mid-16th century, interchangeable with the word 'aldermen'. In 1627, the charter of Charles I actually stated that there should be 12 aldermen to form the council of the borough and assist the mayor. They were to be chosen for life from among the burgesses, and vacancies were to be filled by the remaining aldermen and mayor or majority of them. The aldermen had no specific privileges but they could wield the most formidable political and social power as they chose the burgesses and thus could influence parliamentary elections. They also helped the mayor govern the town, of course. The Municipal Corporations Act of 1835 set the number of councillors at 42, one-third of whom retired, in rotation, every three years, and the number of aldermen at 14, one-half of whom retired every three years, and from amongst whom the mayor was chosen. From 1835, every ratepayer was counted a burgess. In 1974 the number of councillors was reduced to 39 and the aldermanic bench was abolished.

The mayor was chosen originally by the burgesses from amongst themselves. The charter of Elizabeth I laid down that he was to be chosen from amongst the senior and better citizens. By 1627, he was to be chosen by a majority of the aldermen and burgesses, from amongst the aldermen. In 1835, the election of the mayor was vested in the borough council, i.e., the mayor, aldermen and councillors. Today, the nomination is in the hands of the ruling political group on the city council. The mayor has also ceased to be a political figure. The leader of the ruling group, i.e., the party with the majority on the city council, is now the power-broker. However in earlier times the mayor was the leading figure in the community. He presided over the two oldest of the borough courts, the View of Frankpledge and the Court Leet, from probably the mid-13th century. The View of Frankpledge and Court Leet were probably the oldest of the borough courts. By the Statute of Frankpledge of 1325, weights and measures were supervised and presentments made concerning misdemeanours such as encroachments, affrays and bloodshed, breach of the peace and all offences affecting trade in the town. The Court Leet was the equivalent of the court baron of a lord of the manor where tenants were admitted to town lands and took an oath to be true tenants of the mayor, aldermen and burgesses. During the 17th and 18th centuries the criminal work of these courts was assumed gradually by the Justices of the Peace and duties such as the repair and lighting of the streets was taken over by the Improvement Commissions in the 1760s. By the charter of Elizabeth I, the mayor himself became, *ex officio*, a justice.

The mayor enjoyed certain perquisites of office initially, e.g., two bushels of wheat from every boatload that came into Point, and certain fines. In the mid-16th century, these payments in kind were commuted for an annual payment, settled at the election of each mayor, of between £20 and £30. In 1785 a sum of up to £300 was voted from which all expenses of the mayoralty were deducted. The mayor was obliged to organise hospitality on special occasions: from the early 17th century at the time of Sessions and the Friday following, on election days and Michaelmas Day. Many vouchers survive, particularly from the 18th century, giving some notion of the scale of civic hospitality. The mayor also provided a piece of good roast beef on Christmas Day, Easter Day and Whitsunday.

Officers of the corporation included the recorder, whose office was in existence from at least the 1590s. He presided over the Court of Record which was granted formally in the charter of Charles I. Portsmouth's most famous recorder was the notorious Judge Jefferies, recorder in 1685. The chamberlain or treasurer of the corporation was an important post-holder from the 16th century. As well as looking after the corporation's finances, he was responsible for the repair of the town property, e.g. the pound. He was elected annually by the mayor and aldermen. Charles I's charter also made provision for the office of town clerk, which post was also to carry out the duties of clerk of the peace, but by the 19th century these two offices had come to be held separately, which tradition continued until the abolition of Sessions in 1971. The office of serjeant-at-mace is medieval in origin. There were two serjeants from at least the 14th century although by the early 19th century there was only one. The serjeants were responsible for looking after the town hall, summoning members of the council and preserving the peace. The beadle was a lowlier officer whose duties included such matters as cleansing the streets. There was also a hayward who had care of cattle in the common fields and impounded strays. There were constables, early precursors of the 19th-century police force, and the early-modern equivalent of trading standards officers: ale-tasters and searchers of market who were responsible for ensuring that the assize of bread and ale was not broken. There were also water-bailiffs, wharfingers and measurers.

Decisions were taken from earliest times in the various borough courts – as they still are today. The Court Leet and View of Frankpledge has been discussed within the context of the mayor's duties. Other borough courts included the Court of Pie Powder, whose curious name derives from the phrase *pied puldreaux*, which is old French for pedlar, i.e. the dusty-footed itinerant tradesmen who brought their wares from as far afield as Normandy and Holland to Portsmouth's fair, held from the time of Richard I's charter firstly in August and from 1627 in late June-early July. The court regulated the business of the fair and fairmen. Unfortunately no records survive of the court's activities aside from an odd reference to fees for court officers such as the 6s. tax to be paid the mayor and 4s. to the town clerk noted on the cover of the Election and Sessions Book 1638-46.[25] Sessions papers do survive in considerable quantity, however, and it is possible to reconstruct a vivid picture of this particular court and its activities, which were presided over by the mayor himself and his three fellow-Justices of the Peace from the granting of Elizabeth I's charter. This court emerged in the late 16th century when it began gradually to assume the criminal work of the old Court Leet and View of Frankpledge. The only remaining court, the Court of Record, was a civil court with jurisdiction over all personal actions. Its records survive in considerable quantity but are little used, being in Latin.

The records of these courts, aside from the Sessions papers, are somewhat confused. This confusion is not helped by the fact that the borough's medieval records do not survive. The activities of the Court Leet and View of Frankpledge are recorded alongside the elections of mayors, aldermen and burgesses, and meetings of Sessions in a series of single volumes, the Elections and Sessions Books and surviving financial records.[28] Other sources include the records of the Improvement Commissions,[29] which took over the duties of the Court Leet relating to street cleaning, watching and warding from the 1760s. Despite these steady encroachments upon its powers over the centuries, the Court Leet continued to meet up to the passage of the Municipal Corporations Act twice a year on the same day as the Easter and Michaelmas Sessions to carry out what business remained to it: the administration of town property, matters relating to trade, and supervision of weights and measures.

This system of local government was essentially medieval in character. It was not geared to cope with the problems of a growing urban society manifest certainly by the mid-18th century. The population had begun to increase in the late 17th century with the growth of the dockyard and the need for more workers. There was a limit to the number of houses which could be built within the walls of the town and therefore early in the 18th century houses began to be built outside the walls of the town on land, known as Portsmouth Common, to the north of the Mill Pond, and on East and West Dock Fields, to the north of the Common. The area developed rapidly. By 1753 the local population had even secured their own church, St George's, a chapel of ease to the parish church of St Mary's. This rapid development brought its own problems of inadequate drainage, paving, street lighting and cleansing. The corporation was not equipped to deal with these issues. Such was the general dissatisfaction existing locally, however, that *ad hoc* bodies were established by private Acts of Parliament to get to grips with the problems. The residents of the new suburb on the Common were the first to obtain an Act, in 1764, 'for the better paving of the streets and lanes, and for preventing Nuisances and other Annoyances in that part of the parish of Portsea . . . commonly called Portsmouth Common'. A further Act was obtained in 1792 extending the powers of the Portsea commissioners. Public-spirited individuals in Portsmouth obtained an Improvement Act in 1768. A subsequent Act of 1776 not only widened the general powers of the Portsmouth commissioners but – a new departure – empowered them to establish a nightly watch.

The last years of the 18th century and the early years of the 19th century therefore saw the administration of the borough divided between two bodies: the old corporation and the two new sets of commissioners, one for Portsmouth and another for Portsea. The boroughs acquired a new lease of life, however, in 1835, when radical campaigns for the reform of the old corporations and their replacement by popularly-elected municipalities culminated in the passage through parliament of the Municipal Corporations Act. The old oligarchical boroughs were swept away and replaced by councils elected by ratepayers. These new councils could legislate by bye-law and appoint town clerks and treasurers. They would be subject now to Treasury control in matters of loans and sales of assets. They acquired administrative powers over police, finance and property. In addition, henceforward, jurisdiction would be separate from administration, and judicial appointments in boroughs would now be under crown control.

Portsmouth's borough boundaries were extended to include the whole of the parish of Portsea. This new borough was divided into the six wards of St Thomas, St George, St John, All Saints, St Paul and St Mary, and its government placed in the hands of an elected council. From this period can be traced the beginnings of modern administrative government in Portsmouth as the newly-elected councillors, many of whom had in fact been burgesses of the old unreformed corporation, addressed themselves to business. A Watch Committee was established which drew up recommendations for the establishment of a borough police force. The Camber was redeveloped with a view to improving the trade of the borough and a Finance and General Purposes Committee appointed to inquire into the state of the borough's finances and what improvements might be effected in their administration. The council also considered, early on, the question of their own premises and removed themselves very promptly into new accommodation near *The Dolphin* in the High Street. The new Town Hall was opened on 28 June 1838, Queen Victoria's coronation day.

The improvement commissions continued to function independently of the council. In fact both commissions obtained newer and more far-reaching powers in the 1840s over such matters as acquiring land for street-widening, preventing nuisances, for lighting and for regulating hackney coaches. They joined battle with the borough council, however, in the middle years of the century over the issue of the drainage of the borough, and this issue dominated the political life of the borough between 1848, when cholera first broke out in Portsea and spread rapidly during the warm summer months into the poorer districts of Landport, and 1863, when the council voted at long last to adopt the Local Government Act of 1858 which gave them powers to abolish the commissioners and take over their duties, as a local board of health. A borough engineer was appointed, Mr. Lewis Angell, and the effective drainage of the borough begun. In fact, Mr. Angell's scheme, begun in 1865, forms the main trunk system of today. The scheme was gravitational, supplemented by lifting power provided at the pumping station at Henderson Road built in 1868. The introduction of mains drainage was a major contributing factor to the reduction of the death rate in the community in the following one hundred years.[30]

The next major event in the history of local government in the town occurred in 1888 when Portsmouth acquired county borough status with the passage of the Local Government Act, 1888, which established county councils and county boroughs. Portsmouth was one of 61 towns created county boroughs. This meant in practice that henceforward the town was independent of any county interference in its affairs. It was a most efficient unit of local government administration, broken up only in 1974. Another notable feature of the 1880s was the growth of an identifiable civic pride and local patriotism. This pride was reflected not only in the new and splendid town hall constructed in Landport between 1886 and 1890, but also in awakening interest in the city's history aroused by the publication, in 1884, of Murrell and East's *Extracts from the Portsmouth Records* which went into a new and enlarged edition in 1891 edited by East. Interest was taken once again in the corporation plate and several significant gifts were made at this time. Alderman Murrell himself presented in 1875 a replica of the smaller, 1618, Haberley Cup and Robert East, in 1890, an elegant, two-handled cup hall-marked Newcastle 1802.

During the last decades of the 19th century and well into the 20th century the council addressed itself to a wide range of issues concerned with improving the quality of life of the townsfolk and developed itself into a comprehensive multi-purpose authority. The scale of operation grew as the borough's boundaries were extended. The first extension since 1832 took place in 1895, when the borough limits were extended to include the Great Salterns. The boundaries were further extended in 1904 to include the whole of Portsea Island and in 1920 Cosham and Paulgrove were absorbed within the borough boundary. Finally, in 1932, parts of Farlington and Portchester were incorporated.

A feature of 19th-century local government reform had been the creation of a board to tackle each newly-identified problem, e.g. the boards of health established by those councils such as Portsmouth who adopted the Local Government Act of 1858. By the Public Health Act of 1872, the local boards of health became urban sanitary authorities. These new bodies continued to function just as they had done in the past as boards of health. In Portsmouth the new organisations exercised control over drainage, sanitation, roads, the electric light undertaking, after 1890, and from 1891 parks and open spaces. From 1895, however, the distinction between the work of the council in its municipal capacity and in its capacity as the urban sanitary authority ceased to exist and all committees were henceforward appointed by, and reported to one body, the town council.

A not dissimilar rearrangement of authorities took place in 1902 in the field of education. On 5 December 1870 the council had adopted the Elementary Education Act and had set up a school board, one of the first areas in Hampshire to do so. During the Portsmouth School Board's existence, some twenty-seven thousand school places were made available and 11 new elementary schools built. The Board also became involved in higher education, establishing a higher grade school in 1888. The history of this school was fraught, however, and in fact in 1899 such schools were declared illegal. It was the confusion of authorities

42. The borough boundaries were extended to include Cosham and Paulsgrove during the mayoralty of John Timpson, 1920.

in the field of secondary education that was one of the reasons for the establishment of local authorities with general educational powers. The 1902 Education Act abolished school boards and transferred their functions to local authorities such as Portsmouth, where an Education Committee was appointed on 2 June 1903.

The local authority also assumed responsibility during the early years of the 20th century for a number of different aspects of public health and, later, housing. The newly-constituted Health Committee of 1902 tackled issues as diverse as the purification of the city's water supply by filtration, uncontrolled tipping and the provision of a maternity hospital. Many measures were adopted on the recommendation of Dr. Mearns Fraser, who was Medical Officer of Health between 1894 and 1933. On his initiative, a school medical officer was appointed in 1908 and a school clinic opened in 1912, and he spearheaded efforts to protect the meat supplies of the town by sending an inspector to watch neighbouring county markets. All local authorities were advised subsequently by the Local Government Board to adopt similar procedures to protect their meat supplies. A tuberculosis dispensary was opened in 1911 upon Dr. Fraser's recommendation, the first of its kind to be opened in the provinces, and during his period of office nearly one thousand dwelling houses were demolished as unfit for human habitation. The first major slum clearance scheme began in 1910 when Albion Street, Southampton Row, White's Row and King's Bench Alley were demolished and Curzon-Howe Road was erected in their place, a tree-lined street of model artisans' dwellings still standing today.

The corporation continued to develop the town's potential as a tourist resort in the early years of the century. Earlier initiatives had included the construction of Clarence Esplanade, in 1848, and later, in the 1880s, a lease of the land having been obtained from the War Department, the development of Southsea Common: Ladies Mile, Pier Road, the ornamental gardens by South Parade, and Canoe Lake. Now, in 1919, the Beach Committee of the council was constituted.

The corporation entered the field of public transport in 1901 with the acquisition of the Provincial Tramways Company's interests in the town. Electrification of Portsmouth Corporation Tramways, as it was now known, began at once and the first electric cars ran on 24 September 1901. In 1919 the bus fleet was inaugurated and in 1933 the decision was taken to experiment with trolley buses as replacements for the trams. In 1936, the 'Tramways Undertaking' became the Passenger Transport Undertaking.

Less well-known is the corporation's venture into telecommunications. The Municipal Telephone Exchange was established in 1900 when the corporation was granted a 25 years' licence for a telephone exchange and a Telephone Committee was constituted. There were some two thousand five hundred subscribers by 1913 when the service was 'nationalised' by the Post Office – and the service cost much less than that of the National Telephone Company. The council also played an active part in relieving distress in the years immediately following the end of the 1914-18 War. An Unemployment Committee was established and public works undertaken to provide work for the unemployed included extending the

43.   The opening of the new western road, the first by-pass road out of Portsmouth, 26 October 1922. This was one of the public works undertaken to provide work for the unemployed in the years immediately following the Great War.

Esplanade past the Marine Barracks at Eastney, the development of Great Salterns, the construction of new roads from Portsbridge to Southwick Road running to the west of High Street, Cosham, and from Portsbridge across the marshes to the west of Wymering. There seemed in fact to be no limit to the diversification of the corporation's interests. In 1930, it set about acquiring a site for an aerodrome and negotiations were concluded to purchase land in the north-west corner of the island for such a purpose. Much of the work of clearing and levelling the site was done by the unemployed and the Municipal Airport was opened on 2 July 1932.

The prestige of the town assumed new heights in 1926 when the borough was raised to the dignity of a city and again, in 1928, when the title of Lord Mayor was bestowed on the chief magistrate by letters patent. Coincidentally, at this time the Anglican Diocese of Portsmouth was created out of the ancient Diocese of Winchester and the parish church of St Thomas's, Portsmouth, was designated the pro-cathedral.

The city was torn apart during the 1939-45 War when considerable parts of Old Portsmouth, Portsea, Landport and Southsea were devastated by enemy bombs and incendiaries. The town hall, known as the Guildhall since the town was raised to the dignity of a city, was itself destroyed in the terrible raid of the night of 10-11 January 1941. Miraculously, the corporation plate and archives survived the holocaust, secure in the safe beneath the tower of the Guildhall. The city council set to immediately to formulate plans for the future. The Development and Estates Committee was constituted in the bleak early months of 1941 as the Replanning Committee, later Planning and Reconstruction and, in 1948, Development and Estates. In the first few years of the new committee's history, negotiations were begun and brought to a successful conclusion for the purchase of Leigh Park, and the city began facing up to the harsh realities of post-War existence.

Not only had the city been severely damaged during the conflict but there was now a large legacy of sub-standard housing, obsolete development and inadequate road communications. It is not generally appreciated that Portsmouth is one of the most densely-populated urban areas in the country and, because of its unique island location, there is an acute shortage of land. Progress was made, however. Extensive clearance and redevelopment, chiefly public sector housing, took place at Somerstown and Buckland, and environmental improvements at Stamshaw, Portsea and Landport. New industry and commerce were attracted to the area during the early and mid-1960s although the city was faced with recurrent running-down of the defence forces and the decline of the related industries upon which the city was, and has been until very recently, so greatly dependent. The road network was greatly improved too, work beginning on the M27 in 1971. The city also played an active role in the formulation of regional and sub-regional planning policy during these years, most notably the so-called Buchanan Report, *The South East Study*, 1966, and the South Hampshire Structure Plan, 1969-73, which examined ways of accommodating the likely growth of the local population having regard to the environment and the quality of life of existing residents of the area.

Nearer home, the city addressed itself to the redevelopment of the city centre. The Guildhall had been rebuilt during the 1950s to the designs of E. Berry Webber, who had been charged to preserve as much as he could of the shell of the old building. The re-built premises were reopened by H.M. the Queen on 8 June 1959. The city centre itself was not a particularly distinguished area. In 1963, Lord Esher[31] was appointed as a consultant. He proposed a master plan for the city centre in 1964 which the city accepted in 1967. The plan has been substantially implemented. New civic offices were opened in 1976, and new law courts, a new library and new student hostel accommodation, as well as a considerable volume of new office space, have all been built too.

The opening of the new civic offices coincided, however, with the reorganisation of local government in England and Wales which followed the Local Government Reform Act, 1972. England and Wales were divided into local government areas known as counties and districts, six of the counties of which were to be metropolitan counties with metropolitan districts (Greater Manchester, Merseyside, South Yorkshire, Tyneside, West Midlands and West Yorkshire). Portsmouth fought hard during the Committee Stages of the Bill for Metropolitan Status for South Hampshire, but to no avail, and the new authorities assumed their responsibilities on 1 April 1974. It was as profound a change in local government as the great reforms of 1835 and 1888. Portsmouth County Borough was abolished and replaced by a district council, although subsequently the new district was granted the privilege of continuing to call itself a city and style its chief citizen Lord Mayor. The divided administration of 100 years before had grown slowly and laboriously into a comprehensive multipurpose authority. The reorganisation of local government in 1974 produced once again a multiplicity of such authorities tackling as wide a range of issues as ever before in an increasingly complex world. There will be more change in the future as new legislation, e.g., the Housing Act, 1988, and the Local Government Act, 1988, compel local authorities to re-examine their role within the community as they move towards the 21st century.

The politics of the borough from at least the mid-17th century was characterised by a considerable measure of independence, which saw expression initially in radical republican sentiments during the turbulent Civil War years and was refined in later years into what John Field in 'Bourgeois Portsmouth 1815-1875' describes as a strong anti-centralist tradition in local politics.[32] Certainly, in 1659, the townsfolk declared for parliament against the army although, admittedly, they had little choice in the matter with Sir Arthur Hesilrige holding a pistol, literally, at their heads.[33] In 1662, however, some 97 individuals were expelled from the corporation under the provisions of the Corporations Act. Those expelled were not only erstwhile supporters of Hesilrige but men who had fought against him, who were all anti-royalist in the eyes of the commissioners enforcing the execution of the Act. Some notion of the scale of the expulsions in Portsmouth – and possibly of local republican sentiment – can be gauged from the fact that in Chester only 39 individuals were expelled and in Exeter only fourteen.

The most prominent of the ejected burgesses quit the town, for example, Josiah Childs, who went on to become governor of the East India Company.[34] Many had been merchants, however, and they just continued to trade and paid a fine[35] for the rest of their lives. As time went on, though, the most prominent disfranchised men of the younger generation reappeared in the civic life of the town and it is not, perhaps, too fanciful to claim that the prolonged struggle against government control of the borough in the 1770s led by the Nonconformist Carter family,[36] in which the corporation fell finally to the local Whig merchant class and their sympathisers, derived something from the religious and political ideals of the Commonwealth period.

Eighteenth-century Portsmouth acquired much of its wealth from the profits to be made in supplying the armed forces. The Admiralty's hold over the corporation, says Field, was paid for 'with a fat wad of contracts – contracts for beer, bread, ordnance, ropes, stone, candles, timber and bedding'.[37] The role of such contracts in the town's political economy has been reconstructed meticulously and painstakingly by Nigel Surry and James Thomas in their Portsmouth Records Series volume, *Book of Original Entries 1731-51*.[38] They have calculated that during the period they studied, one third of the aldermanic bench engaged in contracts either with the Navy Board or the Ordnance, or both, and occasionally with the Treasury. Relations between the parties were, to quote Surry and Thomas, 'delicate and complex' and under almost constant review. The Carters' triumph in the 1770s lasted well into the 1840s and was a truly remarkable achievement. A number of circumstances combined to produce this long period of political stability. The Carter family's own property in the borough afforded them some influence. Their brewing and distilling trade, with that of the Spicers of Portsea to whom they were connected by marriage, gave them control of two of the largest industrial units in the town outside the dockyard and, according to Field, they owned between them some thirty per cent of the town's public houses.[39] There were no great extremes of wealth or poverty in the town either which could be exploited by any radical elements. Equally, the industrial experience of Portsmouth men was very different from that of their northern counterparts. The Carters represented the party of reform – and local prosperity. It was when they – and the Liberals – ceased to do so in the 1840s that their power in the borough waned and the Conservative star moved into the ascendant.

The Carters' capacity for winning the hearts of all men, aristocrats and radicals alike, in particular the last, also helps to account for the singular weakness of radicalism in the town. The career of Daniel Howard demonstrates this. He was an attorney, born in 1773. He chaired a quasi-Jacobin meeting in November 1795 in protest against the 'Two Bills'.[40] At the same time, he published a pamphlet defending corresponding societies and a few years later, in 1798, he and several other local radicals defended a Portsea carpenter who had 'damned' Pitt[41] and prosecuted some Gosport men who had assaulted the carpenter. According to his obituary, he was the author of several pamphlets which do not, alas, survive, a member of the Portsmouth Corresponding Society and, after the government security clampdown of 1796, he and other Jacobins met in a small boat at Spithead. There was opposition when he became a burgess but he went on to become mayor four times: in 1818, 1822, 1826 and 1830. It is worth noting, too, that the troubles of 1817-20[42] had little impact in the town despite the lay-offs which had taken place in the yard between 1813 and 1820 when as many as fifteen hundred men lost their jobs. There was some radical activity. Early in 1817 William Cobbett[43] and Lord Cochrane[44] addressed a crowd reputedly some twenty thousand in number on Portsdown Hill under the watchful eyes of the county magistrates and the yeomen cavalry. In the same year, James Williams, a Portsea printer, was sentenced to a year's imprisonment and a fine of £100, for reprinting and selling seditious material. But in 1819 attempts to organise a county meeting to condemn the Peterloo massacre ended very tamely with an appeal to leave the question to parliament. Independent radical activity disappeared thereafter for almost twenty years.

The election of 1832 is described by Field as a vindication not only of the Whigs' record on reform but 'in particular . . . a vindication of the Bonham Carters'.[45] It is an apt comment. The closedness of the corporation ruling group had been raised at the hustings but the electors were not deterred. They voted for John Bonham Carter and Francis Baring.[46] They were the only pair of representatives who were elected for the same borough both before and after the Reform Act. The Act itself had been celebrated in grand style in Portsmouth. There was a public dinner in St George's Square of meats, pies, potatoes, plum pudding and beer and a firework display on Southsea Common watched by some thirty thousand. A monster procession made its way through the streets led by an armoured man on a white charger with a sword in one hand and a cap of liberty in the other. To quote Field again, 'it was no time to be a Tory'.[47]

It was almost equally dispiriting for radicals. A pressure group was set up in 1835 by local radicals, William Bilton, Henry Tichborne and others, called the Landport Reform Association. There was a subscription of 1s. a year, and the organisation pledged itself to further the aims of traditional democratic liberalism: to watch registration, defend possible victims of intimidation, extend the franchise, demand triennial parliaments and support the ballot. It was primarily a discussion group but did try to affect local and parliamentary elections. John Sheppard, secretary of the Association, not only stood in the council election of 1839 but was elected unopposed on a manifesto of support for household suffrage and abolition of the Corn Laws. It would be easy, however, to exaggerate the strength of the organisation. If it wished to retain any influence, it had to line up at the end of the day behind the Whigs. The peculiar circumstances of dockyard employment, where a good working relationship existed between yard workmen and their middle-class political leaders, also meant that local radicals could not expect to find any class following there. It is also why Chartism was never strong in the town. Feargus O'Connor[48] addressed a meeting in 1836 to protest at newspaper duties, but only two hundred attended. The meeting at which the charter was adopted was not even organised by a local man and only some eighteen hundred signatures seem to have been obtained. In fact, far from supporting the charter in 1848, yard workers in Portsmouth enrolled as volunteers, acting as guards when the regulars were sent to defend London and making some three thousand truncheons and staves for special constables.

Strong growth of Conservative support in the town can be traced positively from the 1840s. The period saw the emergence of a local Tory press as sales of the Liberal *Hampshire Telegraph* declined. There was general dissatisfaction now with the government, its centralising tendencies and the rise in food prices. In 1857 Portsmouth returned its first Tory M.P. since Admiral Cockburn in 1818:[48] Scottish baronet Sir James Elphinstone. Sir James sat for the borough until 1880 with a break of only four years. The strength of local Conservatism was also reinforced enormously in 1868 when a mass of working-class voters was added to an electorate thoroughly alienated by the enormous cuts in the yard workforce which had taken place some eight months before the election of that year. As Field says, 'Liberal policies of peace and retrenchment were a little insensitive to the needs of a workforce whose prosperity depended upon war and expenditure'.[50] Put another way, Portsmouth workmen began now to vote Tory for the simple reason that nationally the Conservatives were more likely to favour a belligerent foreign policy than the Liberals. The Conservatives also benefited during these years from the steady enlargement of the municipal electorate which virtually doubled under the Small Tenements Rating Act from 3,960 to six thousand, six hundred and sixty.

These changes in the electorate began to alter the nature of the council itself. From the middle years of the century, high status groups began to decline in importance, i.e. the merchants and bankers. By 1874, according to Field, the professional group was confined to lawyers and the council was made up of 'a chamberfull' of retailers, a fifth of whom were in the drink trade.[51] Interestingly, it is also during this period that Dr. Ray Riley has identified a discernible change in the social composition of the inhabitants of Thomas Ellis Owen's Southsea.[52] Inhabited originally by naval and military officers of some affluence, the character of the area was shifting now, subtly, to accommodate what Riley calls a 'service group', i.e. a trading element.

The Liberals were able to hold on to their power, albeit, according to Field, 'unsteadily', in the middle years of the century because both they and the Tories believed the council chamber should be a place where politics was subservient to other needs. The Liberals could also count on the support of the radicals on most issues. By 1885, however, the Conservatives had a clear majority on the council. The Liberals made some substantial advances in the good Liberal years of the late 1880s, and by 1890 the parties were almost evenly balanced. But despite a Liberal revival locally, as nationally, between 1905 and 1907, the period 1895-1914 saw the Conservatives receiving a considerably larger share of the vote than the Liberals and gaining around fifty per cent more councillors. Gregory Ashworth, in his psephological study of Portsmouth's political history, 1885-1945,[53] ident-ifies three trends or themes in the inter-war period: Conservative consolidation of their position as the ruling party in the borough (at the outbreak of the Second World War they had the allegiance of two-thirds of the councillors and aldermen), the annihilation of the

Liberal party and the confirmation of Labour as the permanent organised opposition. These trends were further consolidated after 1945. Right-wing opinion polarised on the southern seaboard and to the north of Portsea Island, and Labour controlled what might be described as the central swathe of the town. Labour has never been able to destroy the Conservatives' hold on the town. Why should this be so? Historically of course, Conservative governments were more likely to support a vigorous foreign policy, i.e. war and expenditure on the machinery of war which meant prosperity for Portsmouth's dockyard workforce. Interestingly, not even recent retrenchments in the dockyard have been able to shake the Conservative loyalties of the city in local elections. There is still, basically, a strong bedrock of Conservative support. The development of Southsea as a seaside resort and the growth of a retired, middle-class, population including large numbers of naval pensioners introduced, in addition, a group whose support of the Conservative interest is still a vital component of that party's local strength.

The fact that there were no great extremes of wealth or poverty in the town capable of being exploited by radical forces combined with the strength of popular Conservatism from the 1880s must account for the fact that the town made virtually no contribution to the history of the trade union movement. Outside the dockyard there was very little organised trade unionism. The only serious movements in the town were those of the building workers, watermen and tailors, and they were never particularly strong or significant.

The parliamentary history of the borough, the voice of the people at Westminster, the seat of government, reflects very much local political resolve. Portsmouth first sent two burgesses to parliament in 1295: Richard de Reynold and Stephen Justice, and since that date the town has returned representatives to every parliament wih few exceptions, chiefly in the 14th century and probably because the burden of the expenses fell on all burgesses. As late as 1597, according to the *Victoria County History*, one representative was paid two shillings a day during sessions of parliament. It looks as if the bailiff and burgesses alone exercised the franchise from the time records survive to the late 15th century. In 1572, the mayor, chamberlains and commonalty of the town voted, and in 1584 burgesses and freeholders but, with these exceptions, returns were always by the bailiff or mayor and burgesses until the charter of incorporation of Elizabeth I, after which returns were made by the mayor, aldermen and burgesses.

For lack of sources, it is not possible to comment on those men who represented the borough before the 16th century. From the mid-16th century, however, it is clear that few men secured seats without the benefit of patronage. It has been calculated that of 16 men who are known to have served as M.P.s between 1529 and 1558, only one, Henry Bickley, who had been three times mayor and owned a substantial amount of property in the town, owed his seat to no one. Some men owed their good fortune to wealthy and well-connected patrons. For example, Geoffrey Lee (1529) was not only connected by marriage to Margaret, Countess of Salisbury,[54] who owned the manor of Warblington, but had an elder brother who was shortly to become archbishop of York. Another member, John Chaderton (1539, possibly 1542 and 1553), was a servant of the lord admiral, Sir William Fitzwilliam,[55] Earl of Southampton. Chaderton's fellow-member in 1542, Christopher Staverton, was a distant relative of the Earl of Southampton. Other Henrician M.P.s were to a man the servants of great men such as Thomas Wriothesley, Baron Wriothesley,[56] and Sir William Paulet, Baron St John, later Marquess of Winchester.[57] Three of the eight Marian M.P.s owed their seats to the latter. In the second half of the 16th century, the governor of Portsmouth was frequently the parliamentary patron and throughout the 17th century successive governors and lieutenant-governors thus maintained the government interest. Samuel Pepys, who was made a burgess in 1662 ('It cost me a piece of gold to the town clerk, and 10s. to the bailiffs, as well as 6s. on a round of drinks for the corporation'), was recommended by both the

King, Charles II, and his brother, the Duke of York, to stand with the governor, George Legge, in 1679. Pepys, however, was assured subsquently of a safer seat at Harwich and gave his interest to Sir John Kempthorne, the resident naval commissioner, who was subsequently returned with Legge.

Naval or military connections were of course advantageous. In the 18th century, when the town was an Admiralty borough, one member was usually an admiral, e.g. Admirals Rowley and Hawke.[58] One of the more colourful M.P.s of the 20th century was naval man Lord Charles Beresford, who was returned to Westminster in the Conservative interest from 1910-16. He was succeeded by another naval man, Sir Hedworth Meux. Several men with military connections were also returned in the period 1885-1918, most notably Sir William Crossman.[59]

By the early 18th century, the town was an out-and-out Admiralty borough managed, in the words of Romney Segdwick, 'by channelling local patronage through the Corporation', i.e. the aldermanic bench who controlled the representation through their power to create the burgesses or freemen.[60] As already noted, it has in fact been calculated by Nigel Surry and James Thomas that between 1700 and 1750 almost one-third of the aldermen were engaged in contracts with the government. The second half of the century was marked by a series of increasingly bitter attempts by the independent element in the corporation, many of whom were Dissenters, led first by John Carter who died in 1794 and afterwards by his son, Sir John Carter, to break up the Admiralty interest. These were exciting years as the Carters and their supporters sought to overturn this influence and assert their own authority. Conflict came to a head in 1774 when the government, irritated by the corporation's refusal to accept their nomination of Peter Taylor on the death of Sir Matthew Featherstonhaugh in 1774, moved successful actions of ouster[61] and left the corporation without a mayor or recorder, with only four aldermen and a few burgesses. A compromise was sought of 'one and one' which operated without too much acrimony until the turn of the century, but to most intents and purposes the Carters' hold on the borough was complete. By 1783 Portsmouth had ceased to be an Admiralty borough and Sir John was now patron. Even after the latter's death in 1808, his family retained their sway and in 1816 Sir John's own son, John Carter, who took the name Bonham-Carter in 1827, came in as M.P. at the by-election occasioned by the death of the veteran Whig, Sir John Miller. John Bonham-Carter continued to represent Portsmouth until his death in 1838. Liberal hegemony was maintained until Sir James Elphinstone's return in the changed political circumstances of 1857. Only in 1874, however, did the Conservatives wrest both parliamentary seats from the Liberals for the first time. Until that year the honour of representing the borough was split between two parties. The Conservatives repeated their success in 1880. There was an Indian summer for the Liberals in the last decade of the 19th century but aside from the year of the Liberal landslide in 1906, the Conservatives' hold on the borough was firm from 1900.

The changed circumstances of 1918 (a new franchise which included women for the first time and the redistribution of the old two-member seat into three new one-member constituencies) produced two Conservative seats in North and South and one Liberal seat in Central. The Liberals held on to the seat until 1924. It was their last parliamentary victory in the city and thus was ended the town's Liberal tradition dating back to the days of Sir John Carter.

Labour captured their first parliamentary seat in the town in 1929: Central, taken for the party by Will Hall. The seat swung back to the Conservatives in 1931. It was regained in the Labour post-war landslide in 1945 when, interestingly, the swing to Labour in Portsmouth was roughly twice the national average in all three seats. North also went Labour, for the first time; South remained Conservative but with a greatly reduced majority. No Liberals even stood. In 1950 the Conservatives won back their lost seats from Labour. There

44. Cartoon from *Punch*, 8 December 1909, referring to the unprecedented parliamentary election activity in Portsmouth 1909-10 when the death of Sir John Baker in November 1909 precipitated an abortive by-election campaign in December. The government declined to move the writ in view of the general election which came in January.

PUNCH, OR THE LONDON CHARIVARI.—December 8, 1909.

PORTSMOUTH ELECTION

TWO MONTHS' HARD.

Charlie Beresford. "ALL VERY WELL DOING THIS SORT OF THING FOR A FEW DAYS, BUT WHEN IT COMES TO WEEKS AND WEEKS AND WEEKS——"

45. Lord Charles Beresford campaigning in Portsmouth, 1910.

had been a rearrangement of the boundaries of the parliamentary constituencies in the intervening period and new names for the seats: West, Langstone and South. The Conservatives held on to all three seats until 1966, when Frank Judd took West from Brigadier Clarke, who had held the seat since 1950. Judd was also Labour's first M.P. for Portsmouth since 1950. In 1974, the constituency boundaries were redrawn once again and Portsmouth was divided now into two seats: North and South. Judd won North and Ralph Bonner Pink South, the seat he had won first in 1966. In 1979, Judd lost North to the Conservative, Peter Griffiths. Griffiths and Pink held their seats in 1983 but in the following year the sudden death of Pink precipitated a June by-election in Portsmouth South and the shock defeat of the Conservative candidate by local councillor and Social Democrat, Michael Hancock. In 1987, however, the Conservative candidate, David Martin, wrested back control of South from the Social Democrats with one of the narrowest majorities of the General Election.

Portsmouth's parliamentary history has been lively and colourful. Figures of national importance have flitted briefly across the local stage from at least the mid-16th century as patrons, party managers and, of course, candidates. Reference has been made already to Margaret, Countess of Salisbury, the Earls of Southampton and the Marquess of Winchester, distinguished 16th-century patrons. In the 17th century both the King, Charles II, and his brother, the Duke of York, took a personal interest in the possible candidature of Samuel Pepys. Eighteenth-century party managers such as the Earl of Sandwich[62] and the Duke of Portland[63] worked hard to ensure that the Admiralty maintained some sort of electoral control over the borough, although finally the town threw off the Admiralty's influence.

The early years of the 19th century were positively quiet by comparison. Few studies have been made yet of the issues and personalities of Portsmouth's 19th-century political past. John Field has done more work than anyone on the Carter hegemony, and took his study up to 1875. Two other recent works: Sarah Peacock's 'The Parliamentary Representation of Portsmouth 1885-1918' in *Hampshire Studies*,[64] and Gregory Ashworth's study bring the story into the mid-20th century. Some themes can be adduced, however. There has always been a strong preference for, and long tradition of, local candidates from the days of the Carters. In the 19th century John Bonham-Carter, local draper John Baker, and solicitor T. A. Bramsdon, whose firm of Bramsdon and Childs is still in existence, all served long apprenticeships in business and often on the town council as well before stepping onto the parliamentary stage. Bonner Pink finished a long career as a local businessman and councillor (he was Lord Mayor in 1961) as M.P. for Portsmouth South, dying in office in 1983.

On the whole, elections in Portsmouth were dominated by national issues. It must be said, however, that local self-interest dictated voting patterns from the late 1850s as working men in Portsmouth turned increasingly to the Conservatives as the party most likely to maintain a strong navy and, of course, it has to be said that in 1910 the constitutional issue scarcely featured in Portsmouth. The naval scare was the key matter from the beginning.

Contested elections were always exciting, rumbustious affairs. While there are no records surviving of excess on the scale of Eatanswill,[65] Rear Admiral Sir George Cockburn's election in 1818 was certainly lively. He swept into town, sought out the 47 electors and, according to W. G. Gates,[66] assured them that 'though a Lord of the Admiralty he would be found an honest man', and won over sufficient number of them to convince one of the former M.P.s seeking election, Admiral Markham, that he was bound to be defeated. The latter withdrew and John Carter and Cockburn were returned unopposed. So pleased was Sir George that the following evening, after a public banquet, he gave a ball at the Green Row Assembly Rooms and before leaving the town gave out several charitable sums including 20s. to each debtor in the borough gaol! His triumph was short-lived, however.

At the next election, in 1820, he was rejected by the electorate indignant at recent reductions in the Navy and unimpressed by his somewhat lukewarm views on reform. Admiral Markham was fielded once again. Markham retired at the next election, in 1826, after a quarter of a century's service to the town, to be replaced by Francis Baring, who went on to serve the town in his turn for 37 years. He held in his time some of the highest offices in the land, being Chancellor of the Exchequer from 1839-41 and First Lord of the Admiralty from 1849-52.

Nineteenth-century newspaper accounts of elections provide a useful picture of events: the receiving of the writ, the nomination of the candidates, the local organisation, the campaigning, the monster public meetings, the issues involved. As the century progressed, letters to the editor, satirical verse, in short, all the paraphernalia of an election campaign as we know it today, became the commonplace. Women too came into their own towards the end of the century as the mainstays of the political machinery of both the Liberal and Conservative parties. Interestingly there were also very active local branches of the various women's suffrage organisations, most notably branches of the National Union of Women's Suffrage Societies (N.U.W.S.S.) and the militant Women's Social and Political Union.[67] The local branch of the N.U.W.S.S. was most active. Led by the Misses Norah and Margaret O'Shea,[68] the branch established an impressive organisation of links in each local

46. Local women's suffrage organisations beginning their march to London, July 1913. They are passing Charles Dickens' birthplace, in Commercial Road.

government ward in the town and mobilised its members with military precision at election times. They had premises in Kent Road and a small library, the remnants of which survive today in the City Records Office.[69] Diaries and newscuttings of their ventures survive as well: a fine record of the early efforts of women to mobilise themselves to fight a situation they perceived as unjust. Women over the age of 30 obtained their right to vote, finally, in 1918. Only in 1928 did all men and women over the age of 21 obtain the right to vote in both local and parliamentary elections.

The scale and complexity of local government has changed considerably over the years and more dramatically than ever in recent times, but the function itself, providing a range of services to the local community, has not changed in essence. The elected representatives of today, both local and parliamentary, are indeed the voice of the people but probably no more so than their predecessors of past centuries. What is indisputable is that a strong and vigorous local government must be not only a cornerstone but one of the surest guarantees of a free democracy.

The house of John Pounds, St Mary Street.

Chapter Nine

Leisure and Pleasure

For many centuries, the leisure activities of most male Portmuthians were based to a large extent on the many inns and alehouses which sprang up in the old town and its suburbs. By the reign of Elizabeth I, some of these hostelries had become extensive establishments specialising in accommodation for travellers. Collectively they were expected to provide 216 of the 252 extra beds which the town was required to have available in times of emergency for special visitors and officials.[1] One of the most famous was the *Red Lion* in the High Street, to which Lieut. Hammond of Norwich went in 1635 and found the hostess to be 'briske, blith and merry, a hansome sprightly lasse'.[2] No doubt she would have met with the approval of Samuel Pepys, who stayed there in 1661 and recalled in his diary that it was the inn where Sir Arthur Hesilrige and his friends had planned the restoration of Charles II, two years earlier.[3]

Prices at these hostelries tended to be high during wartime. One visitor in 1807, reporting that the *Crown* was excessively dear, added, 'I believe all the other inns are liable to the same objection'.[4] Some of the victuallers became prosperous and influential. Before the Civil War at least two were mayors: Darby Savell in 1562-3 and 1571-2, and Thomas Trydles in 1618-19. Andrew Nance, who held the same office in 1854-5, was born at the *Fountain*, which his family kept for many years.[5]

Situated in the High Street, this inn was described by an officer in 1764 as 'the best at Portsmouth', but went on to call it 'both extravagant and dirty'.[6] Nevertheless, its reputation was such that in 1794 a play performed at the Theatre Royal, Covent Garden, contained scenes set there, with the evocative stage directions, 'bells ringing and bustle'.[7] The *George*, where Nelson stayed before leaving England for the Battle of Trafalgar, was another notable High Steet inn until its destruction during the Second World War.[8] These hostelries were mainly the resort of senior officers. The *Blue Posts* and the *Star and Garter* on Point were frequented by those of lesser rank.[9] The *Crown*, with its assembly room and elaborate public baths, although well known during the early 1800s, did not long survive the Napoleonic Wars.[10]

These spacious establishments, serviced by armies of maids, cooks, laundresses, waiters and ostlers, often accommodated very distinguished visitors. In August 1829, for example, apartments were reserved at the *George* for the Queen of Portugal and the Empress of Brazil; the following year the Duchess of Kent stayed there with the young Princess (later Queen) Victoria.[11] Inns were also important venues for many different kinds of social activity, including official dinners, which were held regularly each sessions time, at mayor-making, and on royal birthdays. Bills for some of these civic feasts still remain, eloquent testimonies of the gargantuan appetites and gastronomic preferences of Georgian Portmuthians.[12] There, too, societies and clubs had their headquarters, musical soirées were enjoyed, and cards and billiards played in well-appointed games-rooms.[13] At the *George* there was a Freemasons' Lodge (the *Phoenix*) of which Thomas Telford the engineer, then at work in the dockyard, was in 1786 a founder member, having been initiated into the fraternity at the nearby *Three Tuns* a few months earlier.[14]

The opening of coffee houses, or the addition of coffee rooms to existing inns, was common from the late 17th century. Already in 1715-16 there were three coffee houses on Point and four in or near the High Street,[15] the most famous of which, situated on the corner of Grand Parade, apparently changed its name with each new owner. According to Henry Slight, it was 'formerly the house of the captains of the navy, and in the olden time . . . it was not uncommon to see captains . . . sitting outside this house on forms, smoking long pipes'.[16] It was here, in the 1720s, that some of the more serious-minded inhabitants used to attend the 'Early Club', meeting at four in the morning to drink coffee, read the newspapers and talk politics, before returning to their homes and the daily round.[17]

Ordinary workpeople and servicemen, and villagers from the surrounding countryside, tended to frequent the smaller inns and alehouses which were to be found all over the island, but particularly in the old town and close to the dockyard gates. When these hostelries first appeared in the town records in Tudor times, they were already seen as potential sources of disorder and moral turpitude. Alehouse keepers (tipplers) were licensed by the magistrates, and from time to time those selling an inferior product, using illegal measures or over-charging were fined. As the 17th century progressed there were frequent complaints that trading occurred during divine service. In October 1636, for example, John Smith 'did keep seamen drinkinge and keepinge unruly order in his howse' at such an hour 'and all night and att diverse other times'. The profits attracted an increasing number of unlicensed tipplers, and in 1667 no less than 78 persons were accused of selling drink illegally. In 1702 the drunkenness and other consequences of the 'great number of alehouses, victualling houses, punch houses and other tippling houses in the back streets and by-places of this towne' and its liberties, 'and the dayly increase thereof', caused the authorities great concern. The extent of the problem is confirmed by a somewhat confusing, but nonetheless revealing, survey of the area's many drinking places made in 1715-16.[18] Not surprisingly, the interlopers were greatly resented by the legitimate traders, 'who have chearfully quartered her Majesties forces'.[19] In 1742 it was reported that one man had set up a 'moveable hut or hovell' on waste land outside the town, where 'Geneva and other spirituous liquors' were sold to 'disorderly persons of both sexes both by night and by day to the terror and disturbance' of travellers using the main road.[20] It was a local manifestation of the national craze for spirits which led at this time to the 'biggest orgy of alcoholic over-indulgence ever witnessed in this country'.[21]

In 1784 there were at least 177 hostelries of one kind or another in Portsmouth and Portsea. Broad Street had 26, Queen Street 17 and The Hard thirteen.[22] Towards the end of the century these establishments were reported to be 'perpetually crowded'.[23] Many brewed their own beer, but already tied houses were becoming increasingly a feature of the trade.[24] After the Beerhouse Act of 1830, scarcely an alley or court was without its drinking place. Many were converted private dwellings lacking special facilities, although in some premises, such as the *King's Arms* on Grand Parade, beer-engines had been installed as early as 1800.[25] Business hours, although controlled, were inordinately long. In September 1836 the maximum period of opening permitted on working days was from 5 a.m. until 10 p.m., a limitation which enraged the beershop keepers who called a meeting of protest.[26] The close connection between publicans and the management of brothels was common knowledge, but despite the diatribes of the press and the clergy little seems to have been done to stop the practice.[27]

After 1869, when the Wine and Beerhouse Act brought greater power to the licensing magistrates, the number of drinking places declined despite the upsurge in population. At the same time the quality of premises greatly improved. Some of the new public houses designed by A. E. Cogswell and other local architects at the end of the 19th century were comparatively palatial, with elegant mirrored bars replacing the squalid, sawdusted taprooms of earlier places.[28] Meanwhile, the older inns, such as the *George*, were losing their primacy, partly as a result of the rapid development of the new suburbs, and partly because grander, more up-to-date hotels were being built in response to the growing holiday industry. Already in 1817 the *Bush Inn and Family Hotel*, Elm Grove, was providing 'those comforts not to be expected in the centre of a seaport town', and boasting of its proximity to the bathing machines. Later came the *Portland Hotel* with 'good sea views', and the *Sussex Hotel*, Landport, conveniently close to the main railway station and 'most advantageously and pleasantly situated in one of the principal thoroughfares'.[29] They were among the first of many hotels and boarding houses which transformed the Southsea scene in the decades before the First World War.

The late 17th-century sessions records show that among the diversions enjoyed by patrons of some of the Portsea Island inns was theatrical entertainment. In May 1694, for example, a constable who went into the 'great roome' of the Portsmouth *Queen's Head* in search of a missing sailor complained that he was hampered in his inquries by James Adams, whose players were performing there.[30] Details of the first regular theatre are unknown, but a farce, *A Trip to Portsmouth; or, The Wife's Election*, which was first published in 1710, had been performed at 'the new playhouse',[31] which was probably the building said to have been in Highbury Street, in or near the area now absorbed into the Gunwharf Gate development.[32] The earliest of which we have certain knowledge was on the site of the present 130 High Street. Owned by the Edmonds family, who were bakers, maltsters and builders, and who for a short time in the 1750s ran a playhouse in Pembroke Road, it was successfully leased over many seasons to some of the most reputable London and provincial companies. During the Seven Years War the dissolute young Duke of York and David Garrick, then holidaying at Wickham, separately attended performances there. Soon after redecoration in 1781 the theatre fell into disuse, and its original function ceased in 1794 when it was acquired by a group of Dissenters led by Isaac Carter, who worshipped there for two years before taking over the old synagogue in Daniel Street, Portsea.[33]

In 1761 a rival establishment was built on the opposite side of the road by Mr. Arthur of the Bath Company. Opened amid much excitement during the Free Mart Fair, it remained the town's principal place of entertainment until 1854, when it was demolished to make way for a new extension to the Cambridge Barracks. Never a very attractive building, its fame lies less in the talents of the players who performed there than in its being the theatre immortalised by Charles Dickens in *Nicholas Nickleby*.[34]

During the late 18th century, the company in residence provided a very varied and, for the most part, undemanding repertoire, which culminated each season in a series of benefit nights from which the most popular performers could earn substantial rewards. For a while the two High Street theatres seem to have been run jointly and opened alternately. Thus the old theatre operated from November 1781 until the following March, and the new from April until July 1782.[35] At most of the performances the audience was a cross-section of Portsmouth society and behaved in a comparatively orderly manner, but sometimes the presence of servicemen resulted in such boisterous behaviour that the actors were forced to quit the stage. On one occasion a midshipman, in an excess of dramatic criticism, fatally stabbed the stage carpenter. The nightly misbehaviour was such that frequently about 1800 the magistrates were forced to close the theatre until common-sense prevailed. During an interval of good order it was visited by Charles Dibdin, the Southampton-born composer of *Tom Bowling*. Prostitutes he saw in plenty, but there was less 'bare-faced profligate indecency' than at Covent Garden or Drury Lane, since 'there was a space set apart for them, where they were obliged to conform to rules and orders or be turned out'.[36]

After the peace of 1815 and the post-war euphoria there was a slow decline in the theatre's popularity. Successive managers gambled on their skill to attract audiences. Gala nights sponsored by high-ranking officers and the local gentry, and celebrity evenings, found the

47.   The Portsmouth Theatre, High Street, opened 1761, *c*.1800.

theatre crowded; but too often performances were poorly attended, and even after a complete redecoration in 1838 and attempts during the next few years by William Shalders to recapture some of the old enthusiasm, the response was disappointing. By the early 1850s the theatre was open only one night a week and its eventual demise and demolition surprised few.[37]

The tinsel glamour of the Portsmouth theatre nevertheless persuaded more than one local boy to make the stage his profession. John Bernard, who was born in 1756, embarked on a long career which included some years in the New World, where he was one of the founding fathers of the American theatre.[38] More significant, perhaps, was the decision of young Ben Terry, son and nephew of Portsmouth innkeepers. Having glimpsed life backstage with the assistance of his brother George, who was the leader of the theatre orchestra, he embarked on an acting career in 1838 with his young bride, the daughter of a local builder. They established one of England's greatest theatrical families, which included several of their own children, the most famous of whom was Ellen, and more recently their great-grandson, Sir John Gielgud.[39]

The short-lived Royalty playhouse at the *Dolphin*, *c*.1843-5,[40] and the more successful South of England Music Hall at the *Bluebell* in Gunwharf Road from the 1850s,[41] were the only other theatrical enterprises in Portsmouth town. Entertainment increasingly became associated with the burgeoning suburbs, especially Landport. As early as 1781-3 the so-called Sadler's Wells was opened in what is now Guildhall Walk. Whether it was on the site of the present Theatre Royal or opposite is not clear. There is no doubt, however, that during the early Victorian period a racket-court built *c*.1800 next door to the *White Swan* was converted into the Landport Hall, which was later renamed the Theatre Royal. This building helped to fill the vacuum caused by the demise of the High Steet theatre and the closure in 1850 of the unsuccessful Grecian Saloon (or Landport Theatre) which occupied a site close to the present Central Library.[42] In 1884 it was replaced by the New Theatre Royal with seats for 2,000 patrons. Sixteen years later Frank Matcham presided over a major reconstruction. From 1900 to 1966 this fine building was a mirror of theatrical change: drama, opera, variety, repertory, films, wrestling, dereliction, and finally slow restoration.[43]

In the early 1900s the rapidly growing Portsmouth conurbation provided residents, visitors and the floating population of servicemen with a great range of live entertainment. The old South of England Music Hall (renamed Barnard's Royal Amphitheatre) had been burnt down for a second time in 1890 and its licence transferred to the new Empire Theatre in Edinburgh Road. The entrepreneurial vote of confidence in the future of live entertainment in Portsmouth was reflected in the construction in 1907 of two large new theatres – the Hippodrome (bombed 1941) in Guildhall Walk and the King's in Southsea – as well as the renovation of another of Matcham's designs, the Prince's Theatre (bombed 1940), in Lake Road.[44] The most famous performers of the age appeared on one or other of these stages in the years before the First World War. Already, however, a new form of entertainment, the moving picture show, was exciting widespread interest.

Films first made their appearance at local fairs and halls in the late 19th century. By 1910, when the provisions of the 1909 Cinematograph Act came into force, there were 21 licensed places in Portsmouth where they might be shown. Of these, three were movable fairground booths, two were traditional theatres (the King's and the Hippodrome) which provided mixed entertainment, four were public halls (including the Grand Pavilion on South Parade Pier), two were centres for the armed forces, and the remaining 10 were what might be described broadly as early cinemas. After this rapid development the number of licences issued remained fairly stable for a few years. Most of these early enterprises were run by local people and situated within a short distance of the Guildhall. Among the halls licensed in 1914 was one at St James's Hospital, which provided seats for 400 patients and staff.

The outbreak of war in 1914 brought an influx of servicemen and, with the growing interest in this new form of entertainment, the industry received a great boost. In 1915 Portsmouth's 27 moving picture halls had a total capacity of 17,752, a figure which rose to 18,224 in 1917. By 1927 there were 25 cinemas capable of seating 22,542. A decade later 27 were licensed for 29,784, a total which was only slightly lower in 1947 despite the intensive bombing campaigns of 1940-44.

During the inter-war years some of the local proprietors sold out to national organisations. A few of the earliest cinemas remained open until the 1960s and even later, although often with changed names,[45] but more typical were the new, aptly-named picture palaces with their lavish interiors, modern equipment and resplendently attired staff. Rivalry was intense. The luxurious new Plaza (Gaumont) at Bradford Junction presented the first talkies in Portsmouth on 28 January 1929, and soon afterwards the management braved widespread abuse by introducing one of the first Sunday programmes. Four years earlier, one of the best-known names in the 20th-century film industry, the actor Peter Sellers, had been born a mile or more away in a flat over a shop at the corner of Southsea Terrace and Castle Road.

With declining audiences in the 1960s most of the city's cinemas closed one by one. Since they almost all stood on prime sites in busy thoroughfares, they were soon absorbed into the city's business world. In 1966 only 12 remained, one of which, at the Royal Sailors' Rest in Edinburgh Road, had been first licensed in 1910. Within a few years the number had fallen to three. Even with the introduction of triple screens, they were capable in 1989 of seating in total only 2,737 patrons.[46]

Music of one sort or another must always have enlivened Portsmouth life. In the Middle Ages minstrels no doubt entertained the burgesses at their civic and social gatherings, as they did in other towns;[47] medieval mariners were fond of playing simple wind instruments such as the shawm and tabor pipes which were discovered on the *Mary Rose*;[48] and it was at Portsmouth about 1763 that the first permanent Royal Marines band was formed.[49] Before the Reformation sacred music at St Thomas's church was provided by a simple organ which, in the late 1530s, was played by Thomas Fountayne.[50]

Theatrical programmes in the Georgian period had a strong musical content. Thus the versatile company who performed *Hamlet* at the old High Street playhouse on 25 January 1782 went on to present *A Fig for the French*, a one-act musical piece.[51] During the early 19th century the Portsmouth Theatre was also the venue for concerts by visiting vocalists and instrumentalists, many of whom were internationally famous, such as Paganini and Johann Strauss the elder and his band. At this time there were also occasional musical programmes at the Beneficial Society's hall in Portsea,[52] and, after their opening in 1843,[53] at the nearby Queen's Rooms, where Portsmouth's first 'rock' concert was held in 1846 – '. . . delightfully sweet music elicited from sundry single pieces of solid rock' – as well as at the Green Row Rooms, the scene on 17 August 1840 of a concert by Franz Liszt. In his party was John Orlando Parry, a well-known composer of comic songs who later became a resident of Queen's Crescent and organist at St Jude's church.[54]

In 1824, Madam Catalini sang in an oratorio at St Paul's church, Southsea, at the time of the annual regatta, to which she donated a silver cup.[55] Her visit was due to the initiative of the talented musician Stephen Sibly (1765-1842), who, with his son Edward (?1792-1843), dominated Portsmouth's musical life for half a century or more. Successful recitals and concerts had been held earlier, but there was a greatly increased interest during the Napoleonic War period, due in large measure to the enthusiasm of Sibly senior. From 1801 he organised numerous subscription concerts, the programmes of which reflect his passion for Handel and his desire to provide local enthusiasts with the finest performers available. 'The town owes much to that gentleman', the *Hampshire Telegraph* said of him in 1807, 'for the elegant and delightful amusements in select concerts he has been the sole cause of their frequently enjoying'.[56]

The early-Victorian High Street contained several music shops, including that of the Treakell family, members of which were well known locally as teachers and performers. From the late 18th century numerous glee clubs and musical societies were established, some based at inns such as the *Dolphin*, the *Wellington*, and the *Wheelbarrow Castle*, and at least one in the dockyard. Another feature was the presence in the town of military bands which not only attended the more formal functions but also gave concerts for residents and visitors.[57]

Towards the end of the century popular interest was still strong. New halls were built, notably the Portland in Southsea which survived from 1861 (rebuilt 1877) until the Second World War, where Ole Bull, Thérèse Tietjens, Clara Butt and many other great artistes performed.[58] The Guildhall, rebuilt after its wartime destruction, has at its heart a spacious 2,000-seat concert hall which has become firmly established as the focal point of Portsmouth's musical life.

48. Portsmouth Free Mart Fair, early 19th century, showing the scene on Grand Parade.

Although there is little information about the Free Mart Fair[59] until the mid-18th century, it is clear that by then an event which had once been an occasion for serious trade had been transformed into little more than an annual festival of fun. Stallholders still congregated in the High Street and sold household goods and clothing, but many of the wares on display were cheap and tawdry bric-a-brac. Menageries, circuses, waxworks, theatres, booths containing all manner of freaks and oddities, and roundabouts, swings and other simple amusements were packed closely together each year on Grand Parade. The fair was officially opened by the town sergeants hanging a wooden hand or gauntlet from a public building in the High Street at midnight on 9/10 July in the presence of a large and noisy crowd. After 15 hectic days it was removed. The stallholders packed away their unsold goods and the showmen's wagons rumbled out of Portsmouth and across Portsea Island to Portsdown Hill, where they pitched their tents and opened up their stalls once again ready for the three-day fair which began there on 26 July.

The popularity of the Free Mart Fair fluctuated considerably. In wartime, when large numbers of servicemen were in the area and dockyard wages were relatively high, the stalls sometimes reached from Point Gate near the Square Tower to the top of the High Street. However, the buoyancy of the local economy was not necessarily a guarantee of a busy fair. A 'very hot press' in May 1803, when the town gates were closed and potential recruits rounded up, was responsible, two months later, for the absence of many cautious showmen and able-bodied young men who feared another sortie.[60] Not surprisingly, the two best years on record were 1815 and 1816.

In the late Georgian period the fair was still apparently considered respectable by all classes, but as the years passed it increasingly became subject to hostile criticism. Held in the heart of the already congested town, the Free Mart made life intolerable for many of the local residents, some of whom moved into the country while it was being held. The noise, inconvenience, increase in petty crime and drunkenness were bitterly attacked from the 1830s by the *Hampshire Telegraph*, which had once supported it. The poor were said to pawn their possessions in order to be able to participate in the revelry, and seamen to desert their ships. The Vauxhalls, where dancing and drinking went on into the early hours, were blamed for much of the licentious behaviour. By the mid-1840s few of the more articulate townspeople had much to say in the fair's favour, and in 1847 it was held for the last time. Despite the rumbustious scenes which had once attended it, in later years the Free Mart was remembered with affection by many who could recall the excitement it had occasioned.

Unlike the Free Mart, Portsdown Fair was of comparatively recent origin. Granted in 1715 to Richard Turner,[61] it was held on a beautiful site approximately where Fort Widley now stands, with spectacular views over Portsea Island and the adjacent harbours. A lively trade in horses, cheese and bacon was carried on, mainly on the first day, and in fine weather the large pleasure fair attracted huge crowds. The local gentry, their tenants, labourers and servants, even merrymakers transported by boat from Southampton, joined in the revelry. They bought hot rolls and loaves from the bakers' stalls, picnicked on the grassy slopes or visited the refreshment tents set up by local innkeepers such as Robert Kiln of the *Wellington* in Portsmouth, whom George Meredith immortalised in his novel *Evan Harrington*. Rooms at Widley windmill, which stood close by, were let to 'respectable parties', and the outhouses rented for storage by showmen and caterers.[62] During the late French Wars, the dramatist John O'Keefe, then associated with the theatre at Portsmouth, travelled by coach to the fair in the company of a distinguished naval officer. On their way through Portsea Island they saw 'pork roasting, and great cauldrons of apple sauce'. At the foot of the hill the party dined at a farmhouse and watched the dancing in a large crowded barn. Higher up they found young men and their sweethearts engaged in the game of 'running down the hill', but it ended when one of the participants fell and broke a leg.[63] In 1806 particularly large crowds thronged the fair, and it was said that so many of the three thousand dockyard workers joined in the fun that only a hundred or so turned up for the afternoon call.[64] Captain Marryat described the fair vividly in *Peter Simple*, in which his hero had an adventure with an escaped lioness and helped to set off prematurely the grand firework display.[65] Pickpockets, footpads and tricksters of every kind were active among the stalls and tents and along the neighbouring roads and lanes.[66]

After the passing of the 1860 Defence Act, by which the construction of the Portsdown forts was put in train, the land on the hill was acquired by the state and the right to hold a fair revoked (1862).[67] Although there was an annual pleasure fair on various sites in the Cosham area on many subsequent occasions,[68] the popularity of the event waned. The spirit of the great festive occasion with its social mix was never recaptured. The holiday crowds turned to other forms of amusement.

The sporting activities of Portmuthians before the Tudor period have left virtually no evidence, but by the Restoration such diversions as card playing, dicing, ninepins, shovel-board (an early form of shove-halfpenny), and even billiards, had become popular, despite the stern disapproval of the authorities.[69] Young men were expected to engage in more manly pursuits, such as archery, which benefited the nation. No doubt butts had long been in existence when, in June 1568, the chamberlains were ordered to see to their repair. Swordsmanship was also a valuable skill, but the same month Hew Salt's fencing academy came under scrutiny because it was all too often 'a cawsyan of contryversy betwene man and man'.[70] The shooting of wildfowl was another acceptable diversion to be enjoyed on the marshes or in the fields, but in 1634, presumably for military reasons, it was forbidden in the vicinity of the Round Tower.[71]

By the 18th century cricket was well established in Portsmouth. John Bew, a turner, is known to have owned a bat in 1734, because he was said to have used it to belabour a sailor's wife,[72] and Stewart, a noted Hampshire player who died in 1799, was the landlord of the *Swan*.[73] In the early 1800s teams allegedly representative of the town included such middle-class devotees as Captain Madden, R.M., and Roger Callaway, the town clerk.[74] Matches between teams of craftsmen were popular. In 1845, for example, there was a contest between the bricklayers and the carpenters employed by Thomas Ellis Owen, 'who kindly gave a holiday to all his men on that day'.[75] Women cricketers played at Milton. In 1813 an orange-ribboned team triumphed over the blues by 120 runs to thirty-nine.[76]

The virtues of cricket were extolled by the *Hampshire Telegraph*, and when boys were said to play in the Portsea streets to the danger of passers-by, it was the military who were blamed for having taken away the field where once children had been free to enjoy themselves.[77] Significantly, one of the earliest Southsea taverns was named the *Five Cricketers*, and when part of the nearby Common was put up for sale in 1841, it was suggested that it might be converted into a permanent pitch.[78] This did not materialise, but the Portsmouth and East Hants Club, which was founded about 1847 and had some sixty members by 1859,[79] played on its own ground until it was sold for housing development in the 1880s. Such was the interest in 1882, when the touring Australians played a Cambridge University Past and Present XI at the Officers' Recreation Ground, that more than sixteen thousand spectators were admitted over the three days, at the end of which the University narrowly won.[80]

In the 1880s a leading cricketer was the Portsmouth G.P., Dr. Arthur Conan Doyle. He was also a keen bowls player and footballer who played for the newly-formed town club. Organised soccer was first made popular in the area by such enthusiasts as The Revd. Norman Pares, curate of St Jude's and classics master at the grammar school, who began to arrange matches between local teams during his university vacations. In 1898 the growing interest in the game led to a meeting of six influential local men, including the brewer Mr. (later Sir) John Brickwood, at 12 High Street, at which a professional club with a ground at Fratton was founded. The first league match was played at Chatham on 2 September 1899. Many crises occurred during the next 40 years, but in 1939 Portsmouth won the F.A. Cup at their third appearance at a Wembley final. By that time Fratton Park was one of the finest grounds in the south of England, and all over the world sailors of the Royal Navy followed the exploits of 'Pompey', their 'home' team, with great interest.[81]

Cock-fighting, forbidden in 1721 as a 'barbarous usuage' which caused 'riotts, quarrells, and other mischiefs',[82] nevertheless remained popular. In March 1802, the so-called 'Gentlemen' of Portsmouth challenged their Brighton rivals. Forty-one pairs of birds in silver spurs fought for £10 a time and, exceptionally, £100.[83] Horse racing, sponsored mainly by army officers and the local gentry, drew large crowds to Portsdown Hill in the early 19th century. These town and garrison races later moved to Southsea Common, where the carnival atmosphere often degenerated into a near riot. The sport continued on Farlington marshes from 1891 until the First World War, when the course was requisitioned, and at Portsmouth Park (Wymering) from 1928 until 1939.[84] An annual regatta also developed out of the informal water sports which had long been enjoyed by local ferrymen and longshoremen. Crowds occupied every vantage point along the shoreline to see the various contests, which in 1842 included races between women's crews from Portsmouth and Plymouth. Southsea Rowing Club was founded in 1860 and the prestigious Royal Albert Yacht Club four years later.[85]

Recognition of Portsmouth's potentiality as a watering-place came during the 18th century. The construction by public subscription of a bathing-house on Point in 1754 is evidence of the growing interest in the therapeutic benefits of sea-water. Situated close to the harbour entrance, Quebec House (as it is now called), is 'one of the earliest, if not *the*

earliest extant building connected with sea-bathing anywhere'.[86] Bathing machines were a feature of Southsea beach by the 1770s, with men and women attendants to assist the timid. At much the same time the first of a series of wooden structures where hot baths could be obtained was built close to the morass to the south-east of Portsmouth's defences, but it was not until 1817 that a substantial building able to survive the onslaught of storm and tide became a recognised social centre for the better-off. In 1821 this establishment was purchased by Henry Hollingsworth, who, although not the most scrupulous of men, was one of the makers of modern Southsea. At a cost of some £700 he greatly improved the facilities, so that by the late 1820s there was a leisure complex which not only included suites of baths, but also a library and an assembly room where balls and other social functions were regularly held. The number of subscribers rose from 225 in 1821 to 482 in 1823.[87] The King's Rooms, as they were called after 1830, were the exclusive domain of the

9. Southsea Common and beach by A. Pernet, c.1865. The Clarence Pier (opened 1861) is to the left and the new own of Southsea is in the background.

leisured and professional classes, the local gentry, and the officers. For many years it was the area's most fashionable meeting-place.

For the less well-to-do swimming was an age-old recreation. 'As there are a number of persons constantly bathing at this season of the year in this neighbourhood', the *Hampshire Telegraph* noted in 1809 when a large shark had been seen off Fort Cumberland, 'it may be well to apprise them that it is not always safe to swim far from the shore'.[88] Nude bathing by the poorer inhabitants along the more remote stretches of the beach was socially acceptable, but the presence of unclad male swimmers and the prying eyes of the *hoi polloi* in the vicinity of the King's Rooms were considered offensive. In 1835, 'for the sake of decency', the area within a hundred yards of the gentlemen's bathing machines was forbidden to outsiders, apparently without much success, since attempts at control went on for many years.[89] But it was not only Southsea beach that was frequented. In 1825 a Portsea resident

50. Holiday crowds on the sea-front at Southsea, *c*.1930.

complained that young men and boys, often fifty or more at a time, bathed at Portsea Hard
and 'run about, naked, to and fro, in the public landing place, within twenty yards of the
houses'.[90] In 1875 Portsmouth Swimming Club was formed and soon had 1,700 members,
which made it one of the largest – if not the largest – in existence. For a while it organised
an annual salt-water swimming championship of the world. The first public swimming
bath was built in Park Road in 1883 and not superseded until the completion of the pool
at Victoria Park 80 years later.[91]

In 1842 the old beef stage at the Square Tower was transformed into the Victoria Pier.
Used primarily as a landing place for steamer passengers, it rapidly became a popular
promenade for residents. The Albert Pier was built at Portsea Hard in 1846 and the Clarence
Esplanade Pier near the King's Rooms in 1861. The latter soon assumed the role of
entertainment centre, especially after the construction of a pavilion in 1882, but it remained
a steamer terminus for some years. Leisure facilities were expanded further in 1879 with the
opening of the first South Parade Pier.[92]

About 1870, a more lavish establishment replaced the derelict King's Rooms, but this soon proved to be uneconomical and was converted into the *Esplanade Hotel*, which survived on the site of the later amusement park until the Second World War.[93] The loss of the seafront baths was offset by the new Turkish baths at 24 King's Terrace, Southsea, on the corner of Gold Street. Operating in 1875 under royal patronage, they continued in business until 1936, when Princes House was erected on the site.[94]

The 19th century saw the development of many new leisure pursuits which could be enjoyed by Portmuthians of all classes. For example, gardening as a hobby rather than as an economic necessity developed apace. In one week in July 1824 there were shows for the display of pinks – a very popular flower at the time – at the *Barley Mow*, the *Bush*, and the *Wheelbarrow Castle* public houses in Southsea. An annual dahlia show was also held at Portsea *White Bear*.[95] Those with an interest in photography could join the Portsmouth Camera Club, founded in 1888, while the more adventurous could participate in the new cycling craze. The members of the Port of Portsmouth Bicycle Club, which was formed in 1879, took the sport very seriously. On their outings they were uniformly clad in dark blue serge tunics, knickerbockers, dark grey stockings, and polo caps on which was their elaborate badge, which included the borough crest.[96]

Before the late Victorian urban expansion, Portsea Island, with its scattered villages, rural byways and wild coastline, afforded countless opportunities for pleasant walks. Much of what is now open space, however, such as Southsea Common, was restricted because of the demands of the armed forces. Consequently, whenever an attempt was made to interfere with what were considered to be public rights of way or common land, there was a strong popular response, the best-known occasion being the so-called Battle of Southsea in 1874.[97] The destruction of the fortifications, where generations of Portmuthians had promenaded under the elms, opened up extensive areas of what has since become the inner city, but they remained, and still partly remain, in the hands of the armed forces. However, the creation in 1878 of the first public open space, the Victoria Park, on the former Portsea glacis,[98] gave the residents, workpeople and shoppers a few green acres away from the growing traffic, and ushered in a period of rapid development in almost every branch of recreational activity.[99]

Southsea Rooms and Baths (later the *Esplanade Hotel*), *c*.1875.

Chapter Ten

Portsmouth and Its Past

The charters which Portsmouth acquired over the centuries were among the burgesses' most prized possessions, since without them their right to hard-won privileges might be difficult to prove. From earliest days, therefore, they and the records of local government, together with the town seals and cash, were kept in a secure chest which was the responsibility of the borough cofferers, who, upon taking office, swore to safeguard the keys to ensure that none of its contents 'be stollen or taken out . . . to the prejudice or hurt of this towne'.[1] Until the Second World War, two chests dating from before 1600 were still in the possession of the corporation. One, of stout oak strengthened with iron bands, had four locks, each

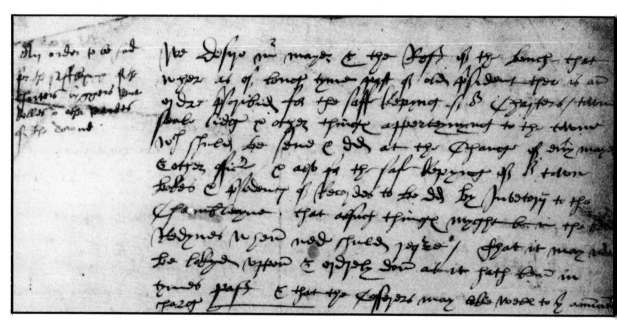

51. Instructions for the safe-keeping of the town records, 1562.

with a different key.[2] In 1562 it was said that strict rules for security had existed 'of long tyme past of old president'.[3] Yet despite all these precautions, documents were sometimes misplaced or lost. In December 1551, for example, Christopher Jervis, a carver, was ordered to return King Henry VIII's charter of 1511 before Pentecost or be fined 20s.[4] The chamberlains, lowly but important town officers who were responsible for financial matters, seem not always to have been respectful of established practice. Thus in December 1560 they were threatened with a fine of £5 if they removed their rolls and accounts from the chest other than 'at the courts and lawdayes except by the consent of Mr Mayer and his Assistantes'.[5]

By the late 16th century the muniments were becoming increasingly diverse, although Portsmouth, still a comparatively small and poor place, was less sophisticated in its administrative records than its neighbour Southampton. Almost certainly they were kept at this period in the town house, which stood in the middle of the High Street opposite St Thomas's church. The more elegant building which replaced it in the 18th century is known to have contained a record room on the upper floor, but it seems that after the completion of a council chamber and strongroom in the new Penny Street gaol, which was opened in 1809, the archives and plate were transferred there.[6] At the time of the Municipal Corporations Act, which drastically changed local government, their future was a matter of concern for the new council, which set up a committee to make recommendations. On 18 January 1836, a detailed inventory was made of the strongroom's contents, and it was decided that in the interests of security and ease of access they should not be moved. Mindful of a clause in the Act which directed that in each borough the town clerk should have 'the charge and custody of, and be responsible for' the muniments, but also concerned to maintain tradition, the committee recommended that the town clerk and the former cofferers should have joint custody.[7] Even after the construction of the new town hall in the High Street (1836-7), the archives and plate remained at the gaol.

Security, however, was at times less rigorous than it should have been. When the Portsmouth artist, R. H. C. Ubsdell, decided to draw the corporation plate about 1840, he wrote to Sir Frederic Madden: 'If you require a sketch of this, Mr. E. Carter has said that I shall have the key of the plate chest in the record room and then I can copy what I require'.[8] The history of the borough archives at Portsmouth, as in so many places, has been bedevilled until this century by the lack of responsibility shown by some of the officers to whose care they were entrusted. The important charter of Charles I (1627), mislaid during the mid-century upheavals, was found among Lord Dartmouth's archives about 1688,[9] and that of Edward II (1313), which was removed before 1836, was not recovered until 1904 at a cost to the council of £45.[10] In 1877 much unnecessary expense was incurred in the *Foreshore Case* in the High Court because the corporation's legal advisers were unaware of a key document which was subsequently discovered in private possession.[11] Even the records of St Thomas's church were not inviolate. On one occasion in 1823 intruders broke in and burnt some of the contents of the parish chest;[12] other manuscripts, including the first register, transcribed in part by Lake Allen *c.*1820, were passed from hand to hand by antiquaries in the 1840s and have now vanished without trace.[13]

Towards the end of the century, however, attitudes were changing. Most significantly, during the mayoralty of Alderman W. D. King (1879-80), the corporation was persuaded to appoint a local brewer, Alderman Richard J. Murrell, assisted by Councillor H. J. Andrews, 'to examine and classify the Borough Records'. That year had seen the death of John Howard, who had been town clerk, and consequently jointly responsible for the muniments, since 1835.[14] Very likely it was considered an appropriate time to review the situation. Murrell, who obviously had a keen amateur interest in archives, promised that he 'would endeavour to repay the trust and confidence' placed in him 'by publishing extracts from the most interesting and valuable documents'. Soon another local resident, Robert East, an inland revenue collector, became deeply involved in the project. He was 'untiring in his efforts to aid me', wrote Murrell, 'both in the difficult task of assorting the documents, and in copying many of the MSS. for the press', and he became joint editor of the extracts which were published in five sections between 1881 and 1884. Sadly, Murrell, aged only 47, died suddenly on 28 April 1884, before seeing the final pages through the press.[15] The work occasioned much local interest and was soon sold out. A *Supplement to Extracts from the Records* was produced by East in 1886, and eventually, in 1891, his efforts culminated in a new and much enlarged edition. These volumes fall far short of the standards demanded by modern scholarship. Many of the transcripts are inaccurate, and the material is badly arranged and inadequately indexed, but nonetheless for the corporation and the amateur editors it was a major achievement. For the first time, the public at large were made aware of the important collection of records preserved in the Portsmouth borough archives.

The town clerk's responsibility for their custody was confirmed by the Local Government Act of 1933,[16] and the sixty thousand or more items which by then had accumulated were housed in the octagonal-shaped muniment room on the ground floor of the late Victorian guildhall, where great protection was provided by the solid, four feet thick walls which formed the base of the clock tower. Additional accommodation was available under the guildhall's main steps. A member of the town clerk's department, known grandly as assistant keeper of the records, was given responsibility for day-to-day management.[17]

Over the centuries the municipal records were searched from time to time for precedents when legal or constitutional issues, such as disputed elections, were matters of civic debate. George Huish, an 18th-century town clerk, is known to have accumulated various papers which were described in 1826 as 'voluminous and exact', but whether these or the local memoranda collected by Alderman Stephen Gaselee were anything more than transcripts made for professional or electoral reasons is not known.[18] Early publications concerning the town were purely descriptive or politically motivated. The most entertaining, *The Borough*,[19] published in 1748, was followed seven years later by Archibald Maxwell's *Portsmouth – A Descriptive Poem in Two Books* which, like most of the accounts of the place written during this period, marvelled at the mushroom growth of the new sister town of Portsea.[20] The great influx of naval and military personnel during the French Wars, and the growing number of visitors to see the wonders of the busy harbour and the ever-expanding dockyard, prompted Dr. Lake Taswell to produce the *Portsmouth Guide* (1775), which was reprinted with revisions in 1790.[21] A few years later came two more substantial works, both of which give evidence of the influence of Taswell's pioneering effort. The first, published anonymously at Gosport in 1799,[22] was compiled by The Revd. R. H. Cumyns, who later became the headmaster of Portsmouth Grammar School.[23] No researcher,[24] but clearly a patriot, his so-called 'history' is little more than a eulogistic description of the town and neighbouring area. Another 'history', published in 1801 by J. C. Mottley,[25] local bookseller, printer and newspaper proprietor, was also anonymous but probably the joint work of Mottley and his employees. Although still largely descriptive and derivative, it has more hard fact, and is a bigger, better and more detailed book than that of Cumyns. Moreover, some attempt was made by the compilers to refer to unusual primary sources, including two manuscripts, now tragically lost, containing descriptions of the Stuart dockyard by Thomas Waite and Isaac Hancock, quartermen, who began work there in 1650 and 1661 respectively.[26]

None of these writers, however, addressed themselves to the task of exploring the historical development of the Portsea Island communities. They thought of themselves as editors, assembling facts for a better understanding by outsiders of the locality as it then was. The value of these works today lies primarily in the light they throw on the physical appearance of Portsmouth and its environs when they were written. As the 19th century progressed, the quest for ready information of this kind was satisfied by a succession of guidebooks and directories produced by enterprising publishers, the most notable locally being Henry Hollingsworth and W. H. Charpentier. For the most part these booklets, like their predecessors, were the work of anonymous hacks who cobbled them together from earlier versions. Occasionally, however, a personality emerges. If an inscription written on an 1828 edition of a Hollingsworth guide is to be believed, it was the work of John Brinton, an assistant or clerk at the publisher's sea-front rooms.[27]

A genuine stirring of interest in antiquarian research is first apparent in Portsmouth during the reign of George III. A letter written in July 1795 by S. Purkis of Brentford, a friend of Sir Joseph Banks, tells of an investigation he had conducted among the records in the Tower of London and elsewhere in pursuit of information about medieval Portsmouth.[28] The recipient of the letter is unknown, but there is evidence that he intended to publish some kind of history. It is possible that it was the young Daniel Howard, whose ambition it was to produce such a work.[29] A similar project was in the mind of the Portsea physician, William Goldson, who was mayor in 1799, 1805 and 1814, and the author of an erudite tome on the North-West Passage which was published in Portsmouth in 1793. A letter written to him in November 1802 and originally containing 'trifling extracts' for 'your intended valuable work' is still extant,[30] but nothing seems to have materialised.

The first real progress came in the years immediately after the peace of 1815, when Portsmouth contained a group of young men with a profound interest in their heritage. One of these, John Bonham Carter, who received part of his education at Dr. Smith's school during the reign of The Revd. For-
rester, was a barrister belonging to the local brewing family, and he represented the town in Parliament 1816-38. His papers contain histori-cal notes, the emphasis being on Portsmouth elections and elec-tors.[31] Local parliamentary history was also of great interest to Daniel Howard, a liberal-minded Portsea lawyer with a penchant for collect-ing statistics, who was mayor on six occasions. Described at his death as 'the consistent, unflinching and energetic advocate of civil and re-ligious liberty',[32] he had the schol-arly mind and concern for fairness and accuracy which might have re-sulted in a valuable work. Unfortu-nately he never found time to realise his ambition, and only his notes remain as a record of his life-long interest.[33]

The key figure during the next half-century was Sir Frederic Mad-den, who became one of the most brilliant palaeographers of the age and from 1837 was head of the manuscripts department at the Bri-tish Museum. Born in 1801 in Portsmouth, where he lived until embarking on his professional career in 1824, he had a passionate interest in the history of the area. About 1817 it was his good fortune to meet and befriend Lake Allen,

52. Sir Frederic Madden (1801-73).

the grandson of Dr. Lake Taswell. Allen, talented but somewhat capricious in his interests, wrote, when barely 18 years of age, a substantial history of Portsmouth,[34] which, although originally intended to be a revised version of his grandfather's guide, was in fact a valuable work in its own right. Allen was far more interested in research than previous writers and, despite its inaccuracies and other faults, his book was a considerable advance on earlier publications about the town's past. Unfortunately Allen died when only 24 years of age, his great promise unrealised,[35] but his companion, despite a busy professional life, went on to amass an extensive corpus of transcripts, notes, playbills, pamphlets, original manuscripts and other material relating to the area, much of which still survives. In addition, particularly during the 1840s, he commissioned a local artist, R. H. C. Ubsdell, to sketch various historic buildings and sites, and to copy any old maps, prints and paintings which might provide a permanent pictorial record of the changing face of the area. Madden was an exacting taskmaster, but Ubsdell fell under his spell, not only throwing himself enthusiastically into the artistic work, but also voluntarily sending him miscellaneous items of historical and architectural information which today are useful in reconstructing the appearance of the Victorian town.[36]

Interest in the past was probably stimulated locally by a number of unusual events during this period. In 1816 a tumulus on Portsdown Hill was excavated and the discovery of several skeletons led to much local debate.[37] Even greater excitement was caused in the 1830s by the diving operations of the Deane brothers, who discovered the wrecks of the *Royal George* and the *Mary Rose* in the Solent mud and recovered many objects which soon circulated in the town.[38] The disputed election of 1820[39] and the inquiry which preceded the Municipal Corporations Act of 1835[40] both stirred up constitutional discussion. A forum for intellectual debate was provided in 1818 by the founding of the Portsmouth and Portsea Literary and Philosophical Society.[41] Although primarily scientifically orientated, it developed an historical section and occasionally included topics dealing with the past in its annual lecture programme.[42]

53.   Dr. Henry Slight (1796-1860).

The launching of the *Portsmouth, Portsea and Gosport Literary and Scientific Register* in 1822 also seemed to augur well. A sixpenny monthly journal full of good intentions, it unfortunately lasted only 12 issues, but it included some interesting historical articles, several of which were by the young Frederic Madden.[43] In the first issue he contributed a letter to the editor on the subject of antiquities, which, he claimed, 'is at present in its infancy among the literati of the town'. Many sources did exist, however, and 'might throw great light on the history of Portsmouth were they properly examined and discussed'. He hoped that the journal would 'become the medium of a communication so long and so hopelessly desired'.

Alas, it was not to be. Madden, sadly disillusioned by the lack of public support, was sharply critical of the publishers, although viewed in retrospect his disapprobation seems a little unfair. There was certainly some inferior material in the *Register*, but it also contained several interesting ideas including a plea for oral history.[44] The suggestion seems to have been ignored, although the *Hampshire Telegraph* occasionally printed the reminiscences of old inhabitants, which now make interesting reading.[45]

That there was a ready market for local history is shown by the publication by subscription of works by Henry Slight, a local medical practitioner. His *Metrical History of Portsmouth* (1820), a bizarre farrago described by David Brent Price as 'a rhyming bagatelle, on the model of Dibdin' and containing 'much curious and useful information',[46] attracted no less than 198 subscribers. Eight years later, when Henry and his younger brother Julian produced the more readable but still rather unmethodical *Chronicles of Portsmouth*, no less than 272 men, including two royal princes, a duke and two earls (but only one woman, Mrs. Bonamy), were persuaded to buy. Some subscribers took multiple copies, including the High Street booksellers W. Crew (100), W. Harrison (100) and M. Comerford (50), so that total sales of about six hundred copies were guaranteed before publication. A decade later, Dr. Henry Slight published in eight instalments his *History of Portsmouth*, which, although including some new ingredients, was essentially the same medicine in a different bottle. These books, which are a bibliographical nightmare, having been reprinted or bound up under different titles on various occasions during the next few years, were bitterly attacked by Madden, who considered Slight 'so ignorant that his histories are contemptible'.[47]

Although Madden had the scholarship and the will, he never found the time to produce the major work on the locality which was one of his ambitions. But his massive collections have been used by many of Portsmouth's local historians, and he himself was generous with help for any genuine scholar who consulted him. His influence was particuary strong on Archdeacon H. P. Wright's *The Story of the Domus Dei of Portsmouth* (1873), which he described as 'a valuable contribution not only to the local history of Portsmouth but to the general history of the county'.[48]

In 1880 appeared *Annals of Portsmouth* by W. H. Saunders, a High Street chemist who had been born, like George Meredith's mother, at the *Vine* on Portsmouth Point.[49] A man 'of genial presence and kindly disposition',[50] who became curator of the town's first public museum, Saunders made extensive collections, some of which survive.[51] The *Annals*, which is more readable than most of the earlier histories, consists mainly of a series of unrelated narrative chapters chronologically arranged, and includes some material from the author's otherwise unpublished memoirs.[52]

The late 19th century saw the inauguration of the ambitious and imaginative scheme to produce the *Victoria History of the Counties of England*. The five Hampshire volumes appeared comparatively early, in 1900-12, Portsdown Hundred with the Liberties of Portsmouth being included in the third volume (1908). The research and writing of this section were entrusted to three very inexperienced young women, who were engaged at a starting salary of 30s. for a working week of about 43 hours. Gladys Arnold Laughton, the only one of the three to have graduated, was educated in Hampshire and at Somerville College, Oxford, where she obtained a Class IV degree in Modern History in 1905. Soon after coming down she was appointed to the *VCH*, principally to undertake research at the Public Record Office. Ethel M. Hartland did not start work until 12 January 1907, having promised to brush up her Latin first,[53] but Lilian Jane Redstone, the last and probably the most talented of the trio, had been working for the *VCH* since 1904, when only 19 years of age. Her contribution to the Hampshire volumes also included sections on neighbouring Havant and Bosmere Hundred. A very skilful researcher, the daughter of an eminent Suffolk local historian who had been trained at King Alfred's College, Winchester, and granddaughter of a mid-Victorian Master of Alton Workhouse, she took an external degree in 1910 and went on to become a distinguished archivist and author of several lively and original books on East Anglian history.[54]

The Hampshire *VCH* committee included Robert East and Alfred T. Everitt, an amateur genealogist who was secretary of a local brewery. East died in 1901, before the Portsmouth research had begun, but Everitt and Saunders were on hand to give advice and information. Despite the comparative inexperience of the three young researchers, they produced the most scholarly short history of the area that had yet appeared.[55] Although investigation at local level seems to have been confined to printed sources, especially East's flawed texts, they made widespread use for the first time of government record publications as well as manuscripts in the national archives.

54. W. G. Gates (1856-1946).

In 1913 came a useful reference work, *Notes on the Topography of Portsmouth* by Alexander N. Y. Howell, a local solicitor. This was followed in the early 1920s by the publication within two years of three works soundly based on a range of original materials. *The Story of Portsmouth* (1921) by Henry J. Sparks, a lecturer at the Municipal College, was intended primarily for use in local schools. Superior to any existing history of the town, it gave for the first time a cohesive and broadly-based account of the community's development and attempted to answer some basic questions. The same year saw the publication of *Portsmouth Parish Church* by Henry T. Lilley and Alfred T. Everitt. Lilley, the gentle, scholarly, former senior science master at Portsmouth Grammar School,[56] went on to produce the slim but informative *Early Portsmouth Defences* (1923).

But by far the most influential and prolific local historian at the end of the 19th century and during the first half of the 20th was the journalist William George Gates. Born in 1856 and soon orphaned, he was admitted to the Royal Seamen and Marines Orphan School and Home on 3 December 1862, from which in 1867 he was transferred to the Greenwich Hospital School. Almost inevitably a period in the Royal Navy followed. In 1877 he began his long career in journalism by joining the staff of the newly established *Evening News*. Except for a brief interval as a reporter on the *Hampshire Post*, he remained with the paper for the rest of his working life, being editor 1892-1926, and editor-in-chief and director thereafter.[57]

Gates's first book, *Free Mart Fair – Sketches of Old Portsmouth*, was published to coincide with the revival of the fair in 1897 to celebrate Queen Victoria's Diamond Jubilee. Three years later he produced the monumental work with which his name will always be associated, the *Illustrated History of Portsmouth* to which Sir Walter Besant contributed an introduction. Originally published serially in the *Hampshire Telegraph*, whose centenary it was intended to celebrate, and eventually by popular demand made into a massive single volume of 91 chapters grouped chronologically, it is a tribute more to the author's immense industry than to his talents as a critical historian. Anecdotal rather than analytical, and based almost entirely on printed sources, it is not a particularly well-organised or attractively written book despite Gates's journalistic experience, but it still fulfils a useful purpose as a major work of reference.

With the exception of a book on spiritualism,[58] in which he believed strongly, all Gates's other publications were collections of historical or topographical notes usually arranged alphabetically or chronologically, the same material often being used repeatedly. The most interesting of his later compilations are *Portsmouth and the Great War* (1919) and the *History of Portsmouth: A Naval Chronology* (1931). Of importance for the future was his inauguration of the *Records of the Corporation* series, the first volume of which listed significant events from 1835 until 1927, most of which had been assiduously culled from newspaper files. After the success of this volume the annals continued to be produced, together with various random historical notes, until 1935, when he passed the laborious task to his son and later to other compilers.[59]

Gates died in 1946 while working on *The Portsmouth That Has Passed* (1949) in which, as in all his books, illustrations played an essential part. The city lay in ruins with many of its most famous buildings destroyed or badly damaged, but in libraries and on countless bookshelves his immense output of books and newspaper articles remained as an inspiration to future local historians. His life's achievement, however, was not only in his publications, with all their imperfections and limitations, but in the influence he was able to exert on the community for almost half a century through his editorial control of the *Evening News*. Without his intense devotion to the city and its heritage, Portsmouth at the end of the Second World War would have been a much poorer place.

The investigation of local antiquities which burgeoned in Georgian Portsmouth was only part of a wider interest that was developing in the study of man's relationship with his environment. Although in earlier times there were no doubt residents with sufficient curiosity to collect unusual botanical and geological specimens, and other interesting objects, which they discussed with their friends, it was James Hay, a Portsmouth mason with little formal education, who was the first local amateur investigator of note, and with whom is associated Portsmouth's first museum. An exceptionally gifted man whose professional work included the original memorial to the victims of the *Royal George* disaster and the design of the Beneficial Society Hall *c*.1785,[60] he had a deep interest in ornithology, botany, conchology, geology, and much else. In 1805 he was elected a Fellow of the Linnean Society of London on the recommendation of three founder Fellows, a rare distinction, especially for a self-educated provincial craftsman.[61] In pursuit of his hobbies he amassed a large number of specimens which were arranged 'with great neatness and taste'.[62] Hay's museum was much admired by the young Frederic Madden, who also spoke warmly of him as a person.[63]

Reader,
With solemn thought
Survey this grave
And reflect
On the untimely death
Of thy fellow mortals:
And whilst
As a man, a Briton and a patriot,
Thou readest
The melancholy narrative,
Drop a tear
for thy Country's
Loss.

On the twenty-ninth day of August
1782,
his Majesty's Ship, the ROYAL GEORGE,
being on the heel at Spithead,
overset and sunk;
by which fatal accident
about nine hundred persons
were instantly launched into eternity:
among whom was that brave and experienced officer
Rear Admiral KEMPENFELT.
Nine days after
many bodies of the unfortunate floted,
thirty five of which were interred in one grave
near this monument,
which is erected by the Parish of PORTSEA,
as a gratefull Tribute
to the memory
of that great Commander
and his fellow-sufferers.

'Tis not this stone, regretted Chief, thy name,
Thy worth and merit shall extend to fame:
Brilliant Achievements have thy name imprest
In lasting characters on ALBION's breast.

55. Memorial to the victims of the *Royal George* disaster, 1782, by James Hay.

Unfortunately, after his death in 1821, all his treasures were sold by auction and consequently dispersed.[64]

By good fortune some of Hay's specimens were bought by the Philosophical Society, which had already begun to develop a museum of its own for the benefit of its members. By 1828 it had acquired upwards of nine thousand items, mainly relating to natural history and geology. When its new headquarters was opened in Old Portsmouth in 1831, it contained a large room specifically designed to house the growing number of exhibits. The quality of the objects on display seems to have been very mixed, since in addition to the butterflies and the birds, the fossils and the antlers, they included two bottles of wine recovered from the wreck of the *Royal George* and a piece of Queen Victoria's wedding cake.[65] Although essentially a private museum, members of the general public were allowed to visit it.[66] When the society was forced to dissolve itself in 1860 and its building was sold to the local Freemasons, the contents of both the museum and the library were offered to the town on condition that the provisions of the Libraries Act of 1850 should be implemented. Unfortunately, the Council was unable to enter into such an undertaking and the valuable collections were split up.[67] A golden opportunity had been lost.

The dismemberment of the society's library, which had been developed over a period of 40 years was, in the long run, an especially grievous loss to the community. It contained a broad range of works including rare learned publications, official reports, catalogues, and other volumes which have only become available again to scholars in Portsmouth in recent years through the development of the inter-libraries loan scheme, and cheap photocopies and microfilms. Fortunately, literate townspeople were able to borrow popular works in plenty from the various subscription libraries that flourished, the most notable being the Hampshire Library, founded in 1805. Originally situated in St George's Square, it later moved to 21 Ordnance Row where, by 1859, it had two reading rooms and a stock of twelve thousand volumes, for the use of which the 140 shareholders paid annually £1 3s. 6d., and the 40 ordinary subscribers a guinea.[68] Not far away at 44 St James's Street, Portsea, Mr. Griffin opened a circulating library of some twelve hundred volumes in 1813.[69] Such establishments, especially those in Portsmouth High Street, were popular meeting places of the local literati.[70] The King's Rooms, the Royal Marine Barracks, the Mechanics' Institute, several of the churches, and many other organisations owned small collections of books which could be consulted or from which members might borrow.[71] When rising costs closed the Hampshire Library, the failure of private efforts to reopen it, and municipal indifference, resulted in the entire collection being sold in 1873 to Wolverhampton for the derisory sum of £200.[72]

It was not until the 1880s that the Council was able to adopt the provisions of the Act of 1850[73] which enabled a local authority to impose a modest rate to establish a free public library if the majority of the ratepayers was in favour. Although a few enlightened inhabitants had pointed out during the intervening years that Portsmouth, one of the largest towns in the south of England, lacked a basic amenity which many much smaller places had long enjoyed, there was a reluctance by most ratepayers to give support. Finally, however, the former residence of the local commanding officer of the Royal Artillery was acquired for the purpose. There, on a site close to that now occupied by the Guildhall, a public reading room was opened in April 1883, followed the next year by a modest free lending library with closed access. The initial stock consisted of about three thousand, two hundred volumes, of which twelve hundred had been transferred from the library of the Borough Police. For a town the size of Portsmouth it was a mean enough provision. Despite some critical comments, the complaint by an indignant councillor that '*youths* used the reading room', and doubts whether ladies should be admitted, the library was soon very popular, with some 500 readers a day.[74] Time was to endorse the comment of the editor of the *Hampshire*

Telegraph at its opening: 'We have done a great thing this week, without perhaps being fully conscious of its importance'.[75]

The first librarian, who received £50 a year and lived on the premises, was an ex-sergeant in the Royal Marine Artillery named Tweed D. A. Jewers. Despite his inexperience, Jewers seems to have done his best, and among his borrowers was Dr. Arthur Conan Doyle, who presented the library with copies of two of his early novels.[76] Soon afterwards the old commandant's house was demolished to make way for the new Guildhall, to which in 1891 the library moved.[77] The following year, 'as an experiment', female assistants were engaged.[78] When, in 1908, the Technical Institute was relocated behind the Guildhall, the library was assigned part of the new premises, and there it remained until 1976. From the first the arrangement was fraught with difficulties, and as demands grew the pressure on space became acute. A young librarian who began work there in 1932 recalled the 'small but densely populated forest of dark green bookcases', and days when 'a ghastly effluvium hung like a pall' over the reading rooms, a blend of 'printer's ink, stale tobacco smoke, embrocation, and perspiration, with subtle undertones of urine, garlic and mouldering cheese'.[79]

Branch libraries were opened in rooms built over the existing police stations at Southsea in 1893 and North End in 1897, but at Fratton a spacious purpose-built library was erected in 1906 largely through the munificence of Andrew Carnegie. At Cosham, where in 1923 the first library occupied the mezzanine floor of the local cinema, and at Milton, where a branch was set up in an old chapel in 1925, it was unfortunately a return to the policy of committing the minimum resources to a much needed amenity.[80] Not surprisingly, a Board of Education inquiry into libraries initiated in 1925 found that Portsmouth had one of the worst services in the country compared with towns of similar size.[81] It was a continuing story of inadequate finance, missed opportunities, bad judgement and lack of vision.

Meanwhile another service had been developing. In the early 1890s, when the old High Street Guildhall became redundant, it was decided to convert the upper floor into Portsmouth's first public museum. An acquisitions fund of £200 was allocated out of the Technical Institute grant which, somewhat mysteriously, was known as 'whisky money'. The building in its new role was formally opened by the mayor on 21 January 1895 amidst much public interest. During the first five weeks there were 10,771 visitors, and attendances remained high throughout the year. The exhibits, which were insured in 1895 for £2,000, were drawn from the heterogeneous municipal collection which had accumulated over the centuries, supplemented by temporary loans from the museums at South Kensington, gifts from wellwishers, and a number of items lent by W. H. Saunders, the first curator. By 1901 the Portsmouth town museum was well established with forty-five thousand or more visitors each year.[82]

In 1903 the Council acquired the birthplace of Charles Dickens in Landport. It was opened to the public the following year, but there seems to have been little enough to see except the building itself. During the first two months there were 10,750 visitors and by the end of the year the total had risen to no less than fifteen thousand, three hundred and thirty-five. This, like the town museum, was free and open six days a week.[83]

When W. H. Saunders died in 1913, he was succeeded as curator by Mr. Seall, the custodian of Dickens's birthplace.[84] It is clear that responsibility for the development of these two establishments was still in amateur hands, and that there was no policy except the acceptance of any objects, however bizarre, that enthusiastic donors offered, regardless of their importance or the space available. In the 'large, lofty, well lighted room' in the High Street museum, collections of knobkerries and stags' heads, 'some of the personal and household effects of King Cetewayo', two cigars from Cuba 'as smoked by the women', and a pipe stopper made from Jack the Painter's mummified finger (insured for £5 in 1897),[85]

56. Portsmouth Guildhall (1838-90) in the High Street, *c*.1850. In 1895 it became the town's first public museum, but was destroyed with all its collections during an air raid in 1941.

were to be found alongside rather more significant exhibits such as the Southsea hoard of Roman coins, models made by French prisoners-of-war at Portchester, and manuscripts from the borough archives. At Dickens's house there was still little to see, although the Council was fortunate early on to acquire 81 first editions of the novelist's work for £35.[86] A trickle of other items of Dickensiana followed. The building also housed a small library of braille books which could be borrowed by the local blind.[87]

In 1924 the post of curator was combined with that of chief librarian. It meant yet again that the two museums were starved of professional expertise, since the first joint incumbent, the existing librarian, had had no specialist training and was noted for his obsession with economy.[88] A steady stream of visitors still gazed at the dusty exhibits in the old Guildhall, but evidently there was a growing demand by interested parties that something should be done to modernise the displays. In 1929 expert advice was finally enlisted. Dr. J. J. Simpson, who was paid £150 to re-arrange and re-label the exhibits, was the highly-experienced former curator of Liverpool Museum, and his report, which probably went much further than the Council had intended, became a landmark in the history of the Portsmouth museum service. He advocated a ruthless weeding out of the huge stock of unregarded, decaying exhibits that had been indiscriminately collected over the years, followed by a major reorganisation. The most valuable items should be divided into three sections: local archaeology and marine, natural history, and ethnology. The High Street museum should be devoted to the first and the other two moved to a separate building.[89]

It was fortunate that the previous year the Council had bought Cumberland House, near Southsea front, for £5,200,[90] and Simpson, no doubt prompted by some local enthusiasts, boldly suggested that it was the ideal building to accommodate the revamped natural history and ethnology collections. 'It is seldom that an old building can be converted into a museum, but Cumberland House is admirable', he explained, and later went on to suggest that an art gallery might be incorporated, too.[91] The Simpson Report was accepted without demur, and the old town museum was re-opened in September 1929. 'Cleared, cleaned, arranged, the new museum is no longer a reproach to the City, but a credit', the *Evening News* commented. With a natural history room on the ground floor and an art gallery upstairs, Cumberland House was ready for the public in February 1931,[92] and provided Portsmouth with its third building devoted to the study of the city's heritage and environment.

On all sides it was recognised that for art lovers Cumberland House was still inadequate. It was 'only a substitute', wrote the editor of the *Evening News*. 'The real art gallery is yet to come'.[93] A small step forward was made in 1932 when Miss A. E. Bashford offered the Council £2,500 in order to build a small extension to the town museum in memory of her parents. With this gift the Bashford Picture Gallery came into being and was opened in 1933, the nucleus of the collection being a gift of six Bashford family portraits. Upstairs the local and marine history exhibits were again reorganised.[94]

The result was a far more cheerful, attractive building with much of interest to see. Even so, Portsmouth still lagged far behind other places of similar size in its expenditure on museums. An article in *The Times* (22 September 1933) revealed that whereas Leicester spent 8d. per head of population each year, Nottingham 7.1d., Plymouth 4.8d., and Salford 3.8d., Portsmouth spent only $\frac{1}{2}$d. It had one qualified full-time member of staff: Leicester had six and Nottingham five.

Portsmouth emerged from the Second World War with its principal museum and art gallery in ruins, but Cumberland House, Dickens's birthplace and the Central Library remained intact. Although the Guildhall had been destroyed during the great air raid of 10 January 1941, the archives and plate stored in the muniment room under the tower miraculously escaped damage.

In 1953 a new-found pride in the locality expressed itself in the formation of the Portsmouth Museums Society 'to encourage research into the local history and archaeology of the district, to arouse public interest in matters affecting records, and to encourage the Local Authority to appoint an archivist'. These aims were pursued with great vigour, and in 1956 an exhibition of documents illustrating the city's history was an overwhelming success, breaking all records at Cumberland House Museum, where it was held.[95] Public consciousness of Portsmouth's rich archival inheritance culminated in the setting up of the City Records Office in the rebuilt Guildhall in 1960 with, for the first time, a full-time professional archivist.[96] In 1967 it became the Diocesan Records Office and in 1976 was moved to the former forces' canteen in Museum Road. At long last, after many vicissitudes, the raw materials of Portsmouth's history were safely housed and made available to researchers in a congenial environment.

Library facilities were slow to improve. Portsmouth, notorious for its meagre service, had a Central Library which had long been considered grossly inadequate. Yet it was not until 1976, when the Guildhall Square and its precincts had been rebuilt, that Portmuthians were at long last provided with a building worthy of the city. The modern Central Library, like a great galleon at anchor in the Square, its decks awash with orange carpet, has its own small concert hall and lecture rooms, greatly-improved facilities for readers wishing to consult the naval and local history collections (a far cry from the 68 books and 27 pamphlets available to local historians in 1895), and a Dickens Room to accommodate the valuable first editions and critical works formerly kept in the novelist's birthplace.

In the late 1930s the lack of an adequate museum and art gallery with ancillary services was widely acknowledged, and a wartime article in *The Times Educational Supplement* commented on the surprise expressed by Portsmouth teachers and pupils evacuated to Salisbury when they discovered the much superior facilities available in that city.[97] Cumberland House, re-opened in 1952, was a wretched substitute for a proper building to display the salvaged collections, although the creation of a schools museums service in 1961 was a move in the right direction. Real progress came in 1967 with the administrative separation of the museums and libraries, and the appointment of the first city curator.[98] Southsea Castle, Point Battery and the Round Tower, acquired from the army c. 1960, were carefully restored, although for a time it seemed that commercial rather than historical interests would determine their future.[99] During the next quarter-century the museum service expanded to include Eastney Pumping Station, Fort Widley, the purpose built D-Day Museum, and a new City Museum and Art Gallery in the former Clarence Barracks. In addition, Portsmouth has the important national museums of the Royal Navy and the Royal Marines, as well as three of the most famous ships in the world: H.M.S. *Victory*, H.M.S. *Warrior*, and the *Mary Rose* (with its own exhibition hall). Portsmouth has admirably fulfilled its ambition to be called 'the flagship of Maritime England'. It is now one of the finest showcases in the country for Britain's naval and military heritage.

Little original research on the history of the city was published between 1930 and 1960. The Portsmouth *Evening News*, however, carrying on the tradition developed by W. G. Gates, printed popular pieces which helped to keep alive an interest in local history among the general public. To Portsmouth and Sunderland Newspapers, Ltd., and its predecessors, which sponsored many of the most important works produced during the Age of Gates, the people of the city owe an immense debt.

The other important patron is the corporation itself, which, from the time of Murrell and East, has shown interest in and helped to finance the printing of local records. In 1966 the city embarked on a remarkable publishing programme which few places can rival. *The Portsmouth Papers*, launched the following year under the editorship of Professor A. Temple Patterson,[100] were intended to provide those interested in the history of the locality with moderately-priced, readable and newly-researched monographs, and have met with great success. In 1971, the *Portsmouth Record Series* was founded, with Professor P. D. A. Harvey as General Editor, to make more easily available some of the principal sources of the city's history, both by printing the edited texts of particularly significant records and, more usually, by means of calendars, bibliographies and other appropriate means. Finally, the publication in 1983 of *Records of the Corporation 1966-74* (edited by R. Windle) continued the project initiated by W. G. Gates. These three series, together with the *Portsmouth Archives Review* produced by the City Records Office, provide the people of modern Portsmouth and scholars at large with a remarkable range of reading matter about the development of the city over the centuries.

During the last few years the widespread interest in Portsmouth's historical and architectural heritage has also been reflected in a multitude of societies, exhibitions, conferences and courses devoted to the subject. Concern for Portsmouth's past is indisputably much alive in Portsmouth present. The narrow path which was trodden by the antiquaries who first set out to investigate the history of their community has broadened during the last two hundred years into an increasingly busy highway.

The ancient coffer in which the charters were formerly kept.

Chapter Eleven

A Changing City

Architecturally, the pre-war city struck many visitors and temporary inhabitants as un-lovely. By 1939 tightly-packed houses covered most of Portsea Island. Older areas contain-ing some attractive streets were soot-begrimed and overcrowded, with metropolitan population densities. Landport's Guildhall (closely modelled on Bolton's Town Hall) and commercial buildings loomed heavily over traffic-laden streets, more typical of the indus-trial north than of other Hampshire towns. The promenades and piers of tidy Southsea provided unsophisticated amusements beside a cold sea and stony beach. The dockyard and fortifications, repeatedly praised by earlier visitors, were either less accessible than before or demolished. Permanent residents seemed strangely complacent among their ugly sur-roundings, surprising those from more fortunate places where even simple buildings were shaped with attention to detail and variety, and where age brought mellow beauty instead of grimy squalor. To thousands of servicemen, however, Pompey was home, where wives and families awaited their return and pubs and prostitutes provided rowdy relief from monotony. The naval tradition was strong, the presence of Nelson's flagship a perpetual reminder of heroism and victory. Battleships slipped in and out of harbour between Blockhouse and Point, while waving friends and relatives gathered along the walls to greet them back or speed them on their way. Naval reviews on the wide stage of Spithead, with royal and foreign visitors and accompanying fireworks and festivities, were lively and impressive. In the nationalistic half-century before 1939 the marching bands of marines and garrison regiments united civilians and servicemen in patriotic pride.

All this changed with the Second World War. Never since the 14th century had Ports-mouth been so laid waste: in 1940-4, 67 air raids showered thousands of bombs on the city, most of the casualties and damage occurring in three attacks in August 1940 and January and March 1941. In the first, over five hundred people died and Southsea's shops were badly hit. A seven-hour raid on 10 January 1941 destroyed many local landmarks, including six churches, the Royal Sailors' Rest, Salvation Army Citadel, Clarence Pier and Hippo-drome. The shopping centres in Palmerston, King's and Commercial Roads fell into ruins. The Guildhall was gutted, leaving only the shell, molten metal streaming down the steps as the main doors melted, and the 200-foot tower blazing like a torch all the following day. Three successive raids on 9-11 March 1941 caused widespread damage, Queen Street and Lake Road suffering badly. To watchers on Portsdown Hill it seemed as though most of the southern part of the city was alight. Raids continued over the next three months, and after two years of warfare most of the older commercial and residential centres had been destroyed.[1]

Recovery was slow. Civic and private offices, magistrates' courts and shops moved into unsuitable accommodation, some staying there for over thirty years. The homeless found refuge with relatives, or moved elsewhere. Villages of prefabricated houses mushroomed around the fringes of the city, many still occupied in the 1960s. As the rubble was cleared people learned new routes across the bomb sites, skirting the gaping cellars where buddleia flourished in succeeding summers. Such widespread destruction gave the planners unpre-cedented opportunities and this, combined with tight governmental building controls and shortage of materials, led to strange delays and anomalies in rebuilding.

57. Bomb damage in Stanley Street, Southsea.

58. Cleared bomb-site around Hyde Park Road.

Some seven thousand homes were destroyed in the raids. Recognising housing as a major post-war priority the council in 1943-4 bought 1,670 acres on the mainland, and nearly half the 22,000 local authority houses built in 1945-74 were in this overspill development at Leigh Park, in attractive countryside outside the city boundary. As critics predicted, many young couples were separated from their families and travelled miles to work and recreation.[2] Moreover, an ageing population remained as a higher proportion of the decreasing numbers in the city, total population falling in 1951-71 from 233,545 to 196,950, while over-60s increased from 38,497 to 43,310.[3] Other municipal housing developments at Wecock Farm and Crookhorn increased the out-of-city population, including some dispossessed by Buckland's redevelopment. Attempts were made to reduce the proportion of Portsmouth's elderly inhabitants by including more one and two-bed units in these areas. In 1966 the South Hampshire Study observed that:

> The record of building operations during the century and a half of rapid urban growth which followed the industrial revolution is not one in which we can take much pride. A great deal of damage has been done, without very much to show by way of recompense in the production of really livable, efficient and beautiful towns.[4]

Conscious of the city's ageing housing stock, the council undertook a vigorous programme of slum clearance and rebuilding, demolishing more houses than were destroyed by bombing. Portsea was transformed from rows of terraces to blocks of flats surrounded by bleak open spaces. Faith in vertical rather than horizontal high-density, fashionable among architects and encouraged by the 1958 Housing Subsidies Act, weakened during the 1960s as evidence of the social and environmental problems linked with high-rise buildings mounted. Nevertheless, parts of Somerstown and Landport were similarly developed. Structural flaws in such system-built flats were tragically revealed by the Ronan Point disaster, and in Portsmouth eight blocks comprising 995 dwellings were expensively remodelled and many people re-housed. The opportunities presented by post-war rebuilding programmes were seldom accompanied by good quality design or construction, and many local authorities soon faced mounting repair bills for unsatisfactory and rapidly decaying buildings. Portsmouth's most notorious case was Portsdown Park, a much publicised development on a choice and conspicuous site on Portsdown Hill. The winning design in a 1963 national competition provided 523 dwellings housing about eighteen hundred people, and construction began in 1968. Early differences with the contractor were soon followed by evidence of persistent water penetration, and despite remedial work, an out-of-court financial settlement and new contractors, the problem persisted. In 1987 the vandalised estate was sold for demolition and replaced by expensive private houses.[5] Similar scandals were common in post-war Britain, but were balanced in Portsmouth by the transformation and improvement of many dirty, overcrowded areas.

As the worst districts were cleared, and resistance by owner-occupiers to destruction of their homes mounted, demolition gave way to improvement, encouraged by the Housing Acts of 1964, 1969 and 1974. It had become clear that properly maintained Victorian and Edwardian terraces, although outwardly monotonous, were more solid and spacious than their post-war replacements. The human scale and familiar social contacts within these streets far outweighed the inconvenience of old-fashioned plumbing in houses stigmatised by planners as substandard. With grant aid, many smaller houses were repaired and improved by local builders, and although the treatment of their façades offended purists, the streets acquired a new gaiety and variety. Similar assistance in conservation areas, including Old Portsmouth and Owen's Southsea, helped owners to keep many listed houses in better condition. Post-war private house-building was severely limited by governmental control, and not until the 1950s did rebuilding allow young married couples and returned

servicemen's families to recolonise Old Portsmouth. Later private housing included development along Langstone Harbour's shores, and on liberated Ministry of Defence land at
Pembroke and Gatcombe Parks and Eastney seafront. In the 1980s redevelopment of the
Old Portsmouth power station site and Anchorage Park on part of the former airport has
crowded gabled houses in the latest redbrick architectural fashion into a maze of tightly-
twisting roads, and redevelopment has also begun in Portsea. High housing densities were
deliberately retained as the city's usually resident population (193,483 in 1971; 175,375 in
1981) dropped still further below the 200,000 envisaged in the South Hampshire Structure
Plan.[6]

Regional planning, 1964-72, tended to be triggered by unreliable forecasts, to generate
wordy reports and to be overtaken by events. Government assumptions that development
around London could be restricted by control of industrial location were invalidated by
the post-1955 birth rate upsurge, and by major expansion in office and non-manufacturing
employment. A search began for development zones to form counter-magnets to London,
and the 1964 South-East Study identified South Hampshire as capable of population increase
of 300,000 by 1981 and 100,000 thereafter.[7] A feasibility report, the 1966 South Hampshire
Study, advised that the Southampton-Portsmouth area might rapidly expand its 1961
population (864,274) to 1,700,000 by controlled development of the coastal corridor (an
area about twenty-five by twelve miles), to become 'one of the great dynamic city-regions
of the latter part of this century'. The preferred structure for this massive expansion,
equivalent to 10 new towns, was a geometric 'directional grid', engulfing small neighbouring
towns like Titchfield, Wickham and Botley. The western end would house the dominant
regional centre, the eastern end providing overspill for Portsmouth, which had one of the
highest population densities outside London. Inferior to Southampton in communications,
business potential and housing, Portsmouth was 'a city with a question mark over it'.[8] The
study was soon shelved, but local councils accepted that south Hampshire should be
comprehensively replanned. By 1970 the Strategic Plan for the South-East saw south
Hampshire as the largest regional growth area, expanding to one million by 1981 and
1,210,100 by 1991, mainly by natural increase: by this time no planned intake of population
was expected. Preliminary studies suggested four choices for development, all involving
impossibly high transport expenditure.[9]

The 1972 Draft Structure Plan, coming closer to reality, saw continued dominance by
Portsmouth and Southampton and conservation of neighbouring agricultural areas. New
urban growth would be concentrated in six settlements, mostly around Southampton.
Offices, industrial estates and shops would multiply in central and outlying areas. A rapid
transit system (not achieved but revived for discussion in 1989) would ease journeys to work.
Better recreational facilities would include swimming pools, sports halls and golf courses,
with particular emphasis on sailing. Portsmouth's problems were accurately identified.
Concentration of jobs in central Portsmouth and long journeys to work created heavy
traffic congestion around ferry terminals and along the two access roads. Persistent male
unemployment was difficult to relieve, new industrial development being hampered by
land shortage. About twenty thousand dwellings were substandard; many schools were
small and old; shopping centres suffered from 'physical and economic obsolescence'. Hotels
to accommodate conferences were needed, as were more sports facilities. Road improvement
was vital, becoming more urgent as employment opportunities increased.[10]

It was primarily due to the energetic efforts of some far-sighted city councillors that most
of these shortcomings were remedied and that employment diversified as never before to
counterbalance peacetime dockyard contraction.[11] In 1945 the dockyard, with a workforce
of 16,820, was the city's principal employer. Post-war cut-back was inevitable, and around
two thousand jobs went by 1948, but refitting and shipbuilding continued and 20 years

later the yard's total workforce was still over twelve thousand. From 1981, however, the government drastically reduced the navy, ended refitting at Portsmouth and cut the dockyard's manpower by nearly two-thirds.[12] This severe blow to the local economy, and perhaps more to local pride, did not fall until 36 years after the war ended, giving ample time, even with planning constraints, for the development of alternative employment. In 1945 this long respite could not be foreseen and Portsmouth's first light industrial estate at Fratton (1948) was followed by others, sited on scattered patches of available land at Hilsea, Burfields, Farlington, Drayton Railway Triangle and the former airport (closed in 1973). Manufacturing employment included plastics and pharmaceutical products, but became increasingly related to high-technology engineering and electronics. Many of these enterprises are sophisticated versions of activities long familiar to the area, like Nautech, making electronic autopilots for yachts, and Marconi, producing equipment for electronic warfare, missile guidance and military and satellite communications. Vosper-Thorneycroft and John Brown, once shipbuilders, diversified to meet changed demands. Many city-dwellers, no longer limited to reaching the dockyard by bicycle or bus, work in the numerous defence-related establishments beween Portsmouth and Southampton, along Hampshire's 'Silicon Valley'. Considerable successes were achieved in the 1970s when IBM established its U.K. headquarters on a polder at North Harbour, and the head office of Zurich Insurance moved into an elegant glass tower near Victoria

59. The Zurich Building from Victoria Park, 1977.

Park. Other major firms were attracted also, and the rebuilt Guildhall area provided a high concentration of city centre office space beside the railway station.[13] Expansion of higher education in the 1960s rapidly increased staff and student members at the city's four colleges, introducing considerable purchasing power and demand for out-of-season lodgings. Portsmouth Polytechnic (designated in 1969) became another large employer with over 1,500 academic, administrative, clerical, technical and manual staff in 1988-9. With a total student population of approximately seven thousand three hundred it expanded to occupy a miscellany of purpose-built and acquired accommodation scattered from Portsea to Milton, with a nucleus near the Guildhall.[14] Seasonal tides of students have replaced pre-war crowds of sailors in the city streets.

As naval activity contracted, the Admiralty at last relaxed its grip, to facilitate commercial use of the harbour. The physical limits of the Camber remained obstinately medieval, and diversification here has transformed former coaling wharves into an Isle of Wight car-ferry terminus, fish markets and a marina with associated housing. The small commercial docks were enlarged by the Albert Johnson Quay (1968) on reclaimed mudlands at Flathouse, subsequently extended and handling container freight traffic and Mediterranean trade.[15] The outstanding achievement in shipping, however, has been the transfer to Portsmouth of Southampton's cross-Channel ferry service, cutting an hour off the journey and escaping Southampton's strike-infested docks. The city council responded rapidly to enquiries in

60. The Continental Ferry Port, 1985.

61. Guildhall Square and Civic Offices, 1985.

1974 from St Malo and various shipping operators regarding roll on/roll off facilities for traffic with French ports. This speculative commercial venture was deliberately restricted to low-cost initial development north of Flathouse on a site capable of easy expansion. Opened in 1976, extended in 1978 and 1983-4, it became the largest south-coast ferry port after Dover, handling over two million passengers and half a million vehicles in 1987.[16]

The M275 road link curves out across reclaimed mudlands and joins Portsmouth to the M27 and A3(M), enabling ferry and city traffic to disperse rapidly into the hinterland. On the western side of Portsea Island, road improvements and rebuilding have obliterated most of the historic settlement pattern, since the new roads reflect current demands. Rush-hour queues inevitably persist since Portsmouth's new breed of salaried workers, more numerous than ever before, often prefer to live elsewhere, and the voluminous inward journey-to-work traffic puts heavy strain on car-parks. The decision to concentrate Portsmouth's main shopping area around the pedestrianised Commercial Road, emphasised by the Cascades development, while logical in many ways, exacerbated the parking problem and damaged Southsea's and Fratton's trade. 'Consolidation' in these areas has generally meant decline in quantity and quality, with the notable exception of Southsea's Waitrose foodstore. The chronic low-wage economy of the past has produced an abiding impression of a city less prosperous and discerning than its neighbours. Some specialist shops, barometers of affluent shopping, have avoided Portsmouth, which suffers also from restricted selection in department stores. The appearance in outer suburbia of hypermarkets and superstores with ample ground-level parking caused some anxiety, particularly since Cosham's shopping and office centre failed to materialise. The mass market is amply catered for, however, and restoration of pre-war standards might capture other customers who habitually go elsewhere for quality and choice.

In the 1970s and 1980s, with much urgent and necessary work completed, Portsmouth developed its leisure and tourist attractions, with four new hotels and various sheltered seaside exhibitions and entertainments clustered around Southsea Castle. In the dockyard the *Mary Rose*, *Victory* and *Warrior* form the nucleus of a maritime heritage centre, and restoration of the surviving fortifications continues. Sports centres, the Crookhorn golf course (1971) and plans to redevelop Portsmouth Football Club's ground provide for more vigorous tastes. Sailing, a traditional Solent occupation, has increased dramatically, with new urban marinas at Eastney, the Camber and Port Solent, where tightly-packed boats resemble car or caravan parks. These and other intrusive water sports, together with waste disposal and reclamation, threaten to encroach on the harbours as the city encroached on the fields.[18] Conservation rather than destruction of buildings and ships is a current preoccupation on Portsea Island. The same policy should be applied to the harbours before further irreversible damage is done. Although homelessness and unemployment persist, it is a measure of the success of Portsmouth's recovery from wartime destruction and the decline of its dominant industry that resources can now be expended on leisure and conservation. To those returning after long absence, the city appears cleaner and more attractive, prosperous and efficient. The rebuilt civic centre symbolises this transformation: grimy, crowded buildings have given way to a stage for civic pageantry. The elegant dark glass of the new offices reflects the familiar Guildhall, reconstructed within its original shell, uniting progress and tradition at the heart of the city.

The ancient seal of
Portsmouth.

Abbreviations

Add. MS. – Additional Manuscript, British Library
ATP – Patterson, A. Temple, *Portsmouth: A History* (1976)
BL – British Library
Bod. L. – Bodleian Library
CSPD – Calendar of State Papers, Domestic Series
East – East, R. (ed.), *Extracts from Records in the possession of the Municipal Corporation of the Borough of Portsmouth and from Other Documents relating thereto* (1891)
EcHR – Economic History Review
EN – Portsmouth *Evening News* (*The News* after 1969)
Gates – Gates, W. G., *Illustrated History of Portsmouth* (1900)
HMC – Historical Manuscripts Commission
Howell – Howell, A. N. Y., *Notes on the Topography of Portsmouth* (1913)
HRO – Hampshire Record Office, Winchester
HS – Webb, J., Yates, N., and Peacock, S. (eds.), *Hampshire Studies* (1981)
HT – *Hampshire Telegraph*
JM – Journals of Sir Frederic Madden, Bodleian Library
LP – *Letters and Papers of the Reign of King Henry VIII*
MM – *The Mariner's Mirror*
PAR – *Portsmouth Archives Review*
PCL – Portsmouth Central Library
PCRO – Portsmouth City Records Office
PP – *The Portsmouth Papers* published by Portsmouth City Council
PRC (1835-1927) – Gates, W. G. (ed.), *City of Portsmouth Records of the Corporation, 1835-1927* (1928)
PRC (1928-30) – Gates, W. G. (ed.), *City of Portsmouth Records of the Corporation, 1928-30* (1931)
PRO – Public Record Office
PRS – Portsmouth Record Series, published by the City of Portsmouth
PTCM – Portsmouth Town Council Minutes
Slight – Slight, H. and J., *Chronicles of Portsmouth* (1828)
VCH Hants – Victoria County History of Hampshire and the Isle of Wight, 5 vols. (1900-12)
White (1859) – White, W., *History, Gazetteer, and Directory of Hampshire and the Isle of Wight* (1859)
White (1878) – White, W., *History, Gazetteer, and Directory of the County of Hampshire including the Isle of Wight* (1878)
Wright – Wright, H. P., *The Story of the Domus Dei of Portsmouth* (1873)

Notes

Chapter One – Marsh and Water

1. Hawkes, Jacquetta, *A Land* (1959), p. 21.
2. *Ibid.*, p. 121.
3. Chatwin, C. P., *The Hampshire Basin and Adjoining Areas* (1960), pp. 86-9, 96-7; Lewis, M., *Spithead. An Informal History* (1972), pp. 17-23; *Atlas of Portsmouth*, Geography Department, Portsmouth Polytechnic, 2.2, 2.3; Admiralty Chart No. 2,631.
4. Hoad, M. J., *Portsmouth – As others have seen it, 1540-1790, PP*, 15 (1972), p. 5.
5. Hoad, M. J., *Portsmouth – As others have seen it, 1790-1900, PP*, 20 (1973), p. 6.

6. Coles, K. Adlard, *Creeks and Harbours of the Solent* (1981), pp. 87, 94, 96.

7. Cunliffe, B., *Studies in Local History: Portchester, PP*, 1 (1967), pp. 11-13.

8. *VCH Hants*, vol. 5 (1912), pp. 360-8.

9. Loomie, Albert J., 'An armada pilot's survey of the English coastline, October 1597', *MM*, vol. 49 (1963), pp. 288, 298.

10. Lockyer, R., *Buckingham* (1981), pp. 366-7, 373-5, 378, 452-4.

11. PRO, SP16/278/38.

12. *CSPD 1637-8*, p. 81.

13. PRO, SP16/278/38.

14. *CSPD 1661-2*, p. 556, *1663-4*, pp. 148, 171.

15. *CSPD 1673-4*, pp. 578, 580.

16. BL, King's MS. 44, ff. 3, 8-9.

17. Hoad, *PP*, 15, pp. 20-1.

18. BL, Maps, K.Top. XIV 86a.

19. Portsmouth City Museum and Art Gallery, 'Two Views in Portsmouth Harbour, looking North and South', *c.*1790, Oil painting attributed to Capt. W. Elliott, R.N.

20. Southsea Castle Museum, oil painting of prison hulks in the harbour, attributed to Louis Garneray, 1810.

21. *VCH Hants*, vol. 3, p. 185.

22. BL, Cotton MS. Aug. I.ii, 15, 81, 117.

23. BL, Add. MS. 16,371C.

24. PCRO, PUH/2/63 vi.

25. PCRO, CCR 1, p. 53.

26. *Ibid.*, pp. 54-5.

27. PCRO, PUH/4/69.

28. 2 & 3 Vic. c. lxxii; PCRO, PUH/4/69; CCR 1, pp. 110-15, 124-6, 154-5, 164-5.

29. PCRO, PUH/4/70, 6/77; CCR 1 pp. 133-48, 154-5; Field, J. L., 'Bourgeois Portsmouth, 1815-1875', University of Warwick Ph.D. thesis (1979).

30. PCRO, PUH/5/74.

31. *See*, for example, PCRO PUH/2/64, 3/65, 6/77; CF 13/1-3.

32. PCRO, PUH/6/76-7.

33. Admiralty Charts nos. 2,045, 2,050, 3,418; PCRO, DC/PM7/8; DC/PM7/19; Adlard Coles, *op. cit.*, pp. 107-17.

34. BL, Maps, K.Top. XIV 57.

35. Thomas, F. G. S., *The King Holds Hayling* (1961), pp. 124-5.

36. PCRO, 320 A/7.

37. PCRO, 906 A.

38. *VCH Hants*, vol. 1, p. 450 *et seq.*

39. Camden, W., *Britannia* (1806 edn.), pp. 170-1.

40. BL, Cotton MS. Titus B v, f. 348.

41. PCRO, GMN/78.

42. PCRO, 387 A/15/2.

43. PCRO, CCR 1836-42, pp. 30-1.

44. PCRO, 387 A/13/1.

45. *Daily Mail*, 10 November, 16, 19 December 1902; Rudkin, D. J., *The Emsworth Oyster Fleet, Industry and Shipping* (1975), p. 32.

46. *PRC* (1928-30), pp. v-vi.

47. PCRO, 1121 A; Winchester College Muniments 15,296-9; White (1859), p. 249; Howell, p. 10.

48. PCRO, P3.

49. PCRO, 320 A/7.

50. PCRO, C/C 19.

51. PCRO, 59/A/1; CF 4/2; L2/8/1, 4; Howell, pp. 29, 41.

52. BL, Cotton MS. Augustus I.ii.15, 117; Halton Thompson, D., *History of Portsmouth and Gosport Water Supply* (1957), p. 3.

53. *Ibid.*, p. 4; BL, Add. MS. 16,371C; East, p. 67; Howell, pp. 48, 53.

54. Hoad, *PP*, 15 (1972), p. 21.
55. Halton Thompson, *op. cit.*, pp. 13-20; Hallett, M., *Portsmouth's Water Supply, 1800-1860*, *PP*, 12 (1971), pp. 5, 13, 15.
56. White (1878), pp. 386-7; Halton Thompson, *op. cit.*, pp. 12, 18, 20, 24, 27-8; Hallett, *op. cit.*, p. 13.
57. Rawlinson, Robert, *Report to the General Board of Health on the Sewage, Drainage and Water Supply of Portsmouth* (1850), p. 94.
58. 20-21 Vic., c. xiv; Halton Thompson, *op cit.*, pp. 38-9, 42-4, 65.
59. BL, Add. MS. 16,371A; PCRO, 36 A/3.
60. *CSPD 1663-4*, p. 329; *CSPD 1664-5*, pp. 72-3.
61. PCRO, GMN/406; DD 417; I 189; *HT* 12 April 1830.
62. *PRC* (1835-1927), pp. 243-4; PCRO, GMN/417; CLC/2/8; CCM 10/3.
63. PCRO, CCM 28; I/126; *PRC* (1835-1927), p. 281.
64. PCRO, 36 A/3; P 116.
65. PCRO, GMN/240; 25 Geo. III, c. 24.
66. *HT*, 7 July 1823.
67. PCRO, GMN/240, pp. 23-4; Howell, p. 50.
68. Charpentier, *The New Portsmouth Guide* (1835), p. 56.
69. *HT*, 17 September 1859; *PRC* (1835-1927), pp. 7, 36, 90, 293; (1928-30), pp. 15-17, 90-1.
70. *PRC* (1835-1927), p. 7; (1928-30), pp. 96-7.
71. PCRO, p. 171; *PRC* (1835-1927), pp. 134, 142; (1931-3), pp. 34, 109.
72. BL, Cotton MS. Augustus I.ii.15; East, p. 484; Slight, Henry, *History of Portsmouth* (1838), part 1, pp. 21-2; *PRC* (1835-1927), p. 132.
73. Ripley, B., *Horsea Island and the Royal Navy*, *PP*, 36 (1982).
74. BL, Add. MS. 16,371A; BL, Maps, K. Top. XIV 18; PCRO, DC/PM2/6B; 36 A/3.
75. PRO, PCC 31 Bennett.
76. Toulmin Smith, L. (ed.), *The Itinerary of John Leland in or about the years 1535-1543* (1907), vol. 1, p. 284.

Chapter Two – Country and Town

1. Hoad, M., 'The Origins of Portsmouth', in *HS*, pp. 7, 16-21.
2. Kitson, Sir Henry, 'The Early History of Portsmouth Dockyard, 1496-1800', *MM*, vol. 33 (1947), pp. 256-8; and *see* Chapter Three.
3. Charpentier & Co., *Illustrated Guide to Portsmouth and Southsea* (1896).
4. Staffs. County Record Office, D(W). 1778/V/1407; and *see* Plate 3: Hodson, D., *Maps of Portsmouth before 1801* (1978), is an excellent catalogue.
5. PCRO, 11A/20/67, 91; East, pp. 720-2.
6. Rawlinson, R., *Report to the General Board of Health* . . . (1850), p. 8. Acreages vary as land was reclaimed and according to whether tidal water and foreshore are included.
7. *PRC* (1931-5), pp. 1-2, 89; PCRO, p. 146; and *see* Plate 4.
8. Hoad, *loc. cit.*, pp. 1-6; Moody, H., *Hampshire in 1086* . . . (1862), and *VCH Hants*, vol. 1 (1900) give the Domesday Book text for the county.
9. Garmonsway, G. N. (ed.), *The Anglo-Saxon Chronicle*, Everyman edn. (1962), p. 15.
10. Chapman, John, *The Common Lands of Portsea Island*, *PP*, 29, pp. 1-10.
11. PRCO, CF 4/1; East, pp. 493-502.
12. PCRO, 1,121 A.
13. PCRO, CLF 9/19; PRO, C205/18.
14. HRO, 44M73/E/P 13, 14, 29; Photocopy 40.
15. Vancouver, C., *General View of the Agriculture of Hampshire* . . . (1813), pp. 86, 146.
16. PCRO, 78A/1/1-2; HRO, 4M53/102/2.
17. PCRO, DC/PM/1/5; CLC 4/13.
18. PCRO, GMN/12; *VCH Hants*, vol. 3, pp. 192-4.
19. Hoad, *loc. cit.*; PCRO, GMN/17.
20. BL, Add. MS. 6,027, f. 106 v.
21. PCRO, GMN/12.
22. PCRO, GMN/12, 16, 38. Although East, p. 666, and Howell, p. 59, print these bounds, both men

appear to imply that they relate to Frodington Heath. Howell, p. 65, identifies 'Schildewell' as North End, but thought that Goldsted was the morass on Southsea Common, p. 39.

23. *VCH Hants*, vol. 3, 165-70.
24. PCRO, AP/10.
25. PCRO, 3A/6/2; CHU 15/4/1, 2; Slight, H., *History of Portsmouth* (1838), part 5, p. 12.
26. Hoad, *loc. cit.*, pp. 18-19.
27. *Ibid.*, pp. 21, 23; East, pp. 1-5, 23-4, 341, 572-7, 624-6, 632-4.
28. *VCH Hants*, vol. 3, pp. 173-87.
29. Hockey, S. F., *Quarr Abbey and its Lands, 1132-1631* (1970), pp. 93-4; Fox, Russell, and Barton, K. J., 'Excavations at Oyster Street, Portsmouth, Hampshire, 1968-71', *Post-Medieval Archaeology*, 20 (1986), pp. 31-255.
30. East, pp. 493-502.
31. Biddle, M., and Summerson, J., in Colvin, H. M. (ed.), *History of the King's Works, vol. 4, 1485-1660* (Part 2) (1982), pp. 492-5.
32. BL, Cotton MS. Augustus I.i.81; Harvey, P. D. A., 'The Portsmouth map of 1545 and the introduction of scale maps into England', *HS*, pp. 33, 43, 45.
33. Toulmin Smith, Lucy (ed.), *The Itinerary of John Leland in or about the years 1535-1543* (1907), vol. 1, pp. 282-4.
34. Hoad, M., *Portsmouth – As others have seen it, 1540-1790*, *PP*, 15, p. 5.
35. BL, Cotton MS. Augustus I.ii.117; Add. MS. 5,752, f. 51; *CSPD* 1547-80, p. 526; East, pp. 673-7; Colvin, *op. cit.*, p. 495.
36. PRO, SP12/38, ff. 82v, 83; PCRO, CF 17/1; East, pp. 133-4, 312-4, 626.
37. BL, Harleian MS. 595, ff. 231, 233, 237-40.
38. Figures kindly supplied by Barry Stapleton, from PRO, E179/176/565.
39. Christie, Peter, 'An analysis of the 1674 Hearth Tax Return for Portsmouth', in Mottershead, D. N., and Riley, R. C. (eds.), *Portsmouth Geographical Essays*, 2 (1976), pp. 22-50.
40. Stapleton, Barry, 'The Admiralty Connection – Port Development and Demographic Change in Portsmouth, 1650-1850', Graph 2. (I am grateful to Barry Stapleton for allowing me to see this paper.)
41. Defoe, Daniel, *A Tour Through England and Wales*, Everyman edn. (n.d.), p. 138.
42. Stapleton, Barry, 'The Population of the Portsmouth Region', in Stapleton, B., and Thomas, J. H. (eds.), *The Portsmouth Region* (1989), p. 91.
43. PCRO, CF 17/1, pp. 9-11, 77, 78, 80, 85, 89, 100.
44. Christie, *loc. cit.*, pp. 23, 26; PCRO, 81A/3/20/1.
45. PCRO, 1,486 A, Sherwood, Cynthia, *The House on the Point*.
46. I am most grateful to Peter Stewart for much of the following information about Point.
47. Gates, pp. 213-4.
48. Mottley, J. C., *History of Portsmouth* (1801), p. 8.
49. PCRO, 81A/3/20/1; East, pp. 730-4.
50. Eley, Philip, *Portsmouth Breweries, 1492-1847*, *PP*, 51 (1988), pp. 10-12, 18.
51. Surry, N. W., and Thomas, J. H. (eds.), *Book of Original Entries 1731-51* (1976), Appendix I, p. 71.
52. East, pp. 228-31, 806; Charpentier's *Stranger's Guide* (1842).
53. PRO, HO107/412, 1658.
54. Charpentier, W. H., *The New Portsmouth Guide* (1839), pp. 27-9.
55. Roscoe, Thomas, *Summer Tour to the Isle of Wight, including Portsmouth ...* (c.1840).
56. 'A Descriptive Account of Portsmouth', from *The Land We Live In* (1847), pp. 212-3.
57. Webb, John, *Sir Frederic Madden and Portsmouth*, *PP*, 47 (1987), p. 20.
58. BL, K.Top. XIV, 43.
59. *CSPD* 1699-1700, pp. 256-7, 362; MacDougall, P., *Royal Dockyards* (1982), p. 87.
60. PCRO, 81A/3/21/1.
61. Particularly in Cramer, James, 'The Origins and Growth of the Town of Portsea to 1816', Portsmouth Polytechnic C.N.A.A. M. Phil. thesis (1985), Chapter 2, *passim*, and especially Figure 18.
62. Emery, J., and Beattie, J., *Correct Copy of the Rate Book, Portsea* (1817).
63. Cramer, *op. cit.*, Figure 18, gives the following totals of rateable properties in Portsea Town: 1709-12: 304, 222, 313, 263; 1786-8: 1,525, 1,762, 1,532; 1799-1801: 2,182, 1,623, 2,119.
64. Defoe, D., *op. cit.*, vol. 1, pp. 138-9.

65. Chalklin, C. W., *The Provincial Towns of Georgian England* (1974), pp. 19, 60, 230-2, 240-3, 262; Chalklin, C. W., and Havinden, M. A. (eds.), *Rural Change and Urban Growth, 1500-1800* (1974), pp. 237-9, 245-8.

66. PRCO, S3B/189.

67. BL, Add. MS. 33,057, f. 555, and *see* Plate 6.

68. East, pp. 289-96.

69. PCRO, G/1CP4.

70. Sadler's *Hampshire Directory* (1784), pp. 115-31.

71. *The Ancient and Modern History of Portsmouth, Portsea, Gosport and their Environs* (1799), pp. 44-5.

72. Hoad, Margaret, *PP*, 20, p. 8.

73. Eley, Philip, *PP*, 51, pp. 12, 15.

74. The table in *VCH Hants*, vol. 5, p. 450, is misleading, although the quoted acreages of Portsmouth (130) and Portsea (4,190) indicate the relevant areas. Gates, p. 248; Chapman, J., 'The Geographical Evolution of Portsmouth', in Bradbeer, J. B. (ed.), *Portsmouth Geographical Essays* (1974), p. 9; Cramer, *op. cit.*, pp. 134, 139, and many other local writers mistakenly credit Portsea town with 24,327 inhabitants in 1801.

75. *Parliamentary Papers, Population 6, 1851 Census* (1852-3), pp. 48-9.

76. PCRO, 1838 Poor Rate Book.

77. *HT*, 16 December 1816; 27 January 1817.

78. Rawlinson, *Report* (1850), pp. 91-3.

79. Post Office Directory of Hampshire . . . (1847), pp. 1,171-8; (1855), pp. 102-10.

80. *Census Summary* (1861), p. 230.

81. PRO, HO/107/636, pp. 58v-59v.

82. PCRO, 11A/30/15; AP 200.

83. *Hard Times, Good Times: Tales of Portsea People* (1987).

84. BL, Add. MS. 16,371C; K.Top. XIV, 11/1; Bod. L., Gough Maps, Hampshire 12; HRO, 44M73/E/P 14; Photocopy 40.

85. Rawlinson, *Report* (1850), pp. 22, 24-5, 37-8.

86. PCRO, CCR/VI/1, Medical Officer of Health, *Report* (1882), p. 3.

87. *PRC* (1835-1927), p. 5; *Post Office Directory, Hampshire* (1847), pp. 1,178-82; Kelly's *Directory of Portsmouth and Southsea* (1940-1). Riley, R. C., *The Growth of Southsea as a Naval Satellite and Victorian Resort*, *PP*, 16 (1972), provides a fuller survey of Southsea's development.

88. I am grateful to Jan Humphrey and Tania Burton for providing material relating to these areas.

89. Preedy, A., and Stewart, I., 'Thomas Ellis Owen (1804-1862), Southsea Architect', Dissertation, Portsmouth Polytechnic School of Architecture (1972).

90. Riley, R. C., *The Houses and Inhabitants of Thomas Ellis Owen's Southsea*, *PP*, 32 (1980). Dr. Riley is mistaken in stating, pp. 4-5, that Owen's 1838 Tithe Map was amended to coincide with the delayed first collection. PCRO holds the working copy map and rearranged transcript of the schedule used by the impropriator's agents, annotated at various times for their own convenience. Compare HRO C/XII/2/3, Portsea Tithe Apportionment, sealed by the Tithe Commissioners, 1845, and accompanied by Owen's 1838 map.

91. British Association, *Handbook and Guide to Portsmouth* (1911), pp. 216-7.

92. Peacock, Sarah, 'A 17th Century Survey of the Manor of Eastney and Milton', *PAR*, vol. 2 (1977), pp. 16-25.

93. PCRO, GMN/361; 43A/1/26; 43A/4/1a, 4a: 78A/1/1-2; *Dictionary of National Biography*, vol. 6, pp. 256-8.

94. Figures calculated from Merewood, Thelma, 'Eastney and Milton, 1832-1872', Dissertation, Portsmouth Polytechnic Diploma in English Local History, pp. 11-12.

95. PCRO, 43A/1/1, 6, 7; GMN/361; Chapman, *PP*, 29, pp. 14-15.

96. PCRO, GMN/361; 43A/2/10; CLC/2/6.

97. PCRO, GMN/361; D334/2; D304/8-19; Merewood, *op. cit.*, pp. 5-6.

98. Gates, pp. 29, 42; Rogers, George James, *Memories of Milton* (1985), *passim*.

99. *VCH Hants*, vol. 3 (1908), pp. 194-5.

100. Chapman, *PP*, 29, pp. 10-11, 14; *VCH Hants*, vol. 3 (1908), pp. 195-6.

101. BL, Add. MS. 6,027, ff. 106-8; PRO, E178/2,059; PCRO, GMN/12, 236, 242; CLC/14.

102. Mottley, *op. cit.*, p. 89.

103. HRO, C/XII/2/3; PCRO, 37A/8; Thomas, Suzanne, 'Living off the Land, a study of Portsea Island agriculture, 1793-1851', Dissertation, Portsmouth Polytechnic Diploma in English Local History (1984-5), p. 53. This study provides much detailed and interesting information about local farming.
104. PRO, HO 107/1,659, pp. 754-7, 863-5; *Kelly's Post Office Directory* (1914-15), pp. 188-91.
105. PCRO, GMN/1, 6, 10, 274, 366; Chapman, *PP*, 29, pp. 15-16.
106. PCRO, GMN/164, 274; 11A/23/9.
107. PCRO, 78A/1/7; CLC 3/9, 10, 12; GMN/366; Thomas, Suzanne, *op. cit.*, pp. 47-8, 51-3.
108. *VCH Hants*, vol. 3, pp. 168-9; PCRO, GMN/386, 357, 405; 11A/31/1; I/309.
109. East, pp. 559-60; *VCH Hants*, vol. 3, p. 193; BL, Add. MS. 16,371A; K.Top. XIV, 11/1, 16; PCRO, 36 A/3; DC/PM2/26.
110. Abercrombie, J., 'Development of Stamshaw', Dissertation, Portsmouth Polytechnic Diploma in English Local History (1979), pp. 2-6.
111. Hoad, M., 'Account Roll of Stubbington Grange, Portsea Island, 1268', *PAR*, vol. 8 (1989).
112. PCRO, GMN/378; Thomas Suzanne, *op. cit.*, pp. 40-2, 47.
113. HRO, C/XII/2/3.
114. Stapleton, Barry, 'The Population of the Portsmouth Region' in Stapleton, B., and Thomas, J. H. (eds.), *The Portsmouth Region* (1989), pp. 101-11.
115. I am most grateful to Anthony Quail for providing these figures.
116. *PRC* (1936-45), p. 78.

Chapter Three – Wooden Walls and Ironclads

1. Horne, R. S., *Her Majesty's Dockyard at Portsmouth. A Chronology* (mimeo 1965), p. 8, citing an extract from the Close Rolls of King John.
2. Horne, *op. cit.*, p. 11.
3. The second dry dock in a naval dockyard was not constructed until 1581, at Chatham.
4. Further details appear in L. G. Carr Laughton, 'Maritime History', *VCH Hants*, vol. 5, p. 371.
5. Until 1871 ship tonnage was related to cubic capacity, the calculation being referred to as 'builder's measure', or bm. The relationship with the later displacement tonnage is slight; long slim vessels could have a high displacement tonnage but a modest bm rating.
6. Goss, James, *Portsmouth Built Warships 1497-1967* (1984), p. 14. All vessel details in this chapter are derived from this source.
7. Carr Laughton, *loc. cit.*, p. 372.
8. *Ibid.*, pp. 375-6.
9. Kitson, Sir Henry, 'The Early History of Portsmouth Dockyard 1496-1800', *MM*, vol. 33 (1947), p. 259.
10. Morgan, L. V., 'An Historical Review of Portsmouth Dockyard in Relation to our Naval Policy', *Transactions of the Institution of Naval Architects*, vol. 90 (1948), pp. 21-2.
11. PCRO, 56 A/5.
12. *CSPD*, 1627-8, 24 April 1627, Sir George Blundell to Buckingham, pp. 148-9.
13. Kitson, *loc. cit.*, p. 259.
14. Marsh, A. J., 'The Navy and Portsmouth under the Commonwealth', *HS*, p. 131.
15. First rates had 80-100 guns, second rates 54-84, third rates 52-72, fourth rates 36-54, fifth rates 26-32, and sixth rates 10-18 guns.
16. A hoy is a small tender used for moving men and stores to and from anchored vessels.
17. Marsh, *loc. cit.*, p. 118.
18. *Ibid.*, p. 120.
19. *Ibid.*, p. 121.
20. *Ibid.*, p. 121.
21. Moore, Sir Jonas, *Map of Portsmouth Dockyard 1667* (PRO, MPE 513); Hodson, D., *Maps of Portsmouth Before 1801*, *PRS* (1978), p. 80.
22. Goss, *op. cit.*, p. 15.
23. Horne, *op. cit.*, p. 23.
24. Further details appear in Riley, R. C., *The Evolution of the Docks and Industrial Buildings in Portsmouth Royal Dockyard 1698-1914*, *PP*, 44 (1985), pp. 3-6.
25. BL, Harleian MS. 4,318; PCRO I/232.

26. Acreage figures are given by Morgan, *loc. cit.*, p. 28, but the accompanying map is inaccurately dated.
27. National Maritime Museum, Add. MS. 9,324.
28. Gattrell, V. A. C., 'Labour Power and the Size of Firms in Lancashire Cotton in the Second Quarter of the Nineteenth Century', *EcHR*, 2nd series, vol. 30 (1977), p. 103.
29. Defoe, D., *A Tour Through the Whole Island of Great Britain*, Everyman edn., vol. 1 (1962), pp. 136-9.
30. Riley, *op. cit.* p. 7.
31. This vessel, launched in 1737, should not be confused with the later *Victory* which is preserved in the dockyard.
32. For details, *see* Coad, Jonathan, 'Historic Architecture of HM Naval Base Portsmouth 1700-1850', *MM*, vol. 67 (1981), pp. 18-21.
33. The term 'double' is used since the upper floors were used for spinning and the ground floor for winding the ropes.
34. Details of the fire are given by Knight, R. J. B., *Portsmouth Dockyard Papers 1774-1783. The American War*, *PRS* (1987), pp. 101-4.
35. *Ibid.*, pp. xlix-liv, provides a detailed description of the yard at this time.
36. The architectural details of these buildings are described in Coad, *loc. cit.*; Lloyd, David W., *Buildings of Portsmouth and its Environs*, Portsmouth City Council (1974); Riley, *op. cit.*, pp. 7-11.
37. Knight, *op. cit.*, pp. liv-lx.
38. Navy Board Quarterly Returns, National Maritime Museum, ADM/B. The numbers broken down by trade for 1774-83 are given in Knight, *op. cit.*, p. 157.
39. Horne, *op. cit.*, Appendix 13.
40. Kitson, Sir Henry, 'The Early History of Portsmouth Dockyard 1496-1800, III Administration of the Royal Dockyards, Seventeenth and Eighteenth Centuries', *MM*, vol. 34 (1948), p. 89.
41. Navy Board Visitation, 20 September 1813.
42. Thomas, James H., 'From Civil War to Waterloo', in Stapleton, Barry, and Thomas, James H. (eds.), *The Portsmouth Region* (1989), p. 63.
43. Kitson, *loc. cit.* Part III, p. 89.
44. Kitson, Sir Henry, 'The Early History of Portsmouth Dockyard 1496-1800, IV The Guardships, Ships in "Ordinary"', *MM*, vol. 34 (1948), pp. 277-9.
45. Further details appear in Riley, *op. cit.*, pp. 11-13.
46. *Ibid.*, pp. 13-14.
47. PRO, ADM/42/1377, Yard Pay Book; Field, John Langston, 'Bourgeois Portsmouth. Social Relations in a Victorian Dockyard Town 1815-70', University of Warwick Ph.D. thesis (1979), p. 24.
48. Admiralty Orders, 29/3/1830; *Parliamentary Papers*, 1831-2, XVII, p. 576; Field, *op. cit.*, p. 24.
49. The Navy Board was abolished in 1832 and replaced by the Admiralty.
50. Laing, E. A. M., *Steam Wooden Warship Building in Portsmouth Dockyard 1832-1852*, *PP*, 42 (1985), p. 3.
51. Select Committee on Army, Navy and Ordnance Estimates, *Parliamentary Papers*, 1847-8, XXI, Pt 1, pp. 778-85; Field, *op. cit.*, p. 24.
52. For details *see* Riley, *op. cit.*, pp. 15-21.
53. Return of the Number of Workmen Employed in Royal Dockyards, *Parliamentary Papers*, 1860, XLII, p. 282; Field, *op. cit.*, p. 24.
54. *See* Riley, R. C., 'Military and Naval Land Use as a Determinant of Urban Development', in Bateman, Michael, and Riley, Raymond (eds.), *The Geography of Defence* (1987), pp. 65-6 for commentary and a map.
55. Colson, Charles, 'Portsmouth Dockyard Extension Works', *Proceedings, Institution of Civil Engineers*, vol. 64 (1880-1), p. 119.
56. *Royal Sovereign* displaced 14,150 tons; *Majestic*, *Prince George* and *Caesar* displaced 14,900 tons.
57. Thomas, F. N. G., 'Portsmouth and Gosport. A Study in the Historical Geography of a Naval Port', University of London M.Sc. thesis (1961), p. 175.
58. King, Ivor E., 'Forty Years of Change at Portsmouth Dockyard with some Notes on Dockyard Organisation', *Transactions of the Institution of Naval Architects*, vol. 97 (1955), p. 396.
59. PCRO 404/A, R. S. Horne Papers.
60. King, *loc. cit.*, p. 396.
61. Morgan, *loc. cit.*, p. 27.
62. King, *loc. cit.*, p. 384.

63. Riley, R. C., 'Urban Conservation or Private Museum. Historic Architecture in Portsmouth Dockyard', in Riley, R. C. (ed.), *Urban Conservation: International Contrasts*, Occasional Paper No. 7, Department of Geography, Portsmouth Polytechnic (1987), p. 12.

64. Kitson, Part III, *loc. cit.*, p. 88.

65. The Commissioners were naval or army officers, with two exceptions: Master Shipwrights John Tippetts and Anthony Deane, respectively Commissioners 1668-72 and 1672-5. Both were eventually knighted. The title of Commissioner was altered to Superintendent in 1823; because the post was held by an Admiral it was often known as that of Admiral Superintendent.

66. The title was changed to Master Shipwright and Engineer in 1863, to Chief Constructor in 1875 and to Constructor Manager in 1904. Kitson, Part III, *loc. cit.*, p. 94.

67. Goss, *op. cit.*, p. 14; *see also* Marsh, *loc. cit.*, p. 131.

68. Kitson, Part III, *loc. cit.*, p. 94.

69. Knight, R. J. B., 'Sandwich, Middleton and Dockyard Appointments', *MM*, vol. 57 (1971), p. 186.

70. Pollard, S., *The Genesis of Modern Management* (1968), p. 171; Field, John, 'Wealth, Styles of Life and Social Tone amongst Portsmouth's Middle Class 1800-75', in Morris, R. J. (ed.), *Class, Power and Social Structure in British Nineteenth Century Towns* (1986), pp. 83-4.

71. Horne (1965), *op. cit.*, p. 19.

72. Kitson, Part I, *loc. cit.*, p. 260.

73. Architectural details are given by Lloyd, *op. cit.*, p. 18.

74. Lloyd, Christopher, 'The Royal Naval Colleges at Portsmouth and Greenwich', *MM*, vol. 52 (1966), p. 145; Sullivan, F. B., 'The Royal Academy at Portsmouth 1729-1806', *MM*, vol. 63 (1977), pp. 311-26.

75. An observation by Captain Montagu Burrows, quoted by Lloyd, Christopher, *loc. cit.*, p. 148.

76. Ranft, B. McL., 'Labour Relations in the Royal Dockyards in 1739', *MM*, vol. 47 (1961), p. 282.

77. *Ibid.*

78. MacLeod, N., 'Wages of Shipwrights in HM Dockyards 1496-1788', *MM*, vol. 33 (1947), pp. 266-7; Knight (1987), *op. cit.*, pp. 62-4.

79. Ranft, *loc. cit.*, p. 285.

80. Knight (1987), *op. cit.*, pp. xliv-v, 44-5.

81. Field, John, 'Work, Wages and Culture. The Journal of Thomas Murphy, a Victorian Dockyard Artisan', *PAR*, vol. 5 (1981), p. 56.

82. MacLeod, *loc. cit.*, p. 269.

83. Ranft, *loc. cit.*, p. 285.

84. Horne (1965), *op. cit.*, p. 80.

85. Field (1981), *loc. cit.*, p. 54.

86. Coleman, D. C., 'Naval Dockyards under the Later Stuarts', *EcHR*, 2nd series, vol. 6 (1953-4), p. 140.

87. *HT*, 29 January 1870.

88. *PRC* (1835-1927), p. 113.

89. Field (1979), *op. cit.*, p. 24.

90. *Ibid.*

91. Lunn, Ken, and Thomas, Roger, *Portsmouth Dockyard, Dockyard Workers and Naval Imperialism 1905-1914*, School of Social and Historical Studies, Portsmouth Polytechnic (1985), p. 17.

92. Patterson, B. H., *A Dictionary of Dockyard Language*, Portsmouth Royal Dockyard Historical Society (1984), p. 26.

93. PCRO 404/A, Horne Papers, p. 90a.

94. Field (1979), *op. cit.*, p. 30.

95. PCRO 404/A, Horne Papers, p. 113a.

96. Field (1979), *op. cit.*, p. 351.

97. Lunn and Thomas, *op. cit.*, p. 18.

98. Coleman, *loc. cit.*, p. 144.

99. Horne (1965), *op. cit.*, p. 17.

100. Carr Laughton, *loc. cit.*, p. 384.

101. Kitson Part III, *loc. cit.*, p. 91.

102. Carr Laughton, *loc. cit.*, p. 384.

103. Horne (1965), *op. cit.*, pp. 71-2.
104. Coleman, *loc. cit.*, p. 144.
105. Slight, p. 137.
106. Horne, R. S., 'Britain's First Co-op in Portsmouth?', *Hampshire*, March 1969, pp. 29-30.
107. Webb, John, *An Early Nineteenth Century Dockyard Worker*, Portsmouth Museums Society, Publication No. 2 (1971), p. 8.
108. Knight, R. J. B., 'Pilfering and Theft from the Dockyards at the Time of the American War of Independence', *MM*, vol. 61 (1975), p. 218. *See also* Knight (1987), *op. cit.*, pp. 65-72.
109. Fourteen watchmen were on the strength in 1684. Horne (1965), *op. cit.*, p. 24.
110. Thomas, *loc. cit.*, p. 62.
111. Horne (1965), *op. cit.*, p. 72.
112. Cramer, James, *The Book of Portsmouth* (1985), p. 61.
113. Slight, p. 160.
114. *Ibid.*, p. 143.
115. Riley, R. C., *The Industries of Portsmouth in the Nineteenth Century*, *PP*, 25 (1976), p. 9.
116. Measom, G., *The Official South Western Railway Guide* (no date), p. 447.
117. Marsh, *loc. cit.*, p. 133.
118. Knight (1987), *op. cit.*, pp. 115, 117.
119. Riley (1985), *op. cit.*, p. 16.
120. Thomas, *loc. cit.*, p. 59.
121. *See* the very detailed exposition of large contracts agreed between 1774 and 1783 in Knight (1987), *op. cit.*, pp. 111-22. *Also* PCRO, PUH/3/65, *An Account of Goods Landed at HM Dock Yard* (May-September 1852). This shows that less than half the coal, one-third of the cement, only one-sixth of the timber, and none of the hemp, iron, chain, bricks and shingle was supplied by local merchants.
122. Riley (1985), *op. cit.*, p. 26.
123. *Ibid.*, p. 15.
124. In 1851 married women outnumbered married men by 1,740; there were 3,160 widows at the time.
125. Riley, R. C., 'The Portsmouth Corset Industry in the Nineteenth Century', *HS*, pp. 259-60.
126. *Morning Chronicle*, 16 November 1849; Field (1979), *op. cit.*, p. 82.
127. *Plans and Sections of Spithead and Langstone Docks and Ship Canal 30 November 1844*, PCRO P/3.
128. In not a single decade after 1830 were more than 3,000 tons launched; in the 1830s and 1880s output was less than 500 tons. *See* Riley (1975), *op. cit.*, p. 11.

Chapter Four – Stone Towers: The Fortifications of Portsmouth

1. *LP*, i (2), 2,574, 14 January 1513.
2. Charles de Marillac, French ambassador.
3. *LP*, 1,091, 1539.
4. Anne de Montmorency, Constable of France.
5. *LP*, xiv (2), 35, 12 August 1539.
6. *LP*, ii (2), 3,952, 15 February 1518.
7. PCRO, Articles of Complaint against Sir Adrian Poynings.
8. PCRO, 11A Madden to Ubsdell, 15 September 1847.
9. Colvin, H. M. (ed.), *The History of the King's Works* (1982), vol. 4. 1485-1660, part 2, p. 492.
10. *LP*, iv (1), 2,123.
11. i.e. walled.
12. i.e. tower.
13. i.e. furrow.
14. Hoad, Margaret (ed.), *Portsmouth – As others have seen it, 1540-1790*, *PP*, 15 (1972), p. 4.
15. BL, Cotton MS. Aug. 1 i 81.
16. HMC, Salisbury i, p. 49.
17. Colvin, *op. cit.*, p. 510.
18. Hoad, *op. cit.*, p. 5.
19. *Ibid.*, p. 6.
20. PCRO, CLF 9/19.
21. Richard Norton of Southwick. Presumably Colonel Richard Norton, at one time an intimate of

Cromwell. Governor of Portsmouth on at least three occasions during both the Commonwealth and after the Restoration when, presumably, he had purged his Commonwealth notions!

22. PCRO, 1430A/1.
23. *Ibid.*
24. Wright, The Late Archdeacon, *The Domus Dei* (n.d.).
25. Saunders, A. D., *Hampshire Coastal Defence since the Introduction of Artillery with a description of Fort Wallington*, The Royal Archaeological Institute (1977), p. 15. (Published originally in the *Archaeological Journal*, vol. 123 (1966), pp. 136-171.)
26. Hoad, *op. cit.*, p. 13.
27. *Ibid.*, p. 14.
28. *Ibid.*, p. 16.
29. *Ibid.*, p. 5.
30. Napoleon III supported the Piedmontese and their king, Victor Emmanuel, in their attempts to drive the Austrians out of Italy. A secret pact was reached at Plombières July 1858. The Franco-Piedmontese War broke out April 1859. Napoleon III was victorious at both Magenta and Solferino although at great cost. Peace was negotiated in July at Villafranca. Nice and Savoy came eventually to France following a plebiscite early in 1860. Napoleon had reached the Alps. Would he now attempt to reach the Rhine and thus create anew fears of further French aggrandisement in continental Europe?
31. Patterson, A. T., *'Palmerston's Folly' the Portsdown and Spithead Forts*, PP, 3 (1980), p. 10.
32. Besant, Walter, and Rice, James, *By Celia's Arbour, A Tale of Portsmouth Town* (1888).
33. PCRO 1430A/1.
34. Thomas Roscoe in Hoad, M. (ed.), *Portsmouth – As others have seen it, 1790-1900*, PP, 20, p. 14.
35. *Ibid.*, p. 16 *et seq.*.
36. *Portsmouth and Gosport Gazette*, 9 December 1745.
37. Gates, p. 283.
38. Rawlinson, Robert, *Report to the General Board of Health on the Sewage, Drainage and Water supply of Portsmouth, 1850.*
39. PCRO, 11A/22/13.
40. Gray, Maxwell, *The Silence of Dean Maitland*, 2nd edn. (1898).
41. Colvin, *op. cit.*, p. 518.
42. For a more detailed account of the history of the Corps of Royal Engineers, *see* Hodson, Donald (ed.), *Maps of Portsmouth before 1891*, PRS, No. 4 (1978), p. xix-xxiii.

Chapter Five – Port and Garrison Town

1. Gates, p. 585.
2. *VCH Hants*, vol. 5, pp. 360 ff.; Hewitt, H. J., *The Organization of War under Edward III* (1966), pp. 45, 85.
3. BL, Sloane MS. 3,233, f. 14; *VCH Hants*, vol. 5, p. 388.
4. Cobb, H. S. (ed.), *The Local Port Book of Southampton for 1439-40*, Southampton Records Series, vol. 5 (1961), pp. xi, l-li. By the compromise the harbour was to remain subject to Southampton's authority, but the local customs were to be divided equally between the two places.
5. PRO, SP12/38, f. 82v.
6. Foster, B. (ed.), *The Local Port Book of Southampton for 1435-36*, Southampton Records Series, vol. 7 (1963), pp. 76-7.
7. *VCH Hants*, vol. 3, p. 174.
8. Lewis, M., *Spithead. An Informal History* (1972), pp. 44-7.
9. Cobb, *op. cit.*, pp. li, liv-lv; Platt, C., *Medieval Southampton. The Port and Trading Community A.D. 1000-1600* (1973), pp. 89-90.
10. PCRO, L 2/1.
11. Marsden, R. G. (ed.), 'Voyage of the *Barbara* to Brazil, Anno 1540', *The Navy Miscellany*, Navy Records Society, vol. 2 (1912), pp. 3-66; Hakluyt, R., *Voyages*, Everyman edn. (1907), vol. 4, pp. 33, 39.
12. Andrews, K. R., *Elizabethan Privateering . . . 1585-1603* (1964), pp. 93-4.
13. Hakluyt, *Voyages*, vol. 6, pp. 162, 196.
14. PRO, E190/822/3, 825/5, 826/2, 826/14, etc.
15. PRO, E190/825/5.
16. PRO, E190/822/6, 826/6.

17. Willan, T. S., *The English Coasting Trade 1600-1750* (1967), p. 210. A Newcastle chaldron contained 53 cwt.
18. Westerfield, R. B., *Middlemen in English Business particularly between 1660 and 1760* (1913), p. 229.
19. PRO, E190/826/2; East, pp. 315, 328, 357; Sainsbury, E. B. (ed.), *A Calendar of the Court Minutes of the E. India Company, 1655-59* (1916), pp. 350, 355; Dymond, D., *Portsmouth and the Fall of the Puritan Republic*, *PP*, 11 (1971), *passim*.
20. *Calendar of Treasury Books, 1676-1679*, vol. 5 (1), (1911), p. 214; *CSPD, 1676-1677*, p. 200.
21. *Calendar of Treasury Papers, 1557-1696*, p. 554.
22. PRO, E190/839/2.
23. PCRO, 11A/20/27a.
24. Westerfield, *op. cit.*, pp. 161-2.
25. Cullen, L. M., *Anglo-Irish Trade, 1660-1800* (1968), pp. 71-3.
26. Fisher, H. E. S., *The Portugal Trade. A Study of Anglo-Portuguese Commerce 1700-1770* (1971), pp. 92-3.
27. Crowhurst, P., *The Defence of British Trade 1689-1815* (1977), pp. 72, 76.
28. BL, Add. MS. 8,133A, ff. 53, 62; *The Hampshire Repository* (*c*.1800), vol. 1, p. 127, vol. 2, pp. 77-8; White (1859), pp. 52, 266.
29. Sainsbury, *op. cit.*, 1660-63 (1922), pp. 228-9.
30. *Commons Journal*, vol. 21, p. 140.
31. Carson, E., *Smugglers and Revenue Officers in the Portsmouth Area in the Eighteenth Century*, *PP*, 22 (1974), *passim*; *HT*, 8 Nov. 1802.
32. White (1859), p. 266.
33. PCRO, CF/16/32.
34. *Report from Commissioners on Municipal Corporations in England and Wales: Hampshire*, p. 819; *British Parliamentary Papers: Fuel and Power. Coal Trade* 1 (1830), Appendices 1, 2.
35. White (1859), pp. 143-7, 265; *Brit. Parl. Papers: Shipping* (1850), vol. liii, p. 380.
36. Information kindly supplied by Mr. Barry Stapleton.
37. *Brit. Parl. Papers . . . Coal Trade* 3 (1871), Appendix to Committee E Report, p. 77.
38. Thomas, J. H., *Portsmouth and the First Fleet 1786-1787*, *PP*, 50 (1987), p. 27.
39. Information kindly supplied by Mr. A. W. H. Pearsall.
40. White (1859), p. 265.
41. Gates, W. G., *The Portsmouth That Has Passed* (1949), p. 439.
42. *Medical Officer of Health Reports* (Port Sanitary Authority), 1893-1935, 1946-7, *passim*; *City of Portsmouth Port Statistics*, 1974, 1987; Barrett, P. F., and Brown, P. J., 'Shipping at Portsmouth', *Marine News: Journal of the World Ship Society*, vol. 17 (1963), pp. 292-3.
43. East, pp. 635-40.
44. BL, Add. MS. 33,278, ff. 4r.-19r.; BL, Harl. MS. 1,326, ff. 39v.-41r., 47r.
45. *Ibid.*
46. Gates, W. G., *Portsmouth in the Past* (1972 edn.), pp. 2, 47.
47. BL, Add. MS. 33,278, f. 9r.
48. Dymond, D., *Capt. John Mason and the Duke of Buckingham*, *PP*, 17 (1972), pp. 7-15.
49. Beloff, M., *Public Order and Popular Disturbances 1660-1714*, 2nd edn. (1963), pp. 108-9.
50. *Ibid.*, p. 109; East, pp. 190-3.
51. East, pp. 190, 282; Slight, pp. 58-9; PCRO, 1,430a.
52. Bod. L., Rawlinson MS. A 201, f. 138v.
53. White (1859), pp. 248-9.
54. Slight, pp. 59-61; White (1859), pp. 246, 249, 260; Lloyd, D. W., *Buildings of Portsmouth and its Environs* (1974), pp. 82, 84; *PRC* (1835-1927), pp. 71-2, 143, 161, 223.
55. *Ibid.*, pp. 91, 213-4, 298-9; Lloyd, *op. cit.*, pp. 82, 84-5.
56. *VCH Hants*, vol. 3, pp. 178, 189; East, pp. 422-34, 686-9; *HS*, pp. 92-3.
57. East, pp. 155, 348.
58. PRO, PCC 49 Hayes; East, pp. 142, 327, 346, 652. *See also* Quail, S., *Civic Pride and Sterling Silver* (1988), pp. 7, 9, 22.
59. East, pp. 166, 314-17, 327-8, 346-68 *passim*.
60. Beloff, *op. cit.*, p. 112.
61. Appleby, J. T., *England Without Richard, 1189-1199* (1967), p. 142.

62. *See* pp. 101-2.
63. Dymond, D., *op. cit.*, pp. 14-15.
64. *The Annual Register . . . 1758*, 9th edn. (1795), p. 85.
65. *HT*, 24 Feb. 1800, 1 July 1811, 1 Aug. 1842, 22 Feb. 1845, 12 July 1845.
66. An Old Naval Surgeon, *An Address to the Officers of HM Navy* (1824), p. 20.
67. BL, Add. MS. 40,001, f. 121r.
68. *HT*, 3 May 1802.
69. *HT*, 21 August 1815, 20 September 1830, 25 September 1843.
70. PCRO, CCM 1/2, pp. 256, 289, 290, 295.
71. Field, J. L., 'Bourgeois Portsmouth: Social Relations in a Victorian Dockyard Town, 1815-75', University of Warwick, Ph.D. thesis (1979), pp. 604-14.
72. *PRC* (1835-1927), pp. 63, 145, 277-8; White (1859), p. 278.
73. *PRC* (1835-1927), pp. 129, 287-8; White (1859), p. 276; Robinson, S., *A Life Record* (1898), pp. 278-9; Robinson, S., *'My Book': A Personal Narrative* (1914), pp. 147-8, 151; Gates, W. G. (ed.), *Portsmouth and the Great War* (1919), p. 116; White (1878), p. 396.
74. Weston, A., *My Life Among the Bluejackets* (1915), *passim*; Gulliver, D., *Dame Agnes Weston* (1971), pp. 19-24, 68-9, 75-6, 130, 142-4.
75. *PRC* (1835-1927), pp. 179, 182, 251.
76. Lewis, M., *Spithead – An Informal History* (1972), pp. 85-8; Gates, pp. 462-8.
77. *PRC* (1835-1927), p. 180.
78. *PRC* (1835-1927), p. 263; Gates, *Portsmouth and the Great War*, pp. 24-6.
79. *Ibid.*, pp. 31-5, 133-233; ATP, p. 136.
80. Lewis, *op. cit.*, pp. 45-7, 53-8; Wernham, R. B., *Before the Armada* (1966), p. 160.
81. Lewis, *op. cit.*, pp. 62-73.
82. Patterson, A. T., *Portsmouth – A French Gibraltar?*, *PP*, 10 (1970).
83. Lewis, *op. cit.*, p. 77.
84. Patterson, A. T., *'Palmerston's Folly': The Portsdown and Spithead Forts*, *PP*, 3 (1968).
85. Webb, J., *The Siege of Portsmouth in the Civil War*, *PP*, 7 (1969).
86. Gates, *Portsmouth and the Great War*, p. 70.
87. Easthope, W. G. (ed.), *Smitten City* (1945), p. 5; for a fuller discussion of Portsmouth's experience during the Second World War, *see* p. 169.

Chapter Six – The Way People Lived

1. Hoad, M., 'The Origins of Portsmouth', in *HS*, pp. 1-30.
2. Bod. L., MS. Top. Hants, e3, f. 13v.
3. Hoad, M., 'Account Roll of Stubbington Grange, Portsea Island, 1268', *PAR*, vol. 8 (1989).
4. Hockey, Dom F., 'The Property and Rents of Quarr Abbey in Medieval Portsmouth', *PAR*, vol. 2 (1977), pp. 9-15.
5. Harvey, J., *The Plantagenets* (1969), p. 101.
6. *VCH Hants*, vol. 3, p. 174; *Calendar of Liberate Rolls, Henry III*, vol. 4 (1959), pp. 30, 423.
7. *Summary Report of Excavations at Oyster Street, Old Portsmouth, 1969-71*.
8. ATP, chapter 2.
9. Hockey, *loc. cit.*, pp. 13-14.
10. For maps of Tudor Portsmouth *see* Hodson, D. (compiler), *Maps of Portsmouth before 1801*, *PRS*, vol. 4 (1978).
11. HRO, Ad. 23; PCRO, CF 1/1, f. 11v.
12. PCRO, L2/2/2; East, pp. 26-34, 116-52, *passim*.
13. *Ibid.*
14. East, pp. 609-17.
15. Fearon, W. A., and Williams, J. F., *The Parish Registers and Parochial Documents in the Archdeaconry of Winchester* (1909), pp. 71-4; Taylor, J., 'Plague in the Towns of Hampshire: the Epidemic of 1665-6', *Southern History*, vol. 6 (1984), pp. 110-11, 115-7.
16. *VCH Hants*, vol. 3, p. 191.
17. PRO, SP12/218/46, f. 71r.

18. Owen Tottye, the wealthiest townsman, left 20s. and two houses to the poor (PRO, PCC 5 Bolein), but this seems to have been exceptional.
19. East, pp. 27, 35.
20. White (1859), p. 246.
21. Howell, p. 9.
22. BL, Harl. MS. 595.
23. PRO, E134/4, James I/Mich. No. 24.
24. BL, Add. MS. 33,281, ff. 64-8; East, p. 312.
25. PRO, E178, 2,059; BL, Add. MS. 6,027, f. 106r.; Corp. of London Record Office, RCE Rentals, 4/1, 6/10.
26. East, p. 690.
27. *See above*, chapter 2.
28. Vancouver, C., *General View of the Agriculture of Hampshire* . . . (1810), pp. 32-3, 111-12, 146, 285, etc.
29. *Pink's Pictorial*, 1, no. 5 (1908), pp. 10-15.
30. ATP, p. 44.
31. Lloyd, D. W., *Buildings of Portsmouth and its Environs* (1974), pp. 38-9.
32. Gates, W. G., *Portsmouth in the Past* (1972 edn.), p. 2.
33. *HT*, 1 April 1816.
34. Part of Portsmouth Polytechnic's Milton campus.
35. Riley, R. C., *The Houses and Inhabitants of Thomas Ellis Owen's Southsea, PP*, 32 (1980).
36. *HT*, 19 June 1847.
37. Foden, F., *Philip Magnus: Victorian Educational Pioneer* (1970), especially chapter 5.
38. Webb, J., *Sir Frederic Madden and Portsmouth, PP*, 47 (1987), p. 21.
39. *Mansfield Park* (1814), chapter 38.
40. *Nicholas Nickleby* (1838-9), chapters 23 and 24.
41. Rawlinson, R., *Report to the General Board of Health on the Sewage, Drainage, and Water Supply of Portsmouth* (1850), *passim*; Slight, p. 17.
42. Hawkes, H., *Recollections of John Pounds* (1884), pp. 10-12.
43. Rawlinson, *Report*, pp. 23, 25, 45, etc.
44. *PRC* (1835-1927), pp. 103, 116.
45. The relevant documents are in the writer's possession.
46. *Pink's Magazine*, 1, No. 6 (1914), pp. 103-7.
47. Osborne, C. E., *The Life of Father Dolling* (1903), chapters 6-17.
48. Rawlinson, *Report*, pp. 50-62, 89; Thomson, D. Halton, *History of the Portsmouth and Gosport Water Supply* (1957).
49. I am indebted to Mr. E. K. Barnard for this information.
50. Rawlinson, *Report*, pp. 62-5.
51. BL, Harl. MS. 58(1), 34; Add. MS. 17,861; Bod. L., MS. Top. Hants, e3. f. 13v.
52. Gates, *Portsmouth in the Past*, p. 91; White (1859), p. 323; *PRC* (1835-1927), p. 306.
53. Webb, J., *Portsmouth Free Mart Fair – The Last Phase, 1800-1847, PP*, 35 (1982), p. 3.
54. Lloyd, *op. cit.*, p. 46.
55. Webb, J., *An Early Victorian Street. The High Street, Old Portsmouth, PP*, 26 (1977), *passim*.
56. Field, J. L., 'Bourgeois Portsmouth: Social Relations in A Victorian Dockyard Town, 1815-75', Univ. of Warwick Ph.D. thesis (1979), p. 101.
57. *EN*, 7 November 1933, 1 April 1966.
58. *EN*, 9 August 1939; White (1859), pp. 314, 331.
59. Gieve, D. W., *Gieves and Hawkes 1785-1985* (1985), *passim*.
60. Patterson, A. Temple, *Portsmouth Nineteenth-Century Literary Figures, PP*, 14 (1972), p. 4.
61. *Ibid.*, pp. 12-13.
62. Horne, R. S., 'Britain's First Co-op in Portsmouth?', *Hampshire*, vol. 9, No. 5 (March 1969), pp. 29-30; White (1859), p. 278.
63. Mihell, J. H., *A Record of the Formation, Progress and Present Position of the Portsea Island Mutual Co-operative Society Ltd to 1919* (n.d.), pp. 1-5.
64. Gates, pp. 373-4; East, p. 737.
65. HRO, 17M57/10-11; *HT*, 10 November 1800, 10 May 1802.

66. Eden, Sir Frederic M., *The State of the Poor* (1928 edn.), ed. Rogers, A. G. L., pp. 196-9.
67. Gates, p. 375.
68. *Ibid.*; White (1859), pp. 232, 248, 352.
69. White (1859), pp. 19, 248; Gates, p. 375; Slight, H., *The History of Portsmouth* (1838), pp. 46-7.
70. White (1859), pp. 275, 278; Gates, pp. 376-80; *HT*, 10 March 1800, 16 December 1816.
71. *PRC* (1928-30), pp. 87-8.
72. *The Portsmouth and Gosport Gazette*, 17 February 1746.
73. Goldson, W., *Cases of Smallpox subsequent to Vaccination . . . read before the Medical Society, at Portsmouth, March 29, 1804* (1804).
74. *HT*, 21 October 1816.
75. *Report of the Medical Officer of Health* (1914), p. 22.
76. Lipscomb, F. W., *Heritage of Sea Power* (1967), pp. 132-3.
77. *Portsmouth Gazette and Weekly Advertiser*, 6 October 1794.
78. Noon, J., *King Cholera Comes to Portsmouth* (1972), pp. 3-4, 6, 12.
79. Gates, W. G., *Free Mart Fair: Sketches of Old Portsmouth* (1897), pp. 49-56; Sargeant, H., *A History of Portsmouth Eye and Ear Hospital 1884-1970* (n.d.), pp. 2-3; *PRC* (1835-1927), pp. 140, 152, 198, 232, 255.
80. *Ibid.*, pp. 98, 124, 232, 262.
81. i.e. smallpox, measles, scarlet fever, diphtheria, whooping cough, typhoid, diarrhoea.
82. *Report of the Medical Officer of Health* (1914), p. 22.
83. *Ibid.*, p. 9; *Report of the Medical Officer of Health* (1879), p. 1; Rawlinson, *Report*, p. 29.
84. Smith, F. J., 'Portsmouth and Education', *Portsmouth N.U.T. Conference Souvenir* (1926), p. 85.
85. Anon., *Portsmouth Grammar School 1732-1878* (1927), Introduction.
86. *Ibid.*
87. East, pp. 55-6.
88. Anon., *op. cit.*, p. 1.
89. Washington, E. S., and Marsh, A. J., *Portsmouth Grammar School 1732-1976* (1978), pp. 5-9.
90. *Autobiography of Sir Walter Besant* (1902), p. 46.
91. Washington and Marsh, *op. cit.*, pp. 10-15.
92. Gatt, L. V., *The Portsmouth Beneficial School 1755-1939*, *PP*, 46 (1986), *passim*.
93. Slight, pp. 224-5.
94. White (1859), p. 274.
95. Stanford, J., and Patterson, A. Temple, *The Condition of the Children of the Poor in mid-Victorian Portsmouth*, *PP*, 21 (1974), p. 9.
96. Slight, H., *A Personal Inspection of the Schools within the Borough of Portsmouth*, reprinted from the *Guardian*, 1851.
97. Hawkes, *op. cit.*, *passim*; *The Penny Magazine*, 23 February 1839, p. 67.
98. White (1859), pp. 316-7.
99. Kipling, R., *Something of Myself* (Penguin edn. 1977), pp. 9-18.
100. Field, J. L., 'Private Schools in Portsmouth and Southampton, 1850-1870', *Journal of Educational Administration and History*, vol. 10, 2 (1978), p. 11.
101. Niven, D., *The Moon's a Balloon* (1972), pp. 23-7.
102. PCRO, G/SB/1/1 (between pp. 54-5). I am indebted to Mr. J. A. Fox for this reference.
103. Noon, J., *Centenary of 1870 Education Act* (1970), pp. 9-12; White (1878), p. 395; *PRC* (1835-1927), p. 213.
104. Washington and Marsh, *op. cit.*, pp. 18-30, 40-2.
105. PRO, PCC 26 Nevell.
106. Gatt, *op. cit.*, pp. 10-11.
107. Howell, M., and Mitton, J., *A Century of History: Portsmouth High School 1882-1982* (1982), pp. 1-4.
108. Noon, *Centenary . . .*, pp. 14-15; *PRC* (1835-1927), pp. 166, 219.
109. Magan, M., *Cradled in History. St John's College, Southsea, 1908-76* (n.d.), pp. 12-15, 22-3.
110. Davison, E. W. J., 'Education in Portsmouth', *Portsmouth N.U.T. Conference Souvenir* (1937), pp. 97-8.
111. *Ibid.*, pp. 99-101; *PRC* (1835-1927), pp. 227, 230; Windle, R. (ed.), *Records of the Corporation 1966-74* (n.d.), pp. 64-9.
112. White (1859), pp. 275-6; Slight, pp. 31-4; *PRC* (1835-1927), pp. 90, 113; *PRC* (1928-30), p. viii.
113. Stavert, G., *A Study in Southsea. The Unrevealed Life of Dr. Arthur Conan Doyle* (1987), pp. 41-8, 57.

114. Albert, W., and Harvey, P. D. A. (eds.), *Portsmouth and Sheet Turnpike Commissioners' Minute Book 1711-1754, PRS*, vol. 2 (1973), pp. xvii-xix; Gates, pp. 469-73; White (1859), p. 267.

115. Burton, L., and Musselwhite, B., *Crossing the Harbour* (1987), pp. 13, 15, 41-5, 49-53, 79, 81; White (1859), pp. 266-7.

116. Bishop, G., *Portsmouth Pageant* (1983), pp. 38, 50, 57.

117. Watts, E., *Fares Please. The History of Passenger Transport in Portsmouth* (1987), pp. 7, 25-43, 49-77, 114-16; *PRC* (1835-1927), pp. 28, 105, 205; *PRC* (1936), pp. 25-6.

118. Shute, N., *Slide Rule. The Autobiography of an Engineer* (1954), pp. 181-249; Windle, *op. cit.*, pp. 90, 92, 160.

119. *PRC* (1835-1927), pp. 157, 169, 190, 203, 207, 252.

120. PCRO, 468A/8/1; *HT*, 15 February 1802; *Portsmouth Chronicle*, 1 January 1803; White (1859), p. 276.

121. C. J. B., 'The First Published Plan of the Battle of Trafalgar', *MM*, vol. 31 (1945), p. 168.

122. Briggs, Sir John H., *Naval Administration 1827-92* (1897), p. 71. I am indebted to Dr. J. L. Field for this reference.

123. Chapman, R. W. (ed.), *Jane Austen's Letters* (1969), p. 258.

124. *HT*, 15 September 1823, 13 May 1854, etc.; *Parliamentary Papers*, 1844, xxxii, p. 424; Read, D., *Press and People 1790-1850* (1961), pp. 64, 211.

125. *The Book of Jubilee: Evening News, Portsmouth, 1877-1927* (1927), pp. 1-8; *The News Centenary Supplement*, April 1977; *Portsmouth Times*, 30 March 1928, p. 9.

Chapter Seven – The Way People Worshipped

1. Winchester College No. 17,377C.

2. Hoad, Margaret, 'The Origins of Portsmouth', *HS*, p. 15.

3. Chapman, John, *The Common Lands of Portsea Island, PP*, 28 (1979).

4. BL, Cotton MS. Aug. 1.ii.117.

5. PCRO, CF4/1.

6. PCRO, CE1 f. 40.

7. Survey of Common Fields of Portsmouth made by Richard Palshid *temp.* Henry VIII (*c.*1531) Winchester College No. 15,250. Available in photocopy in the PCRO, 1,121A/1/1.

8. Molyneux, Moleyns or Molins, Adam (d.1450), Bishop of Chichester and Keeper of the Privy Seal, *Dictionary of National Biography*, vol. 13.

9. Wright, The Late Archdeacon, *The Domus Dei*, Portsmouth (n.d.).

10. BL, Cotton MS. Aug. 1.ii.117.

11. HRO, Al/18 Vol. 2.

12. HRO, Southwick Priory Registers, IM/54.

13. Lilley, Henry T., and Everitt, Alfred T., *Portsmouth Parish Church*, Portsmouth (1921). This is a most useful secondary source for any student of medieval church history in Portsmouth.

14. Toulmin Smith, Lucy (ed.), *Itinerary of John Leland 1535-43* (1964), vol. 1, pp. 282-4.

15. *VCH Hants* (1903), vol. 2.

16. Hockey, Dom Frederick, 'The Property and Rents of Quarr Abbey in Medieval Portsmouth', *PAR*, 2 (1977).

17. PCRO, CF4/2.

18. *Valor Ecclesiasticus Henr. VIII, A.D. 1535*, vol. 2 (1814).

19. *VCH Hants* vol. 2, (1903).

20. Hockey, Dom Frederick, 'The First Post-Dissolution account of the Domus Dei of Portsmouth', *PAR*, 4, 1979-80.

21. For an account of this incident, *see* Townsend, G., *The Acts and Monuments of John Foxe*, VI, 1846.

22. Stephen Gardiner (*c.*1493-1555), Bishop of Winchester 1531-1555.

23. A church-ale was a festive gathering held in connection, as here, with a church.

24. PCRO, CHU 3/2A/1.

25. PCRO, CHU 3.

26. PCRO, CHU 2.

27. HRO, 24M 54/14.

28. The Main Guard stood on Grand Parade.

29. Sir George Legg was governor in 1678.

30. PCRO, CHU 3/2A/1, 12 April 1664.
31. The Declaration of Indulgence of 1672 suspended all penalties against Nonconformists.
32. Cohen, Sheldon S., 'Thomas Wren: Ministering Angel of Forton Prison', *The Pennsylvania Magazine* (1979). There is a photocopy of this article in the Portsmouth City Records Office.
33. The Act of Toleration, as it was popularly known, allowed Protestant Nonconformists who believed in the Trinity to have their own places of worship, provided they met with unlocked doors and certified the place of meeting to the bishop, the archdeacon or quarter-sessions. They were allowed to have their own teachers and preachers if they took certain oaths and declarations, to which none of them had in fact any objection.
34. The Compton Census of 1676, so-called after Henry Compton, then Bishop of London, provides by parishes numbers of Anglican communicants, Protestant dissenters and Roman Catholic dissenters. Returns were made to the archbishops of Canterbury and York. Original returns survive at Lambeth Palace, the William Salt Library, Stafford, and at the Bodleian Library, Oxford. Returns for the County of Southampton are in the William Salt Library. The returns for the whole country have recently been published: *see* Whiteman, A. (ed.), *The Compton Census of 1676: A Critical Edition* (1986).
35. HRO, B2/1725, Drokensford Deanery, Portsea and Porsmouth.
36. *Ibid.*
37. Surry, N. W., and Thomas, J. H. (eds.), *Book of Original Entries, 1731-51, PRS*, vol. 3 (1976), pp. xlv-xlvii.
38. BL, Harl. MS. 595, ff. 237-40.
39. Gates, pp. 333-6.
40. *Ibid.*, pp. 336-9.
41. HRO, 35M 48/11.26.
42. HRO, Bs/1725.
43. HRO, 35M 48/11.43.
44. There is an original copy of Archdeacon Wigram's *Letter on the Spiritual Necessities of Portsea* (London 1851), in the Cope Collection, Southampton University Library. There is a photocopy in the Portsmouth City Records Office, PCRO 800A/2.
45. For a more detailed account of this period, *see* Yates, Nigel, *The Anglican Revival in Victorian Portsmouth*, *PP*, 37 (1983).
46. Merewood, Thelma, 'Letters from a Portsea Parsonage 1872-75', *PAR*, 6 (1982).
47. *Ibid.*
48. *Ibid.*
49. Yates, *PP*, 37.
50. Garbett, Cyril (ed.), *The Work of a Great Parish* (1915).
51. The writer has been able to discuss these issues only briefly with the present vicar of St Mary's, Canon Michael Brotherton, and leading lay figures in the parish. For Southam's own thoughts *see* parish magazines in Portsmouth City Records Office, PCRO CHU 3/5.
52. The other is the cathedral church of St Edmundsbury and Ipswich, Bury St Edmunds, Suffolk.
53. *Church Building*, Winter 1986.
54. *See The News*, October-December 1988.
55. Dwyer, Gerald, *Diocese of Portsmouth Past and Present* (1981).
56. Weinberg, Aubrey, *Portsmouth Jewry*, *PP*, 41 (1985).
57. PCRO, Rate Books 1732.
58. Records of the local Jewish synagogue are held at the synagogue in The Thicket, Southsea. Students should remember that the bulk of this material is in Hebrew.
59. For a detailed history of local Methodism, *see* Cooper, W. Donald, *Methodism in Portsmouth 1750-1932*, *PP*, 18 (1973).
60. For details of George Bayne's career, *see* newscuttings in PCRO, 109A/1/12.
61. *Gates*, p. 660.
62. *HT*, 1 May 1897, p. 6.
63. *PRC* (1956-65), p. 59.
64. Details of the ecclesiastical conflict in Wymering and Farlington can be found in Yates, Nigel, *Ritual Conflict at Farlington and Wymering*, *PP*, 28 (1978).
65. Information supplied by the Statistical Unit, Church House, Westminster.

66. *Diocese of Portsmouth Year Book 1988*, Diocesan Information Office, St Edmund House, Edinburgh Road, Portsmouth.

Chapter Eight – The Voice of the People

1. Alderman Frederick Power (1837-1927), described in PRC (1835-1927), p. 318, as 'the grand old man' of the city council.
2. For surviving correspondence, newscuttings, etc., relating to this matter, *see* PCRO, C1/14.
3. For details of his life, *see* Webb, John, *Sir Frederick Madden and Portsmouth*, *PP*, 47 (1987).
4. Alderman Sir Thomas Scott Foster (d.1918), active in borough politics from 1875 as councillor, alderman and mayor.
5. PCRO, C/1.
6. Hoad, Margaret, 'The Origins of Portsmouth', *HS*.
7. Kersey was a kind of coarse narrow cloth, usually ribbed, woven from long wool.
8. Broadcloth was a fine twilled woollen cloth.
9. The Court of Record was a civil court having jurisdiction over all personal actions. The surviving records may be consulted in Portsmouth City Records Office under PCRO R.
10. Hoad, *loc. cit.*
11. The 'farm' of the borough was the fixed sum payable in medieval times annually by way of composition for all regular royal revenues derived from the town.
12. In feudal land law, land reverted or escheated to the lord if the tenant died without heirs or committed a gross breach of the feudal bond. It was also a prerogative right of the king's to confiscate all lands of a person convicted of high treason of whatever lord they held. John de Gisors' land escheated to the crown for the part he played in the rising of Prince John in 1194.
13. PCRO, CE1/2.
14. Sir Christopher Hatton (1540-91), Lord Chancellor of England, 1587, and a favourite of Queen Elizabeth.
15. Sir Julius Caesar (1557 or 8-1636), English judge. Held many high offices during reigns of Elizabeth and James I. Famous for his bountiful acts of generosity and charity. Amassed a remarkable collection of manuscripts, many of which are now in the British Library.
16. General George Monck, 1st Duke of Albemarle (1608-69), soldier. Played a decisive role in the restoration of Charles II in 1660 by securing London and enforcing the dissolution of parliament.
17. Samuel Pepys (1633-1703), diarist.
18. John Byng (1704-57), British admiral. Tried by court-martial, condemned to death and shot at Portsmouth, 14 March 1757, for failing to do his utmost against the enemy, the French, off Minorca.
19. For more details of the history of the Corporation's plate, *see* Quail, Sarah, *Civic Pride and Sterling Silver. The Civic Plate and Insignia of The City of Portsmouth* (1988).
20. Payments due for passing over or using bridges, ferries, markets, ports or any other similar facilities.
21. The shire was an ancient division of England from at least the seventh century, composed of several hundreds and administered by this time by the sheriff. The shire court was the general assembly of the people of the shire and was convened by the sheriff twice a year.
22. A hundred was a group of townships in pre-Norman and Medieval England. It had a court which met monthly, presided over by the sheriff or his deputy.
23. Forests were originally areas set apart for royal recreation. Forest law originated under King Cnut. Codified at the Assize of Woodstock (1184), it was a body of law quite distinct from common law.
24. PCRO, 3A/1. A copy made 1727 of 13th-century customs and usages in Portsmouth.
25. PCRO, CE1/5.
26. PCRO, CE1/1-16.
27. PCRO, CE6/1-4.
28. PCRO, CF.
29. PCRO, G/ICP (Portsea); G/ICQ (Portsmouth); G/ICL (Landport and Southsea).
30. For a brief history of the newly-reformed borough, *see* Peacock, Sarah, *Borough Government in Portsmouth 1835-1974*, *PP*, 23 (1975).
31. Lionel Gordon Baliol Brett, 4th Viscount Esher (b.1913), architect and town planner. Lists the Civic Offices, Portsmouth, as amongst his principal buildings.

32. Field, John, 'Bourgeois Portsmouth: Social Relations in a Victorian Dockyard Town, 1815-1875', Univ. of Warwick Ph.D. thesis (1979).

33. For details of this episode and Hesilrige's career, *see* Dymond, Dorothy, *Portsmouth and the Fall of the Puritan Republic*, *PP*, 11 (1971).

34. Josiah Child (1630-99), English merchant, economist and governor of the East India Company.

35. The privilege of trading freely in the borough was confined to those individuals who were freemen or burgesses. Those who traded but were not free were amerced or fined. Lists of those fined can be found in PCRO, L2/1-8, 1550-1753.

36. *John Carter (1672-1732)*, a Presbyterian and wealthy merchant. *John Carter (1715-94)*, only son of the above John Carter and first of the family to enter the corporation. Known as Alderman Carter. Burgess 1732, alderman 1744 and mayor 1747. As leader of the independent party in the corporation, he was the moving spirit in the struggle to rid the borough of government control. *John Carter (1741-1808)*. Known as Sir John Carter. Knighted by George III in 1773 on occasion of latter's first visit to Portsmouth. Eldest son of Alderman Carter. Fought alongside his father to secure the independence of the borough. Mayor nine times. *John Bonham-Carter (1788-1838)*, only son of Sir John. A barrister, he became an M.P. for Portsmouth in 1816. Took the name of Bonham in 1827 when he inherited the fortune of his cousin, Thomas Bonham. Represented Portsmouth until his death in 1838. *See* Bonham-Carter, Victor, *In a Liberal Tradition* (1960).

37. Field, *op. cit.*, p. 121.

38. Surry, Nigel, and Thomas, James (eds.), *Book of Original Entries 1731-51*, *PRS*, vol. 3 (1976).

39. Field, *op. cit.*, p. 255.

40. The 'Two Bills' were the Seditious Meetings Act and the Treasonable Practices Act.

41. William Pitt (1759-1806), English statesman. Son of William Pitt, Earl of Chatham. England's youngest prime minister, 1783.

42. The most prominent of the 'troubles of 1817-20' were the events at St Peter's Field, Manchester, on 16 August 1819 (the Peterloo Massacre), the agitation occasioned by the 'Six Bills' introduced to prevent, if possible, revolutionary outbreaks, and the Cato Street conspiracy.

43. William Cobbett (1766-1835), Radical and irascible English politician and writer. Most noted today for his *Rural Rides* (1830).

44. Lord Cochrane, Radical M.P. for Westminster 1807-18. A sailor and 'patrician revolutionary', according to E. P. Thompson in *The Making of the English Working Class*, who resigned his seat in 1818 to enlist as a democratic free-booter in the South American wars.

45. Field, *op. cit.*, p. 280.

46. Francis Thornhill Baring (1796-1866), M.P. for Portsmouth 1826-65. Chancellor of the Exchequer 1839-41 and First Lord of the Admiralty 1849-52. Created Baron Northbrook 1866, the barony being converted into an earldom in 1876. A member of the eminent family of English financiers and bankers, Baring Brothers.

47. Field, *op. cit.*, p. 280.

48. Feargus O'Connor, the Chartist leader.

49. Sir George Cockburn, Bart. (1772-1853), British admiral. Played a prominent part in the American War 1812-14, including the capture of Washington. In Autumn 1815 in the *Northumberland*, he carried out the sentence of deportation to St Helena which had been passed upon Bonaparte.

50. Field, *op. cit.*, p. 337.

51. *Ibid.*, p. 338.

52. Riley, Ray, *The Houses and Inhabitants of Thomas Ellis Owen's Southsea*, *PP*, 32 (1980).

53. Ashworth, Gregory, *Portsmouth's Political Patterns 1885-1945*, *PP*, 24 (1976).

54. Margaret, Countess of Salisbury (1474-1541). Widow of Sir Richard Pole. Executed in 1541 for alleged complicity in abortive conspiracy.

55. Sir William Fitzwilliam (*c.*1490-1542), Lord High Admiral of England. Created Earl of Southampton 1537. Boyhood companion of Henry VIII. Left no sons, so his titles became extinct on his death.

56. Thomas Wriothesley (1505-50), created Earl of Southampton 1547. Loyal servant of Henry VIII, richly rewarded with monastic spoil, obtaining large tracts of land between Southampton and Winchester.

57. Sir William Paulet (*c.*1470-1572), statesman who served four Tudor monarchs: Henry VIII, Edward VI, Mary and Elizabeth. In his time, Lord President of the Council and executor of Henry's

will, Lord Treasurer after the fall of the Protector Somerset, speaker in two Elizabethan parliaments, Marquess of Winchester 1551.

58. Edward Hawke, Baron Hawke (1705), British admiral. Elected M.P. for Portsmouth in 1747. Represented the borough for 30 years though he must rarely have been in his place.
59. For details of the Portsmouth parliamentary careers of Beresford, Meux and Crossman, *see* Peacock, *HS*.
60. Sedgwick, Romney, *The House of Commons 1715-1754*, 1 (1970).
61. Ouster: dispossession.
62. John Montagu, 4th Earl of Sandwich (1718-92). For much of his official career, he was First Lord of the Admiralty. He was not a distinguished First Lord. Corruption was rife and the navy singularly ill-equipped to fulful its role fighting its country's battles.
63. Henry Cavendish Bentinck, 3rd Duke of Portand (1738-1809), Prime Minister 1783 and 1807-1809. Also served his country at various times as Lord Chamberlain, Lord-Lieutenant of Ireland, Secretary of State for the Home Department, President of the Privy Council.
64. Peacock, Sarah, 'The Parliamentary Representation of Portsmouth 1885-1918', *HS*, pp. 267-308.
65. Eatanswill was the borough featured in Charles Dickens's *Pickwick Papers*.
66. Gates, p. 96.
67. For more details of the women's suffrage movement in Portsmouth *see* Peacock, Sarah, *Votes for women: The Women's Fight in Portsmouth*, *PP*, 39 (1983).
68. According to information given to the author by local people who knew them, Norah and Margaret O'Shea were the daughters of Kitty O'Shea, mistress and, after her divorce from Captain O'Shea, wife of Charles Stewart Parnell (1846-91), Irish nationalist leader.
69. PCRO, 753A.
70. For references to these sources *see* Peacock, *PP*, 39.

Chapter Nine – Leisure and Pleasure

1. East, p. 681.
2. Hoad, M. J., *Portsmouth – As others have seen it. Part 1, 1540-1790, PP*, 15 (1972), pp. 6-7.
3. *Ibid.*, p. 8.
4. Hoad, M. J., *Portsmouth – As others have seen it. Part 2, 1790-1900, PP*, 20 (1973), p. 10.
5. East, pp. 312-14, 322, 326, 343, 345.
6. BL, King's MS. 213.
7. BL, 11,778g(22), *Arrived at Portsmouth*, an operatic drama in two acts.
8. Webb, J., *An Early Victorian Street. The High Street, Old Portsmouth, PP*, 26 (1977), p. 6.
9. Parkinson, C. N. (ed.), *Portsmouth Point: The Navy in Fiction 1793-1815* (1948), pp. 98-102; *HT*, 7 June 1802.
10. *HT*, 7 January 1805, 2 November 1807, 18 July 1814.
11. *HT*, 17 August 1829, 1 November 1830.
12. PCRO, CF 2/25.
13. Webb, *op. cit.*, pp. 6-7.
14. Howell, A., *History of the Phoenix Lodge, no. 257, 1786-1893* (1894), pp. 10-11, 13, 18, 268.
15. PCRO, S3 B/189.
16. Slight, H., *The History of Portsmouth* (1838), Part 1, p. 30.
17. Hoad, *PP*, 15, p. 13.
18. East, pp. 31, 34, 46, 68, 93; PCRO, S3 B/189.
19. East, p. 94.
20. East, p. 110.
21. Monckton, H. A., *The Story of the British Pub* (1982), p. 12.
22. Sadler's *Hampshire Directory* (1784), pp. 99-112, 115-31.
23. *The Universal British Directory of Trade, Commerce and Maintenance*, vol. 4 (1798), p. 194.
24. Riley, R. C., and Eley, P., *Public Houses and Beerhouses in Nineteenth-century Portsmouth, PP*, 38 (1983), pp. 5-6.
25. *HT*, 24 November 1800.
26. *HT*, 12 and 26 September 1836.
27. Riley and Eley, *op. cit.*, pp. 12-13.

28. *Ibid.*, pp. 12-26; Lloyd, D. W., *Buildings of Portsmouth and its Environs* (1974), pp. 100-101, 103, etc.
29. *HT*, 19 May 1817, 21 March 1846, 30 September 1848.
30. PCRO, S3 B/112.
31. The playwright was Essex Waller of Portsmouth. The farce was republished in 1822.
32. Slight, p. 30.
33. *Ibid.*; PCRO, 39A/5, 9, 10, 13; Hare, A., *The Georgian Theatre in Wessex* (1958), pp. 15-16, 41, 49-50; Sargeant, H., *A History of Portsmouth Theatres, PP*, 13 (1971), pp. 2-5; Carter, I., *The Wonder! Or the Life of Isaac Carter* (*c*.1823).
34. Hare, *op. cit.*, pp. 55-6. The new theatre changed its name on several occasions. The Portsmouth Theatre became the Portsmouth and Portsea Theatre during the Napoleonic Wars, and later the Theatre Royal.
35. Webb, J., 'The Portsmouth Theatre Account Book, 1771-4', *PAR*, 4 (1979-80), pp. 44-60; BL, Playbills, 298, 426.
36. Hare, *op. cit.*, pp. 23-6, 36, 171-3; PCRO, S3/85; *Portsmouth Gazette and Weekly Advertiser*, 26 January 1795.
37. Sargeant, *op. cit.*, pp. 11-16.
38. Bernard, J., *Retrospections of the Stage* (1830), *passim*.
39. Steen, M., *A Pride of Terrys* (1962), *passim*.
40. Webb, J., *PP*, 26, p. 19.
41. Offord, J., *The Theatres of Portsmouth* (1983), p. 11.
42. Slight, pp. 30-1; Sargeant, *op. cit.*, pp. 7-8, 15, 16; Butcher's *Portsmouth Directory* (1874-5), p. 119; White (1859), p. 277.
43. Offord, *op. cit.*, pp. 51-63.
44. *Ibid.*, pp. 11-12, 20-7, 43-5, 63-6.
45. Notably the Eastney Electric (Essoldo), Apollo (Classic) in Albert Road, and Shaftesbury (The Tatler, etc.) in Kingston Road.
46. *PTCM*, 1910 onwards give details of licensing applications. *See also* Barker, J., Brown, R., and Greer, W., *The Cinemas of Portsmouth* (1981).
47. Cf. Davies, J. S., *A History of Southampton* (1883), pp. 216-7.
48. Rule, M., *The Mary Rose* (1982), pp. 98-9.
49. Information from the Royal Marines Museum, Eastney.
50. East, p. 120.
51. BL, Playbills, 426.
52. Webb, *PP*, 26, pp. 16, 18.
53. White (1859), p. 277.
54. *HT*, 5 September 1846; White (1859), p. 304; Webb, *PP*, 26, p. 16.
55. *HT*, 5 July 1824.
56. *HT*, 25 May 1807.
57. Webb, *PP*, 26, pp. 15-16; *HT*, 10 May 1830, 4 October 1830, 8 June 1840, 26 February 1848, etc.
58. I am greatly indebted to Mr. Frank Warren for this and other information.
59. The paragraphs that follow are based on my *Portsmouth Free Mart Fair: The Last Phase, 1800-1847, PP*, 35 (1982).
60. *Portsmouth, Portsea and Gosport Journal*, 9 May and 25 July 1803.
61. *VCH Hants*, vol. 3, p. 171.
62. White (1859), p. 243; *HT*, 29 June 1818, 2 August 1824, 26 July 1830, 28 July 1834, 10 July 1843; ATP, p. 106.
63. O'Keefe, J., *Recollections of the Life of John O'Keefe*, vol. 1 (1826), pp. 376-7.
64. *HT*, 4 August 1806.
65. *Peter Simple* (1834), Chapter 9.
66. *HT*, 17 August 1801, 2 August 1802, 30 July 1827, 29 July 1833, 25 July 1836.
67. *An Act for the Discontinuance of Portsdown Fair*, 25/26 Vict., c. xxxiv.
68. *PRC* (1835-1927), p. 97; Brown, R., and Greer, W., *Fairdays and Tramdays: The Story of Cosham* (1982), pp. 28-32.
69. East, pp. 52, 56, 61, 128.
70. PCRO, L2/2/2.
71. East, p. 44.

72. PCRO, S3/101.

73. *HT*, 16 December 1799.

74. *Portsmouth Chronicle*, 21 and 28 August 1802.

75. *HT*, 13 September 1802, 2 September 1816, 16 August 1845.

76. PCRO, 4A; *Hampshire Courier*, 24 May 1813.

77. *HT*, 11 May 1840, 5 February 1844.

78. *HT*, 31 May 1841.

79. White (1859), p. 278. The ground was in the area of the modern Wimbledon Road.

80. *PRC* (1835-1927), p. 148.

81. Neasom, M., Cooper, M., and Robinson, D., *Pompey: The History of Portsmouth Football Club* (1984), pp. 7-11, 20, 43-7.

82. East, p. 717.

83. *Sussex Chronicle and Chichester Advertiser*, 10 March 1802.

84. *HT*, 15 July 1816, 19 September 1836, 29 August 1842, 26 August 1848: *EN*, 14 December 1962; *Southsea Holiday Guide*, 1933, p. 15.

85. *HT*, 25 July 1825, 10 October 1831, 11 July 1842, 1 August 1842; *Royal Albert Yacht Club: Rules and Regulations* (1924), p. iii.

86. Lloyd, *op. cit.*, p. 51.

87. *The Portsmouth Guide* (1775), pp. 20-1, 75; Slight, pp. 27-9; *HT*, 19 September 1803, 16 June 1817, 25 June 1821; JM, 1823, p. 218, 1821, p. 172.

88. *HT*, 3 July 1809.

89. *HT*, 22 June 1835; Field, J. L., *The Battle of Southsea*, PP, 34 (1981), p. 5.

90. *HT*, 25 July 1825.

91. Stevens' *Directory of Portsmouth* (1887), pp. 47-8; *PRC* (1835-1927), pp. 131, 151; Lloyd, *op. cit.*, p. 120. Hilsea Lido was opened in 1935.

92. White (1859), p. 266; *HT*, 1 and 29 August 1842; *PRC* (1835-1927), pp. 93, 140, 148; Field, *op. cit.*, pp. 8-11; Lloyd, *op. cit.*, p. 112.

93. Riley, R. C., *The Growth of Southsea as a Naval Satellite and Victorian Resort*, PP, 16 (1972), p. 16; Field, *op. cit.*, pp. 10-11.

94. Butcher's *Portsmouth Directory* (1874-5), p. 49.

95. *HT*, 5 July 1824, 26 September 1831.

96. Chamberlain's *Directory* (1879), p. 65; Stevens' *Directory of Portsmouth* (1887), p. 60.

97. Field, *op. cit.*, *passim*.

98. *PRC* (1835-1927), p. 138.

99. For an excellent account of leisure and culture in 20th-century Portsmouth *see* Nicholas Fox's chapter in Stapleton, B., and Thomas, J. H. (eds.), *The Portsmouth Region* (1989), pp. 179-205.

Chapter Ten – Portsmouth and Its Past

1. PCRO, CE 8/2.

2. East, p. 657; Gates, W. G., *The Portsmouth That Has Passed* (1949), p. 44.

3. PCRO, L2/2/1.

4. PCRO, L2/1, f. 8v.; East, p. 342.

5. PCRO, L2/1, f. 50r.

6. East, pp. 806-9; Slight, pp. 18, 44.

7. PCRO, CCR/1, pp. 1-8; *HT*, 1 February 1836.

8. PCRO, Ubsdell Correspondence, no date.

9. *VCH Hants*, vol. 3, p. 177.

10. *PTCM*, 1904, pp. 381, 384.

11. *PRC* (1835-1927), p. 134.

12. *HT*, 30 June 1823.

13. PCRO, Ubsdell Correspondence, 19 September 1847, 24 March 1848, 16 April 1848, etc.

14. *PRC* (1835-1927), p. 141.

15. Murrell, R. J., and East, R. (eds.), *Extracts from Records in the Possession of the Municipal Corporation of the Borough of Portsmouth; and from other documents relating thereto* (1884), pp. i, ii, v, vi.

16. 23-24 Geo. V, c. 51 (part xv).

17. PCRO, Box I/14, Rea, H. G., *The Civic Records of Portsmouth*, an address given 7 February 1937.
18. PCRO, CC7/45/2.
19. Reprinted in Surry, N. W., and Thomas, J. H. (eds.), *Book of Original Entries, 1731-51*, PRS (1976), pp. 70-8.
20. A copy of this rare book is in the Local History Collection, PCL.
21. Webb, J., 'Young Antiquaries: Lake Allen and Frederic Madden', in *HS*, pp. 201-2.
22. *The Ancient and Modern History of Portsmouth, Portsea, Gosport and their Environs* (1799).
23. Washington, E. S., and Marsh, A. J., *Portsmouth Grammar School, 1732-1976* (1978), pp. 11, 90.
24. JM, 1823, p. 126.
25. *The History of Portsmouth . . . with an Account of the Towns of Portsea, Gosport . . . and the Isle of Wight* (1801).
26. *Ibid.*, pp. 44-5.
27. The copy is in the Local History Collection, PCL.
28. PCRO, CC 7/43.
29. PCRO, CC 7/45/2.
30. PCRO, CC 7/44/2. For Goldson *see above* p. 91, and East, pp. 319, 332, 388.
31. HRO, 94 M72/F29-31; *PRC* (1835-1927), p. 22.
32. *HT*, 16 February 1850.
33. PCRO, CC 7/51-3; BL, Add. MS. 40,001.
34. *The History of Portsmouth; containing a full and enlarged account of its ancient and present state . . .* (1817).
35. For Allen and his friendship with Madden *see HS*, pp. 201-24.
36. Webb, J., *Sir Frederic Madden and Portsmouth, PP*, 47 (1987).
37. *HT*, 23 September and 7 October 1816.
38. McKee, A., *King Henry VIII's Mary Rose* (1973), pp. 93-108.
39. PCRO, PE 7.
40. *Reports from Commissioners on Municipal Corporations in England and Wales: Hampshire*, pp. 801-20 *passim*.
41. *See above*, p. 95.
42. *HT*, 23 January 1847.
43. *Register*, nos. 1 (pp. 5-8), 2 (pp. 17-23), 5 (pp. 98-107), 8 (pp. 161-72), 9 (pp. 185-94).
44. *Register*, no. 4, p. 66n.
45. E.g. *HT*, 9 May 1842, 'Narrative of a Portsmouth Coachman'.
46. *Register*, no. 3, p. 61.
47. BL, Add. MS. 33,283, f. 410r.
48. *Ibid.*, f. 447.
49. *PRC* (1928-30), pp. 40, 43.
50. *PRC* (1835-1927), p. 253.
51. PCL, Saunders Collection (942.27); PCRO, 11A/22/3-6.
52. PCRO, 11A/22/3 *(Things I have seen; men I have known; A Portsmouth Retrospect)*.
53. For the above information I am greatly indebted to Mr. C. R. Elrington, General Editor of the *VCH*, and Miss P. A. Tattersfield who kindly examined the records.
54. Scarfe, N., 'Memoir: V. B. Redstone and Lilian J. Redstone', in Thirsk, J., and Imray, J. (eds.), *Suffolk Farming in the Nineteenth Century*, Suffolk Records Society (1958), pp. 7-13.
55. *VCH Hants*, vol. 3, pp. 165-202. *See also* vol. 5 (1912), pp. 359-408, for Laughton, L. G. C., 'Hampshire Maritime History', in which Portsmouth figures prominently.
56. Washington and Marsh, *op. cit.*, p. 29.
57. PCRO, 827/A/1/2(1); *EN*, 25 March 1946; Gates, W. G., *The Portsmouth That Has Passed* (1949), pp. 278, 405.
58. *The Secret of Death* (1944).
59. *City of Portsmouth Records of the Corporation:* volumes include 1835-1927 (1928); 1928-30 (1931); 1931-5 (1936); 1936-7 (1938), compiled by G. Singleton Gates and E. C. Bloomfield.
60. Slight, pp. 29-30, 51, 236-7; PCRO, 857A, p. 355.
61. My thanks are due to Mr. J. H. Fiddian-Green, Executive Secretary of the Linnean Society of London, for searching the Society's records for me.
62. Slight, p. 237.
63. JM, 1821, p. 275.

64. PCL, Madden Newspaper Cuttings, vol. 3, p. 177; *JM*, 1822, p. 29.

65. *Reports of Portsmouth and Portsea Lit. and Phil. Soc.*, 1824-5, pp. 17-25, 1839-40, p. 20; Slight, p. 32; White (1859), p. 275.

66. *HT*, 30 June 1828; *The New Portsmouth . . . Guide* (1839), p. 33.

67. *PRC* (1835-1927), p. 90.

68. White (1859), p. 276; Slight, p. 223.

69. PCRO, 857A, p. 341.

70. Webb, J., *An Early Victorian Street – The High Street, Old Portsmouth, PP*, 26 (1977), p. 20.

71. *Ibid.*; White (1859), p. 276; *JM*, 1819, p. 95; Slight, p. 28.

72. *PRC* (1835-1927), p. 125.

73. 13-14 Vict., c. 65: *An Act for enabling Town Councils to establish Public Libraries and Museums.*

74. Ollé, J. G., 'The First Public Library', *Portsmouth Reader*, vol. 10, no. 3, pp. 35-7; Ollé, J. G., *Portsmouth City Libraries, 1883-1983; A Century of Service*, typescript, PCL, pp. 10-11, 14.

75. Quoted by Ollé, *Portsmouth Reader*, vol. 10, no. 3, p. 37.

76. Ollé, *Portsmouth City Libraries*, pp. 12-14, 20.

77. *Ibid.*, pp. 14-15.

78. 'Sixty Years: A Library Chronology', *Portsmouth Reader*, vol. 7, no. 2, p. 20.

79. Ollé, *Portsmouth City Libraries*, pp. 17-18, 32-4.

80. *Ibid.*, pp. 15-17, 29-30.

81. *Ibid.*, pp. 28-9.

82. *PTCM*, 1895-7 *passim*, 1901, pp. 269, 751; *EN*, 27 September 1929; *PRC* (1835-1927), p. 184.

83. *Ibid.*, pp. 212-13; *PTCM*, 1904, pp. 72-3, 685, 1905, p. 217.

84. *PTCM*, 1913, p. 420.

85. PCRO, 11A/22/4, Saunders' notebook with details of loans to the museum, 1893-1900. For exhibits *see also PTCM*, 1913, pp. 518-19, 1916, pp. 359, 374, 735; Saunders, W. H., 'Portsmouth Free Museum', *NUT Conference Souvenir and Guide* (1904), pp. 237-41.

86. *PTCM*, 1904, pp. 383-4.

87. *PTCM*, 1905, p. 869.

88. Ollé, *Portsmouth City Libraries*, pp. 28, 30.

89. *PTCM*, 1929, pp. 579, 652-5.

90. *PTCM*, 1928, pp. 133-4, 165.

91. *PTCM*, 1929, pp. 655, 686.

92. *EN*, 20, 27 September 1929, 6 February 1931.

93. *PTCM*, 1911, pp. 1,050-1; *EN*, 6 February 1931.

94. *EN*, 2 May 1932, 13 May 1933, 31 May 1933.

95. *EN*, 26 March 1956, 21 April 1956, 30 May 1956.

96. This was Miss Betty Masters. An experienced part-time archivist (Mrs. Margaret Hoad) had been appointed temporarily in an advisory capacity in 1956.

97. 9 December 1939.

98. Ollé, *Portsmouth City Libraries*, p. 59; *PCR* (1966-74), p. 128.

99. *Ibid.*, pp. 38, 94.

100. His *Portsmouth: A History* (1976), written on traditional lines, usefully, in brief compass, reassessed the city's development in the light of post-war research.

Chapter Eleven – A Changing City

1. *PRC* (1936-45), pp. 153-6, 183-90, 285; *Smitten City* (1945).

2. *PRC* (1936-45), pp. 292-4; (1966-74), pp. 20-3, 25.

3. Windle, R., 'Post-War Developments', Table 2, p. 209, in Stapleton, B., and Thomas, J. H. (eds.), *The Portsmouth Region* (1989).

4. Colin Buchanan and Partners, *South Hampshire Study* (1966), p. 2.

5. *PRC* (1956-65), p. 121; (1966-74), pp. 28-9; Report to Housing and Health Committee, 12 February 1985; *Sunday Times*, 6 December 1987, p. 4.

6. *PRC* (1966-74), pp. 86-7; *A Census Profile of Portsmouth* (1983), p. 3.

7. Ministry of Housing and Local Government, *South East Study* (1964), p. 72; Bateman, M., 'Portsmouth –

Growth Pole of the South East?', in Bradbeer, J. B. (ed.), *Portsmouth Geographical Essays* (1974), pp. 42-58.

8. *South Hampshire Study*, pp. 15, 26, 88, 98-107, 113, 154-6; Appendix to City Council Minutes, 20 February 1968, pp. 149-55.
9. South East Joint Planning Team, *Strategic Plan for the South East* (1970), pp. 80-2, 95, 107.
10. South Hampshire Plan Advisory Committee, *South Hampshire Draft Structure Plan* (1972), pp. 254-69.
11. Blanchard, V., *et al.*, 'Portsmouth: post-war recovery and progress', *The Municipal Journal*, no. 3,254 (1955), pp. 1,741-73; 'Portsmouth: a special report', *The Times*, 3 March 1970; *The Changing Face of Portsmouth* (1971); *Progress in Portsmouth* (n.d.); *PRC* (1936-45), pp. 263, 267.
12. *PRC* (1966-74), p. 88; Stapleton and Thomas (eds.), *op. cit.*, p. 169; Statements by Leader of Portsmouth City Council, 16 June, 8 July, 6 October 1981, City Council Minutes, pp. 361-7, 375-83, 523-7.
13. *PRC* (1966-74), p. 82; *City of Portsmouth Official Handbook* (n.d.), pp. 7, 38-43; Stapleton and Thomas (eds.), *op. cit.*, pp. 213-7.
14. Figures kindly supplied by Portsmouth Polytechnic Registry and Personnel Office.
15. *PRC* (1966-74), p. 90; City of Portsmouth Official Handbook (n.d.), p. 47.
16. *PRC* (1966-74), p. 137; Transportation Committee, Appendix to City Council Minutes, 29 April 1975, pp. 55-61; *City of Portsmouth Annual Report* (1986-7), p. 36.
17. *PRC* (1966-74), pp. 93-4; Planning Services Committee, Appendices to City Council Minutes, 25 July 1978, pp. 109-15; 13 February 1979, pp. 99-103.
18. Ashworth, G., and Bradbeer, J., 'Portsmouth's Recreational Resources', in Bradbeer, J. B. (ed.), *Portsmouth Geographical Essays* (1974), pp. 83-103; Tubbs, C. R., *Langstone Harbour: a review of its ecology and conservation objectives* (1975); Planning Services Committee, Appendix to City Council Minutes, 4 January 1977, Langstone Harbour Study, pp. 107-16; Haynes, F., and Stranack, F., 'Aquatic Flora and Fauna', in Stapleton and Thomas (eds.), *op. cit.*, pp. 156-64.

Select Bibliography

Besant, Sir Walter, *Autobiography* (1902).

Besant, Sir Walter, and Rice, James, *By Celia's Arbour: A Tale of Portsmouth Town* (1878).

Burton, Lesley, and Musselwhite, Brian, *Crossing the Harbour* (1987).

Chalklin, C. W., *The Provincial Towns of Georgian England, 17401820* (1974).

Coad, Jonathan, *Historic Architecture of H.M. Naval Base Portsmouth, 1700-1850*, reprinted from *MM*, vol. 67 (1981).

Colvin, H. M. (ed.), *The History of the King's Works*, 4 vols. (1963-82).

Dolling, Robert R., *Ten Years in a Portsmouth Slum* (1896).

East, Robert (ed.), *Extracts from Records in the Possession of the Municipal Corporation of the Borough of Portsmouth and from Other Documents relating thereto* (1891).

Field, John L., 'Bourgeois Portsmouth: Social Relations in a Victorian Dockyard Town, 1815-75', University of Warwick Ph.D. thesis, 1979.

Garbett, C. F. (ed.), *The Work of a Great Parish by Nine Portsea Men* (1915).

Gates, William G., and successors (eds.), *City of Portsmouth. Records of the Corporation, 1835-1974*, 7 vols. (1928-83).

Gates, William G., *Illustrated History of Portsmouth* (1900).

Gates, William G. (ed.), *Portsmouth and the Great War* (1919).

Gates, William G., *Portsmouth in the Past* (1926, reprinted 1972).

Gates, William G., *The Portsmouth That Has Passed* (1949).

Goss, James, *Portsmouth Built Warships, 1497-1967* (1984).

Hare, Arnold, *The Georgian Theatre in Wessex* (1958).

Hawkes, Henry, *Recollections of John Pounds* (1884).

Howell, Alexander N. Y., *Notes on the Topography of Portsmouth* (1913).

Lewis, Michael, *Spithead: An Informal History* (1972).

Lilley, Henry T., and Everitt, Alfred T., *Portsmouth Parish Church* (1921).

Lipscomb, Frank W., *Heritage of Sea-Power: The Story of Portsmouth* (1967).

Lloyd, David W., *Buildings of Portsmouth and its Environs* (1974).

Offord, John, *The Theatres of Portsmouth* (1983).

Oppenheim, M., *A History of the Administration of the Royal Navy and of Merchant Shipping in relation to the Navy, 1509-1660* (reprinted 1961).

Osborne, C. E., *The Life of Father Dolling* (1903).

Patterson, A. Temple, *Portsmouth: A History* (1976).

Portsmouth and Sunderland Newspapers, *Smitten City. The Story of Portsmouth in the Air Raids, 1940-1944* (1981).

Portsmouth Archives Review (1976-).

Portsmouth Geographical Essays, 2 vols. (1974 and 1976).

Portsmouth Museums Society Local History Series, 1-8 (1970-77).

Portsmouth Papers, The (1967-).

Portsmouth Record Series (1971-).

Quail, Sarah, *Civic Pride and Sterling Silver* (1988).

Quail, Sarah, Barrett, George, and Chessun, Christopher (eds.), *Consecrated to Prayer: A Centenary History of St Mary's, Portsea, 1889-1989* (1989).

Saunders, A. D., *Hampshire Coastal Defence Since the Introduction of Artillery*, reprinted from *The Archaeological Journal*, vol. 123 (1967).

Sparks, Henry J., *The Story of Portsmouth* (1921).

Stapleton, Barry, and Thomas, James H. (eds.), *The Portsmouth Region* (1989).

The Victoria History of the County of Hampshire and the Isle of Wight, 5 vols. (1900-12).

Webb, John, *The City of Portsmouth and the Royal Navy* (1984).

Webb, John, Yates, Nigel, and Peacock, Sarah (eds.), *Hampshire Studies* (1981).

Wright, H. P., *The Story of the Domus Dei of Portsmouth* (1873).

Index

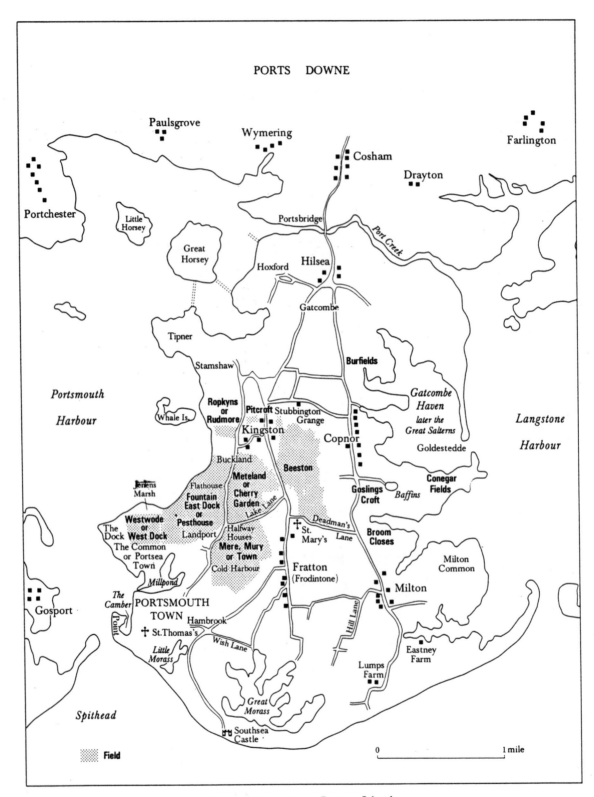

PORTS DOWNE

Paulsgrove

Wymering

Farlington

Cosham

Drayton

Portchester

Little
Horsey

Portsbridge

Port Creek

Great
Horsey

Hoxford

Hilsea

Gatcombe

Tipner

Portsmouth

Harbour

Stamshaw

Burfields

Gatcombe
Haven
later the
Great Salterns

Langstone

Harbour

Ropkyns
or
Rudmore

Pitcroft

Stubbington
Grange

Whale Is.

Kingston

Copnor

Goldestedde

Buckland

Beeston

Conegar
Fields

Jenens
Marsh

Flathouse

Meteland
or
Cherry
Garden

Goslings
Croft

Baffins

Fountain
East Dock
or
Pesthouse

Lake Lane

Westwode
or
West Dock

Landport

Deadman's
Lane

Broom
Closes

The
Dock

Halfway
Houses

St.
Mary's

The Common
or Portsea
Town

Mere, Mury
or Town

Milton
Common

Cold Harbour

Fratton
(Frodintone)

Millpond

Milton

Gosport

The
Camber

PORTSMOUTH
TOWN

Point

Hambrook

Hill Lane

St. Thomas's

Wish Lane

Little
Morass

Eastney
Farm

Lumps
Farm

Spithead

Great
Morass

Southsea
Castle

0   1 mile

Field

Early settlements on Portsea Island.